D0742237

APPALACHIA IN THE SIXTIES

APPALACHIA IN THE SIXTIES

Decade of Reawakening

Edited by David S. Walls
& John B. Stephenson

The University Press of Kentucky

ISBN: 0–8131–1259–1 (cloth)   0–8131–0135–2 (paper)

Library of Congress Catalog Card Number: 78–160052

Copyright © 1972 by The University Press of Kentucky

A statewide cooperative scholarly publishing agency serving Berea College, Centre College of Kentucky, Eastern Kentucky University, Kentucky State College, Morehead State University, Murray State University, University of Kentucky, University of Louisville, and Western Kentucky University.

Editorial and Sales Offices: Lexington, Kentucky 40506

To *DAN GIBSON*
RUPERT B. VANCE
the memory of JUANITA BAIN

Contents

Part Three
Lessons in Fighting Poverty

Preface

More than ten years have passed since John F. Kennedy's visit to West Virginia during the campaign for the 1960 presidential primary, the visit which precipitated a declaration of war against the social, economic, and human problems of the Appalachian Region. Ten years have passed since the research was carried out which led to the publication of *The Southern Appalachian Region: A Survey.*

In that volume, and in a later article reprinted in this book, Rupert Vance suggested a decennial follow-up on the problems and progress of the region. How far have we come in ten years? There is no study comparable to the survey on which to rely for an assessment. Despite the absence of quantitative data, despite the lack of scholarly research on the matter, information is available which could lead us to a tentative answer. This information is found in the observations, impressions, and evaluations of journalists, field workers, local residents, politicians, and social scientists who have lived with, worked with, watched, and written about the problems they have seen and the programs established to cope with them. These mostly frontline reports come in a variety of published forms, from national literary magazines to action-group house organs, from articles in famous dailies to letters to the editors of county weeklies. What follows is a selection of such reports about what happened in Southern Appalachia in the 1960s.

The Appalachian Region is itself an elusive entity, as can be seen from the number of conflicting definitions given it by scholars, reporters, natives, and politicians over the years. How many counties in which states are included? For the most part, we are concerned here only with the southern portion of the region, and within that portion we have concentrated mainly on the coalfields of West Virginia, eastern Kentucky, southwestern Virginia and north-central Tennessee. These are the areas that first attracted the attention of the nation in the early sixties; they seem to have been the places where there was the greatest depression, the greatest concentration of antipoverty efforts, the most heightened response to local, state, and federal programs, and the greatest degree of organization around common interests by the end of the decade. What has been written about central southern Appalachia applies in varying degrees to mountainous areas which are further north or south, lower in altitude or more "piedmont" in nature, based more on agricultural economies, or which have not had the complicating factor of coal added to their otherwise broadly comparable histories. It should certainly not be thought that places like western North Carolina and much of eastern Tennessee are not truly Appalachian in their culture, character, and problems; it is only that less is known about them, and that what is known suggests that settlement patterns, economic history, and current prospects are different enough for other Appalachian subregions to require a separate accounting. Something registers when you tell many Americans about places called Hazard and Bluefield, but who knows of Spruce Pine or Erwin? The presence of coal seems to be an important common denominator of central southern Appalachia, and perhaps it is coal that has made this area unique, both in its history and in its uncertain future.

Mass unemployment caused by mechanization in the coal industry forced Appalachia to the attention of the nation at the beginning of the sixties. Theorists of the automation revolution prophesied that Appalachia foreshadowed a national employment crisis. Hazard became a symbol for the New Left of the sixties as Harlan had been for the old Left of the thirties. The violence associated with the roving picket movement in eastern Kentucky dramatized the need for intervention by the federal government. By the end of the decade it became clear that coal had been one of the most labor-intensive, technologically backward sectors of the economy, and the Appalachian crisis had not been as representative of the national economy as some had imagined. The roving picket movement thus turned out to be the last gasp of the old era of labor struggles in the mountains. The movements of the later sixties, in contrast, were premised on the existence of a mechanized mining industry and a permanent welfare state designed to care for the industry's casualties.

The Area Redevelopment Administration, established in 1961 with a program for stimulating private industrial development, quickly proved inadequate to the problems of depressed areas in America. The Economic Opportunity Act of 1964 packaged a patchwork of liberal proposals, including a public employment program disguised as "work experience and training," and the dramatic Community Action Program with its call for "maximum feasible participation" of the poor. The much criticized work experience program, concentrated disproportionately in eastern Kentucky, managed—together with the food stamp program—to defuse the violence that had haunted the coalfields in the early sixties.

A few far-sighted individuals called for an Appalachian version of the Tennessee Valley Authority as a solution to the chronic problems of the southern mountain region. This idea had little widespread support at the beginning of the sixties, however, and proposals for public ownership and development of the region's resources were quickly scuttled by the coal industry and private utilities. Instead of a new TVA, the Appalachian Regional Development Act of 1965 created the Appalachian Regional Commission as a funnel for federal money into the mountains. Overshadowed by the more controversial Office of Economic Opportunity programs in the middle sixties, the ARC by the end of the decade had firmly established its network of local development districts as the focus of developmental activities for the early seventies. Perhaps as many as half of OEO's community action agencies had maintained some independence of local courthouse and school-board political machines for three or four years, until amendments to the Economic Opportunity Act whittled back the scope of the program and returned control to local public officials. The ARC's development districts never presented any such embarrassments, as they were dominated by their respective local establishments from the start. Up for renewal in 1971, the ARC won an overwhelming endorsement from Congress, despite opposition from the Nixon administration, which wished to substitute its own revenue sharing proposals for the regional development plans.

At the end of the sixties, some of the focus of grassroots activities had shifted from Kentucky to West Virginia. The Association of Disabled Miners and Widows began legal action to obtain benefits they claimed were due them from the United Mine Workers of America. The Black Lung Association led a wildcat strike that took 40,000 men out of the mines, shutting down the coal industry in West Virginia until the state legislature passed a measure providing adequate compensation for coal miner's pneumoconiosis. The Miners for Democracy movement attempted to restore self-government to the districts of the UMWA. Sparked by Kentucky's Appalachian Group to Save the Land and People, the opposition to strip-mining spread to West Virginia and was the subject of major legislative battles. In the mountain areas of both states welfare rights organizations were concerned with a wide range of issues from free school lunches to disability criteria. Many of these activities had been stimulated by OEO's community action and VISTA programs. A small number of the organizers and lawyers who were attracted to Appalachia by the War on Poverty stayed on past the demise of these programs as forces for change and made their homes in the region, continuing to give support to grassroots social movements.

We draw two generalizations from our survey of the Appalachian scene as of this writing in 1971. First, there are few if any grounds for optimism regarding "victory" (or even moderate success) in the "war" on the region's problems. Second, to measure progress in 1971 by reference to problems defined in 1960 is misleading, because neither the manner in which problems are currently defined nor the yardsticks by which change is gauged are the same as a decade earlier. Our impression is that the quantity of human suffering, privation, degradation, and confusion, and the extent of environmental rape and devastation in Appalachia have not decreased significantly. These problems represent a kind of absolute standard by which to judge the well-being of a region. Beyond them, and the very minimal kinds of expectations which they connote (for example, that people should have decent housing and should not be victims of malnutrition), there are significant dissimilarities in the ways problems, solutions, and progress were viewed at the beginning and at the end of the decade.

This change may simply reflect changes occurring in the rest of society during that ten years, especially among people concerned with programs of social action—civil rights and minority protest, the antiwar movement, and the youth, consumer, women's, and ecology movements. The major aspect of this change has been that what were initially brought to consciousness as problems-in-themselves are now seen as symptoms of more fundamental, underlying conditions. These problems are now viewed as incomprehensible when not taken in their relationships with other problems and conditions. Thus what once might have been praised as progressive, forward-looking, and humanitarian programs of social and economic amelioration are derogated as "bandaids" and "aspirins." Individuals and families in suffering are looked upon as casualties of an unjust social and economic system which is itself the *real* problem.

Thus, solutions to the problem of Appalachia today are cast in terms of reconstruction, not amelioration, and the signposts to progress are marked in political and organizational mileage instead of numbers of new privies, schoolhouse repairs, or even increased median incomes. If there is to be a movement for progressive change in Appalachia, the evidence of this volume suggests it would result from a diverse coalition: poor people's grassroots groups, conservationists, a revitalized UMWA, teachers and parents concerned for better education, dedicated students willing to work for constructive change, and church bodies committed to social action.

In our view, what signs of optimism and hope there exist for the future of the Appalachian region grow out of this very redefinition of the problem. The sixties witnessed the awakening of a spirit of self-determination within the mountain region; whether this "Appalachian nationalism" will find wider acceptance will be seen in the seventies. We see the possibility that the people of the mountains may come together in new social forms which will permit and encourage them to have a real say in the directing of their futures. Without such consequential collective participation in their own fates, a large portion of the people of the region can be expected to remain as powerless and resigned as they have been since before the days of Campbell and Kephart, and we can expect to continue to roll bandages and nurse wounds instead of reducing injuries through democratic, preventive social engineering.

We hope this collection of articles can be put to several good uses. Reports on the contemporary scene in Appalachia are available, but they are widely scattered. Few but the hardiest scholars will bother to mine the libraries and the newspaper morgues for such sources. This set of articles, we hope, will make the job of staying informed about Appalachia—at least as of the late 1960s—easier for the general reader, the politician, the planner, the community action worker, and the student. We are very encouraged by the increase in the number of regional schools and colleges, and in the numbers of students at these institutions, who show interest in and concern about the region in concrete ways. Several high schools, colleges, and universities now offer courses in Appalachian studies. Preparing this collection of articles on problems and prospects for today's Appalachia is at once a response to this growing concern on the part of young people and, we hope, a way of encouraging even more interest.

The cast of characters in the unfolding drama of Appalachia in the 1960s is a large one. Representatives of churches, governments, private citizens groups, colleges and universities, industries, and the national media were there. Acronyms were abundant: EKRDP, ARC, FNS, FOCIS, AV, VISTA, NWRO, OEO, CORA, CAP. Some organizations, such as the Frontier Nursing Service and the Eastern Kentucky Resource Development Program were there before 1960, while others such as the Federation of Communities in Service and the Appalachian Regional Commission were newcomers. It was impossible to keep track of all problem-solving organizations and activities in the region for a time, and it is still difficult. To the extent possible, this set of articles reflects the involvement of all parties, although we recognize that because of what is available in the way of published materials not every group receives the attention it deserves.

The editors wish to thank everyone who made helpful suggestions and criticisms of this volume. In particular we extend our appreciation to Arlene Johnson and Loyal Jones. Our thanks also go to the staff, past and present, of *Mountain Life and Work* for their cooperation.

Part One

The Early Sixties

Recognition Again

THE LOST APPALACHIANS
Harry W. Ernst and Charles H. Drake

The teaching principal, her face lined with the creases of old age, had been called out of retirement to take charge of the three-room school that no one else wanted. She turned to her pupils and said: "Would you like to sing for these gentlemen?"

With childish embarrassment, they opened their song books. One child suggested they sing "America" and the teacher agreed.

"My country 'tis of thee; sweet land of liberty. . . ."

They sang with the detached innocence of childhood. Their voices carried beyond the frame schoolhouse and into the unpainted shacks that blight the bleak hollows of West Virginia's coal-mining country.

In this sweet land of liberty, these are the shaggy, shoeless children of the unwanted—the "hillbilly" coal miners who have been displaced by machines and largely left to rot on surplus government food and the small doles of a half-hearted welfare state.

"Children, how many of your fathers are working?" the teacher asked. Thirteen of the thirty pupils raised their hands. "These are the

From *The Nation*, May 30, 1959. Used by permission of the publisher. This article won the Sidney Hillman Prize in 1959.

nicest and most timid children I've ever taught," she murmured. "Yet they're destitute. How can they be so nice?"

The freshly-painted school they attend near this prosperous capital of West Virginia has no hot-lunch program. The teacher buys some bread and peanut butter and brings it to school to make sandwiches for the children who come without lunches.

Suffering isn't a newcomer to these hills and hollows. The school is located on Kelly's Creek, where the grandfathers of its pupils fought for the right to be human in the bloody mine wars from 1912 to 1921.

But the suffering may be even worse today. "When times were hard before, things were cheap," said eighty-seven-year-old W. L. Hudnall, a retired miner, logger and handyman who lives near the school. "Flour was $3 a barrel during the depression; it's $16 a barrel today. Without my old-age pension, I don't know what would happen. FDR give us that. Since he's gone, things have been wrecked. Today it's worse than it was under Cleveland."

"Look up any hollow and you'll find hungry, unemployed people," said George R. Cook, Jr., who owns and operates a funeral home at nearby Cedar Grove, a mining town of about 1,500 persons. He waved to a half-dozen men who were cleaning the town's streets. "See those men? We have a municipally-owned water company and they're cleaning the streets to pay off their water bills. We've reached the point of no return. All we have is the coal mines and they're closing or laying off more miners. The situation is even worse than most realize. If you've got a job, you can't realize what people are facing in these hollows. There's going to have to be a change somehow—and soon."

To the isolated hollows that twist crazily throughout the Appalachian South, the misery of Kelly's Creek is familiar enough. An estimated eight million people live in this impoverished area, which comprises 257 counties hugging the Appalachian mountain range and sprawling over nine states from West Virginia to Alabama. They eke out a marginal subsistence on their small, hilly farms or by chopping down what remains of the area's depleted timber resources. A dwindling number work in the coal mines which have done so much to shape the region's enigmatic character.

"The Southern Appalachian area apparently has been characterized by an interplay between stability and change, isolation and contrast, the primitive and progressive," says Dr. Earl D. C. Brewer, professor of sociology at Emory University's School of Theology in Atlanta. "Where else can one find such contrasts as Elizabethan folklore and atomic reactors, planting by the moon and scientific agriculture, medieval demonology and modern medicine, beliefs that God sends floods to wipe out the sinful as in Noah's time and TVA, the primitive Protestant emphasis on individualism and the overloaded welfare rolls?"

The tiny mountain communities with the queer names, such as Prosperity and Czar, consist of a few houses scattered around a general store with a gasoline pump in front. Dirt clings to the coal camps and towns like coal dust to the miner's pores. Cramped clusters of company-built shacks, with washing machines on their front porches, lie over every hill of the mining country. Many of the shacks have been boarded up and abandoned.

Narrow, bumpy paved roads dissolve into muddy trails, connecting the Appalachian South's bleak hollows with the world beyond. Sprawled along the Kelly's Creek Road in West Virginia are dilapidated shacks, rusting oil and gas wells, crumbling coal tipples. The creek winds its way through rotting piles of garbage and old tires. With spring, the hillsides explode into bright colors, providing an ironic background for the misery of Kelley's Creek.

Occasionally the winding roads lead to islands of industrial prosperity, such as Charleston, where the per capita income is among the highest in the nation. In the river valley dominated by this city, the region's natural resources—including coal, natural gas, salt and water—have blended to create one of the nation's largest and most prosperous complexes of chemical plants.

Elsewhere poverty blights the Appalachian South. In 1949, more than 60 percent of the families and individuals in two-thirds of the mountain counties had cash incomes of less than $2,000. Full-time farmers had an average net income of less than $500. Unemployment in West Virginia climbed to 15 percent this year, and 300,000 West Virginians—one-sixth of the state's population—depend partly or wholly on "mollygrub" (as surplus government food is called) to stay alive. Many of the unemployed have now exhausted their "rockin'-chair money," the mountaineer's vivid phrase for unemployment pay.

On a counter in the O. A. Dunbar & Sons General Store on Kelly's Creek was a cardboard box with "Food Donation for Molly Workman" printed in crayon on its side. Molly, an elderly woman who lives with her daughter and five children in a three-room shack they rent near the store, was in bed when we visited her. "What we need is food in this house," she said.

On the thin walls of the crowded, squalid room were pictures of Jesus and His disciples, clipped from the religious calendars which are a favorite of the Bible Belt. Wrapped in dirty cloths on a bed in the adjoining room was a small baby. The bones in his forehead protruded unnaturally when he cried, the skin tightening over his long, thin face.

Rev. Ralph Keenan, pastor of Ward Community Church and operator of a small service station at Cedar Grove, leaned on the car window and ran his fingers through his gray hair. "It couldn't be any worse than it is at the present time," he said. "Even with the welfare, people aren't getting enough to eat. If nothing is done, you're going to drive them to stealing."

An upsurge in crime has been reported throughout the coal country. In a recent six-month period, Charleston police revealed that 1,500 parking meters had been robbed. U. S. Treasury agents are working overtime to keep up with one of the region's favorite modes of free enterprise—moonshining and bootlegging. More than 200 inmates at the West Virginia Penetentiary are eligible for parole but can't be released because no jobs are available.

A frustrating interplay of such forces as obsolete agriculture, depleted timber resources, a high birth rate, rapid mechanization of coal mining, the declining demand for coal, short-sighted and selfish political-business leadership, and scarcity of industrial jobs have coalesced to create the chronic poverty of the Appalachian South. In this predominantly rural area, with few cities over 50,000, too many children are born for too few jobs. In 1950, about 20 percent of West Virginia's families had three or more children under eighteen, as compared with 12 percent of the families in Illinois.

Employment in the coal mines has declined at least 50 percent since 1950. In West Virginia, the nation's largest producer of bituminous coal, machines and shrinking markets have reduced the number of miners from 125,000 in 1948 to about 47,000 today. Few jobs are available for these displaced miners; there are more factories in Cincinnati, for instance, than in all East Kentucky.

Writing in *Farm Policy Forum*, Dr. William H. Nicholls, professor of economics at Vanderbilt University, traced the historical reasons for the Appalachian South's chronic backwardness:

. . . An early date of settlement followed by a long period of economic and cultural isolation, brought the establishment of a pioneer pattern of small subsistence farming which has been very slow to change. . . . Frequently, such communities also suffered from the political neglect of their transportation and educational needs by their own state governments, which tended to be dominated by the interests of the larger and wealthier landowners in more favored parts of their respective states.

This analysis snugly fits West Virginia, which has a larger portion of mountain counties than any other Appalachian state. While the state ranks fifteenth among states in basic wealth added to the nation, it is thirty-eighth in per capita income. As a producer of raw materials which, for the most part, profit out-of-state firms, it fails to reap the advantages of school and road funds which ordinarily flow from finished products. And West Virginia never has had a full-fledged severance tax on its abundant natural resources.

Meanwhile, the familiar poverty-breeding pressures of population and unemployment—intensified by the decline of traditional jobs in the mining and timber industries—have pushed an estimated 800,000 mountain people onto the highways in the past decade alone. Most migrated North, but some turned toward growing Southern cities, such as Atlanta, to stake their claims for a better life. In 1950, an estimated 275,000 Kentuckians and 103,000 West Virginians were living in Ohio alone. They've been settling in Cincinnati, just across the state line from Kentucky, for the past thirty years. H. L. Mencken wrote of the horrors of hillbilly migration northward to work in defense plants during World War II.

To these "poor, proud and primitive" people (as they appear to city observers), their mountain homeland, as contrasted with the prosperous America they hear of elsewhere, offers them only a bleak future of grinding poverty. So they head North to knock on the doors of industrial prosperity. Then, when prosperity stumbles in Chicago or Cleveland, many of them periodically pack up and head home. They move in with relatives or set up housekeeping in abandoned shacks, tightening their belts to live off rockin'-chair money and mollygrub until another recession ends. But some, with acquired skills and years of seniority providing them a measure of job security, have become solid citizens of Midwestern cities, where their recently arrived cousins are considered alarming social problems.

This nomadic existence causes heartbreak and headaches for all concerned—the nomads, the industrial centers to which they migrate, and the impoverished communities to which they return during hard times.

When stagnating economies force mountaineers to abandon their mountain homes for urban industrial jobs, they leave behind a way of life radically different from the one the city offers them. Their semi-Southern accents and strange behavior brand them as "hillbillies" in cities always eager to exploit new arrivals. Although white Protestants of old American stock, they face the same prejudice that traditionally has made life uncomfortable for strangers in new lands.

Dr. Roscoe Griffin, sociologist at Berea College in Kentucky, has sketched a profile of the typical mountaineer. From his writings emerges the portrait of a man who takes life easy, adjusting to its demands rather than striving to master his environment. Fear of failure doesn't disturb him. He prefers "eternal salvation" to earthly rewards, naturally, since few of the latter are available to him in his mountain homeland. A stubborn individualist who respects differences in others, he reacts violently when his own rights are infringed.

There's nothing wrong with hillbillies—a description which mountain people loathe—that a strong dose of equal opportunity wouldn't cure. Applying every yardstick of social well-being, their Appalachian homeland emerges a sordid blemish on the balance sheet of the wealthiest nation in history. You name it—schools, health services, housing, per capita income—and the Appalachian South stacks up as an underdeveloped region which produces citizens incapable of realizing their human potential in the complex twentieth century. Their stunted growth not only saps the vitality of the mid-South, but also weakens the nation. Unprepared migrants become burdens on cities already bulging with social problems. Today's inferiorly educated children of Appalachia are Ohio's citizens of tomorrow.

Many economists believe migration from the Appalachian South will continue even if the region becomes more industrialized. With mechanization increasingly eliminating coal miners and marginal farmers, enough new jobs won't be created to satisfy the demands of a traditionally high birth rate.

Although some continuing migration may be desirable, what the Appalachian South desperately needs is a domestic Point Four program combining federal, state and local resources. Only with federal help—similar to the economic aid Uncle Sam sends to underdeveloped nations abroad—can the region receive its share of the national wealth. The eighty-fifth Congress took a step in this direction when it passed a bill designed to help chronically depressed areas finance industrial development. But President Eisenhower vetoed the measure. A repeat performance, with even less support in the supposedly more liberal current Congress, is shaping up. Senator Douglas (D.-Ill.) reintroduced a $390 million measure to aid depressed areas, but it barely squeezed through the Senate, 49 to 46, almost beaten by that ancient killer of liberal dreams—the familiar coalition of Republican and Southern conservatives. Ironically, the South probably would have profited most from the bill. If the House approves a similar measure, President Eisenhower is expected to veto it again. He commended aid to depressed areas costing only $53 million.

Depressed areas such as the Appalachian South also need much more generous federal grants to improve their public schools and highways and to provide better health, library and employment-service facilities. Federally-subsidized research into coal's vast potentialities, such as chemical conversion into synthetic fuels, and Congressional adoption of a sensible national fuels policy to give coal an even break with other fuels, also would ultimately help the coal country.

State and regional development commissions have been organized to woo industries into the region. The most extensive effort is probably under way in Kentucky, where rural sociologists and the State Department of Economic Development have begun a comprehensive program aimed at rebuilding rural communities and attracting private industry. The Kentucky emphasis is on people and their needs rather than factories at any cost.

A $250,000 study of the Appalachian South now under way may be helpful in developing a program to aid mountain migrants and in determining the direction of a domestic Point Four program. Financed through the Ford Foundation through Berea College, it is the first comprehensive survey aimed at determining the needs of the region's eight million people.

The Council of the Southern Mountains, the only region-wide organization dedicated to improving the quality of life throughout the nine-state area, recently called upon the region's governors to establish an interstate commission to study problems unique to the Appalachian South and to recommend solutions on a regional basis.

The achievements of TVA indicate what could be done if federal resources were used to help develop the entire region. By following TVA's example, a Point Four assault on the region's poverty could bring a better life to the long-ignored people of Appalachia. Migration could be reduced and in future years mountaineer migrants would cease to become costly social problems for American industrial centers.

The alternatives are clear—either mountaineers will continue to go to industry or industry must come to the mountains. In the long run, bringing suitable industries to the Appalachian South would be much less expensive, both in dollars and human misery.

IN HAZARD
Dan Wakefield

I would just as soon forget about Hazard, Kentucky, a desire I share with a number of its unemployed residents, the large U. S. coal companies, the United Mine Workers of America, and the Federal Government. I went there in late March for a large national magazine on an assignment that did not, for innumerable and irrelevant reasons, work out. I was there for four days—rather longer than most visiting journalists, sociology students, or candidates for elective office usually stay before issuing authoritative reports on the place (twenty-four hours is par for this course)—and I have not been so happy to leave a strange town since the time I departed from Montgomery, Alabama, after being set upon by Confederate patriots following a White Citizens' Council meeting.

The effect of automation on the coal industry is not the only burden that has come to rest on the weary, stripped hills of Hazard and the surrounding countryside, but it is the latest and most basic of the problems that have earned the whole Appalachian region the title of "the nation's number one depressed area." Appalachia—which Thomas B. Morgan described as our own "underdeveloped country" in an excellent brief account of the place in *Look* last winter—is an 80,000-square mile mountain region stretching south and west from Virginia

From *Commentary*, September 1963; © 1963 by Dan Wakefield. Used by permission of the author.

through Kentucky, North Carolina, Tennessee, and into the upper tips of Georgia and Alabama. Long geographically landlocked by the mountains and poor roads, and largely known to the outside world as the home of colorful mountaineers or hillbillies, Appalachia is more its own place than a part of the states through which it extends. Hazard and surrounding Perry County (both of which are named after Oliver Hazard Perry, and not, as some imaginative journalists have written, after the "hazards" of coal-mining) present neither its worst nor best face, but are representative of the region.

Hazard became the center of attention in Appalachia's troubles because of a wildcat strike of coal-miners that erupted throughout the Appalachian fields at the end of summer in 1962. The strike—which was discouraged by the United Mine Workers, the union to which the majority of the men belonged—petered out in most places, but in four or five counties of eastern Kentucky, the strikers managed to keep going, sent out "roving pickets" in automobiles to shut down mines, and called weekly meetings in Hazard that are still being held. What has since become known as "the Hazard strike" drew special attention because of its accompanying violence, which of course was perpetrated by those now nationally famous "extremists on both sides" who are having such a field day in our moderate land. Both striking miners and coal operators—as well as people known to be supporting one side or the other—have been victims of arson, beatings, and shootings, and have had their homes, cars, and equipment dynamited. By December of last year there had been fifty such acts of violence, after which officials stopped counting.

Unemployment is ordinarily a dull subject, but violence titillates everyone, and I imagine it was this aspect of the Hazard situation that drew so many of us reporters—like vultures circling in on the wounded town—to what had previously been an unknown place. By the time I arrived, Hazard had been visited by representatives of such assorted media as the *New York Times*, the Washington *Post*, CBS, *Life*, *Tass*, *Newsweek*, FM station WBAI of New York, a West German documentary film crew (later rumored to be really *East* German), and something called *Progressive Labor*, which published a special issue largely devoted to the "class struggle" in Hazard. There had also been several people posing as representatives of these and other media, including a man claiming to be from *Newsweek* who preceded a man who really *was* from *Newsweek*, and a girl who preceded me claiming to be from the magazine I had been sent by. When I reached Hazard, confusion was at a maximum and hospitality at a minimum.

The first thing I did after registering at Hazard's Grand Hotel on Main Street ("a phone in every room") was to call Fred Luigart, a reporter and Hazard resident who is Eastern Kentucky Bureau Chief for the Louisville *Courier-Journal*. The first thing he did, with apologies, was call the New York office of the magazine that had sent me to make sure I really was the person I said I was. After satisfying himself that I "checked out," Luigart performed the essential service of taking me around to the leading local officials and participants in the battle and personally vouching for my credentials. Hurrying along behind his brisk pace as we went from stores to offices to homes through a rainfall that made the drab town even grayer and muddier, I felt rather like a U.N. mediator must feel when he comes to some remote troubled land whose warring factions have long since grown disillusioned with the aid of outsiders.

Late in the afternoon we tracked down Berman Gibson, the principal leader of the strike, and though he was glad to see me—for the strikers, unlike the owners, want all the outside publicity they can get—he, too, was suspicious because I had met the town business, police, and civic leaders, the hostile "other side" in the battle. "Oh yes, "he burst out later in redfaced indignation, "you see them folks on Main Street, they'll wine ye and dine ye and show ye a good time." He hadn't of course considered the fact that just as he knew I had been talking with them, they knew I was talking with him and his troops, and were not about to wine and dine me—in some cases weren't even about to talk to me. (At one point during my stay, a businessman noted some mud on my shoes as a sign of my having consorted with the strikers.) Going back and forth from the town to the union hall where the strikers had their headquarters, or from union hall to offices or homes of business people, was nearly as tense a business as going back and forth between Negro and white communities in Alabama or Mississippi during a racial crisis. (You give the address, the cab driver makes that slow turn of the neck to look you over, perhaps spits his comment out the window, and grinds his gears in a way that suggests he would like to be grinding you.)

That evening was the weekly meeting of the strikers at the union hall (the local, made up of retired UMW men, was still allowing the strikers to use their hall, but later, in April, town officials discovered a "fire hazard" and the strikers had to be turned out). The union hall was a building as barren as the brown hills seen through its windows, and decorated mainly with a large glowering portrait of John L. Lewis. The strike was in its sixth month by then and everyone was tired, including Gibson, who pounded the table as he had so many times before and shouted against the injustice of "the coal operators, keeping the poor people down—them with two Cadillacs in their driveway and kids here going without any shooooooes!"

Yet it hadn't been a lack of shoes or the money to buy them that originally triggered the strike. Wages had been falling steadily in the area and there were fewer jobs, but these conditions seemed inevitable in Appalachia's sick coal industry, and the miners had not protested against them. What, then, caused the strike? The best answer I could find to that question was in the story of Riley Hicks, a sixty-year old coal-miner, who came up after the meeting to talk to me about what had been going on. Like many of the men of this region, Hicks has lived and worked as a miner here all his life. Even though he was getting only $10 and $12 a day, instead of the union scale of $24.25, he did not quit his job. But in August of 1962 he was one of some 4,000 miners in the Appalachian fields, most of them older men, who without warning received a letter from the United Mine Workers Welfare and Retirement Fund informing them that the "hospital card" which entitled them and their families to free medical treatment would no longer be valid after September 1, 1962. The letter explained that these medical benefits were being taken away from the men because their employers were not paying into the welfare fund the royalty of 40 cents for every ton of coal produced, as provided by the union contract. Riley Hicks went to his boss of thirteen years, six months, and three days, and when the boss said he couldn't pay the royalty and still stay in business, Hicks walked off the job. So did hundreds of others like him in eastern Kentucky, Tennessee, and finally, West Virginia.

More followed a few months later when the union announced that it was not only taking hospital benefits away from its members, but their hospitals as well. In 1955 the UMW Welfare Fund had built ten modern, superbly staffed and equipped hospitals in the Appalachian coal region where adequate medical facilities had not previously been available. Last fall, after cancelling the hospital cards of so many of its members in the area, the union announced that not enough members were eligible for treatment any longer to justify the operation of all the hospitals. The union gave notice that it was offering for sale four of the hospitals in eastern Kentucky, including the one at Hazard, and would have to close them down if they were not purchased by July 1, 1963. The Presbyterian church led efforts to raise funds for purchasing the hospitals, and just before the July 1 deadline a grant from the federal Area Redevelopment Association and an appropriation from the Kentucky state legislature guaranteed the continued operation of the four hospitals for at least another year. The union is completely out of the picture now, and the hospitals will be administered by a non-partisan Appalachian Regional Hospital Association.

The Fund and hospitals were not only a matter of security to the members but a matter of pride—created out of their own sweat to adorn the barren landscape. The emotions of many of the men about "their" hospitals were voiced by "Preacher Bill" Bailey, one of several lay ministers among the striking miners, who rolled up his sleeves and shouted to the weekly meeting at the union hall: "I helped build that hospital in Hazard, and now I can't even go there and get a pill!"

But most of the strikers are reluctant to blame the union for taking back these blessings so briefly bestowed. The UMW, after all, once brought these men the only benefits they have known in a lifetime of grueling work, and even though the union says that it cannot support their strike, their loyalty is still in most cases unshakable. "We can't blame the union for this," Gibson told the strike meeting as he so often had before. "It's our fault for letting this happen, letting these operators get away without paying royalty or scale," and the men called back, "That's right, our fault!"

It is almost as if they saw the strike and the sacrifice attendant upon it as an atonement for their sins, a gesture to propitiate the distant union god, so that he might finally smile upon them and grant their plea, which is, as Gibson puts it to answering applause, "to get the union back like it once was." Yet it is hardly the fault of these men that union contracts were not enforced and that the operators were able to slide out from under them as times got worse. In many cases the men knew that payment of scale and royalty by these small fringe operators would mean closing down and the end of their jobs, and they preferred working for low, non-union wages to not working at all.

Who, then, can be blamed for this mess? Prevailing opinion in Hazard was most aptly summed up by Rader "Preacher" Smith, another miner-minister, who told a visiting reporter that "some kinda something has gone wrong here that the men haven't got a fair deal from someplace."

The real forces behind the upheaval in the Appalachian coal fields are vast, complex, and locally invisible; but invisible dragons cannot be slain and men in crisis must go forth against some tangible enemy. How can a working man fight automation? In the first crisis of the Industrial Revolution, the weavers smashed the looms; but the looms in this case—the new machines that can mine hundreds of tons of coal in a day—are not to be found in Hazard. One of the main reasons the coal industry is sick in this region is that the seams of coal in the Appalachian fields are generally too thin to be mined by the huge new machines that are operating in western Kentucky and the northern coal fields. So in the absence of machines to blow up, the men are blowing up—and in turn being blown up by—their fellow citizens. And in the absence of the real villains, villainous roles have been assigned by each of the two "sides": the ones who have jobs and ones who don't.

The warlike rhetoric from each of the sides, flavored with the Biblical imagery of a God-fearing region, is as bitter as any that ever accompanied the old family feuds for which these mountains are famous. "Oh, I've lived in many a town," Berman Gibson says, pacing the platform in the meeting hall, "but I've never seen one as bad as this. The way this thing is, I'd like to see fire and brimstone rain down on Hazard and wipe it all out." The women gasp and say, "Oh no!" as if they feared that his word might release the fury then and there, and he says, "Oh yes, my house with it, yessir, my house too!" Nor is the bitterness limited to the miners. A successful local businessman told me that a bunch of troublemakers had caused all the trouble and that "There'll have to be some funerals and fires before this thing is settled."

But the funerals of a few "troublemakers"—whether they are rich or poor—will hardly bring relief from the problems plaguing this region. When one of the miners, who is personally aware of the sentiments of some of the enemy camp (his home was dynamited), assured a meeting of the strikers that "They can't kill us all, there's too many of us," they chanted back their "Amens" and "Yessirs" with confidence. "Us" doesn't include only the strikers, whose numbers dwindle and rise as some go back to work to make enough to lay off again; nor does it mean only the miners of this region whose working conditions and pay have grown steadily worse. It means all these plus the many more able-bodied men left in the area who either cannot find work at all or who must work for pay that doesn't suffice to keep them and their families in food and shoes. The strike, with its drama and violence, became an outlet for and a means of protest against the bitter frustrations that have been building up here for a decade. In fact, a few of the men who have joined the strikers and their erratic picket lines are not even miners, and never have been. They are men who have long been out of work, some of them high-school dropouts who took all their savings and pinched their way to Detroit or Chicago, where as "hillbillies" they got into trouble in the strange urban slums and then returned more broke and hopeless than before.

Each of the men who gathered those long afternoons at the union hall to sit and talk and boil coffee on the potbellied stove had his own story to tell, and most of them were eager to tell it to anyone who wanted to listen. In general they tended to be older men, but there were some young ones, like Manuel Stidhan, who at thirty-three had been to Detroit but came back because this was home. "I've worked in these mines around here for $4 a day," he told me, "and that wasn't 1930, brother, that was 1961. You hear these fellas talk about the 'old days,' but I want to tell you the old days are back." One man known as "Hoss," toothless and in his late fifties, had left his job when the strike first began, and when I asked why, he paused for a moment and then said frankly: "Well, I tell you boy, I've worked in these mines all my life, and to tell you the truth, I was tired." Another miner who had a wife and three children showed me his last paycheck stubs for $10 a day: "It's tooth 'n' toenail just gettin' by on that, and without the hospital card you can't make it." He said he'd worked in Utah for a while on a farm and "I dunno why I ever come back to this dry old mountain. Way things is, I'd like to get me in one of them jets and go, far as it'd take me outa here—anywhere."

Though not by jet, a million people with similar sentiments have left Appalachia since 1950, twelve thousand of them (out of a 1950 total of 46,500) from Hazard's Perry County. It is sometimes said here that

"Them with get up and go, got up and went." Those who have stayed behind are mostly the older men, many of them men with no other skills but "swingin' a pick and slingin' a shovel"—skills for which there is constantly less demand and less pay. In eastern Kentucky the number of workers employed in coal-mining—the area's main industry —has dropped from 57,000 in 1950 to 25,000.

The only alternative to "funerals and fires" their more affluent fellow citizens seem to have found so far is the hope that more of the miners will decide to leave. Mrs. Martha Nolan, the business manager and unofficial "spokesman" of the Hazard *Herald*, a woman sincere in her prejudices, who was born in these mountains and is dedicated to them by her own lights, expressed a widely held sentiment in the business community when she said of the strikers: "These people are like a cancer on us. I believe a great many of these fellas are on the picket line because of their unskills for other jobs. They've picked up the torch for jobs that just aren't here."

While Mrs. Nolan sat in the small front office of the *Herald* discussing the local "cancer" with me, a man came in to announce that "the Walters boys were dynamited last night." The Walters boys, I was told, are two brothers who own several of the hundreds of small truck mines that are now the principal type of operation in the Hazard coal fields. Eager to see what a local battleground looked like, and where the "coal kings" lived, I accepted Mrs. Nolan's invitation to go see the damage.

The Walters lived a few miles out of town just off the main road in small-frame one-story houses that could hardly be described as the grand homes of wealthy business tycoons. The brothers are fairly typical of the operators in these fields today; they are sons of a retired member of the UMW and former miners themselves who scraped a little money together after the war and "went into the mining business." There were no Cadillacs in the driveway. A small creek strewn with garbage ran in front of the house, and a muddy path served as a sidewalk. A workman was putting new glass in a broken window and hunks and splinters of shattered glass sparkled in the yard. Mrs. Nolan knocked at the door of one of the houses and it was partially opened by a young woman wearing slacks and a sweater who held her arm protectively around the shoulders of a small boy. The woman, Mrs. Luke Walters, explained that the house of her brother-in-law, Mark Walters, next door, had suffered the most damage. The blast had shattered the glass in the window of the room where Mr. and Mrs. Walters were sleeping, and only a drawn venetian blind had saved them from injury. Mrs. Nolan expressed her sympathy, and Mrs. Walters nodded. "It's gettin' so you're scared just to go to bed at night," she said.

I didn't sleep too well myself in my room at the Grand Hotel that night. The sense of crisis was heightened by the casual presence of more guns than I have ever seen outside of a military installation. The state of Kentucky outlaws the possession of a "concealed deadly weapon," but it is legal to have guns that are not concealed, and in the homes both of owners and miners, guns were lying everywhere—on coffee tables and on the tops of television sets—as well as on the seats of cars. The local clergyman seemed to be right: this conflict was "pure war."

It is, however, a peculiarly American war. The *New York Times* has reported that in Hazard "the class struggle is a reality," to which I would add that it is also an illusion. One of the incidental tragedies of the situation in Hazard is that a complex upheaval whose origins lie outside the region should have been interpreted in the "class-struggle" terms of which the *Times* speaks, in an attempt, perhaps, to make it more comprehensible and more familiar—a re-enactment of the battles of the 30's when the poor miners were rising up against the rich mine owners. The wrong people are being fought here for the wrong reasons, and perhaps even for the wrong goals.

This, then, was the general picture I got during my stay in Hazard. But there are also things to be learned from looking at some of the people who have been caught up in the conflict and who have a special interest in the course it will take. Here are five of them:

Harley Caldwell lives in Hazard with his wife on a UMW pension that was cut, as they all were several years ago, from $100 to $75 a month. Caldwell is a proud, straight-backed man who was born in Perry County, worked thirty-five years in the mines, and married and raised three children here. The children are grown and gone to distant states, and the Caldwells live quietly in a small immaculate house, saving a little out of their pension to indulge once a year in a fishing trip. When the trouble began last August, Caldwell was one of a number of retired miners who contributed what money they could from their pensions to help the strikers, wrote away to men in other locals to ask for help, and collected food and clothing for the families of the men who had left their jobs.

Caldwell does not blame the union for the current problems, any more than do most of these men, who credit what little they have from a life of hard labor to the UMW. "If it wasn't for the unions," Caldwell told me, "I couldn't have built myself a small house and educated my family. When I started in the mines I loaded coal for 22¢ a ton—you had to load ten tons of coal to make $2.20 a day. Out of that you had to buy your own powder to shoot the coal and your own carbide and lamp. When the union first came in we got a 15 percent over-all raise with the contracts and fringe benefits, and it kept going up till the scale is $24.25 a day now."

He explained that his own local, which is made up now of retired men, "is sympathetic with the pickets as long as they're lawful. We gave them moral and financial support and we still do." But Caldwell differs with some of the strike leaders, for he feels that any money coming in ought to go "for food, not for lawyers' fees." As one of the fund-raisers for the strikers, he has been contacted by people in New York, Chicago, and Philadelphia offering help, and though grateful for it, he feels that "some of these people who have come in here are using the miners for guinea pigs, as scapegoats for their own ends. I won't accept anything unless I know where it comes from. I have to be thoroughly convinced of that first—I wouldn't suck an egg to find out whether it was rotten."

Milton Rosen lives in New York City, where he edits a monthly called *Progressive Labor*. I don't know whether or not he has actually been to Hazard, but he has written to the editors of the Hazard *Herald* offering to come to Hazard and "debate publicly—in front of the miners—your alleged prolabor record." Mr. Rosen's angry letter was in answer to a story in the *Herald* called "Communism Comes to Kentucky," in which it was alleged that "Reds" had moved into Hazard to aid the striking miners. Mr. Rosen was incensed at this charge because representatives of the Progressive Labor Movement had been in Hazard to help the strikers, and *Progressive Labor* had put out an issue which had been distributed there to explain the true meaning of the strike to the unsophisticated townspeople. As Mr. Rosen explained in his letter to the editors of what he called "Your rag," "The coal kings have provoked the strike. . . ." He was angered by the "hypocrisy" of the *Herald*, assured them that *Progressive Labor* was not trying to mislead the strikers, and was disgusted with the charge that Communists had come to Kentucky.

Where, indeed, did the editors of the *Herald* get such an idea? Perhaps it was from reading the January, 1963, issue of *Progressive Labor* —the one that was distributed in Hazard—for inside, on a page called "PL Action," was a reprint of a story from the University of North Carolina's *Daily Tarheel* which attributed the following direct quote to Mr. Rosen in a speech before the "New Left Club" in Chapel Hill:

"We American Communists are few in number and the stakes are high," said Rosen, "but if we are to take advantage of the state of discontent and the injustices in the U. S., we must press the socialistic movement at all costs. We must maintain the outlook of smashing the ruling party."

The intrusion of an element so identified into the already greatly confused Hazard mess is unfortunate, for it enables the enemies of the strike to call the whole thing a "Communist plot," an interpretation as erroneous, albeit as convenient, as *Progressive Labor*'s view of the troubles as a class war precipitated by the local "coal kings." It has also created factions among the miners themselves—who of course don't want to be called "Reds"—at a time when they need all the cooperation and mutual trust they can muster. I heard the miners discuss this issue at their meeting, and most of them had some trouble even pronouncing the word "Communist." It came out something like "Commus." One angry man said: "Hell no, we're not any Commuses, we're not smart enough!"—a statement which brought gasps and cries of "No, don't say that" from the women. Most of them have learned their lessons well enough to refuse help from the Reds—but how are they to know who is who and what is what in the sudden inundation of parties, organizations, publications, and committees with their strange and confusing names?

By the time I arrived in Hazard, the town had already been visited by representatives of *Progressive Labor*; the Young People's Socialist League; the Socialist Party (one YPSL complained that an SP man had been sent to make sure that the YPSL people would come back with the right political interpretation of the situation); several New York union locals; various student groups from various colleges; and a couple of actors from the Living Theatre. In New York, the General Strike for

Peace, an anti-bomb group, had held a rally for the striking miners of Hazard at the Living Theatre, featuring a showing of Eisenstein's movie *Strike*. A young lady activist who had been to Hazard explained that it wasn't "quite" like the film.

The term "coal mine" elicits in the breast of the average liberal the same thrill that the word "Polaris" brings to the contemporary right-winger, and Hazard has accordingly given many liberals a nostalgic cause and a chance to get out the guitar and sing about the miners again. (*Progressive Labor* has reprinted some of the words of a 30's song, "Which Side Are You On?" written about the struggle in Harlan County, which contains such timely lyrics as: "You are either a union man or a thug for J. H. Blair.") Yet in spite of their illusions, and in spite of the confusion they have brought, all the groups mentioned above also brought food and clothes and money to the Hazard miners: and who else came to this far-off province to offer them any help?

Berman Gibson had never been outside Appalachia until by default and determination he became the principal leader of this protest. Now he has spoken at Cornell University, attended a Teamsters' square dance in Brooklyn, and generally expanded his cultural horizons. His blunt and angry speech-making has won food and clothing and money from political groups as well as from sympathetic locals of the Teamsters, Steelworkers, and Longshoremen. He has somehow held the thing together, maintaining his leadership over the "moderates" who want to give food and clothing to everyone who needs it instead of just strikers, as well as over the "radicals" who want to bring in Jimmy Hoffa instead of waiting any longer for the ghost of John L. Lewis to appear.

Gibson is a big man with slightly protruding upper teeth and an ex-panding waistline, a man whose rages are brief and quickly change to smiles and back-slapping. He faces several dangers as leader of the strike: one is that he or his home will be blown up, and another is that he will be dressed up in blue jeans and a miner's cap and paraded through colleges and rallies to the tune of guitars and forgotten songs, a kind of living relic to be patted and admired and misrepresented.

Gibson comes not so much out of the mines as out of the transient underside of American life that is so seldom written or talked about and so often experienced. He has moved from town to town in the Appalachians, working as a farmer, a miner, and a truck driver; his last job was driving an ice-cream truck for the Dixie Bell dairy in Hazard. In some places Gibson has got into "labor trouble," as in Carr Creek when his house was shot at during a strike, and his son, a star basketball player, used to drive home from games with an axe on the front seat of the car beside him for protection—a bit of Americana that surely deserves preservation. But towns wanted the Gibsons because of the son's ability at basketball, and his performance on the court for Hazard High School made the name Gibson well-loved by all. Then he went off to college (the University of Kentucky having given him a scholarship) and the Gibson name became known in a different way as his father kept attending the strikers' meetings, where he talked loud and angrily and found that men would listen. Gibson's daughter, a high-school cheerleader, comes to the meetings and cheers for her father on the platform just as she does for her brother on the basketball court.

Dewey Daniel is president of the People's Bank in Hazard and served as state Republican chairman for Kentucky when John Sherman Cooper ran for the Senate. He is obviously a man who moves with ease in the great world beyond the mountains, but his cosmopolitanism seems hardly to have tainted his social views, which are mostly reminiscent of *Dead Souls*. When I talked with him, Mr. Daniel seemed amazed by the fact that after a CBS-TV program on Hazard (which he felt was distorted) people throughout the country sent food and money and clothes to the poor. It especially chagrined him that a Hollywood studio had sent in a plane-load of toys at Christmas. "Can you imagine," he asked, "giving toys to those mountain kids?"

Mr. Daniel has helped raise money to save a small charity hospital in the town which may also close (its load was very heavy, for the union hospital did not take charity patients), but like most of the town businessmen, he appeared unconcerned about the probable loss of the large, modern Miners' Hospital. "If they built too expensive a hospital, that's their problem. This town was here before the hospital was, and it will be here after it goes."

Mr. Daniel was the only Hazard businessman who talked with me openly and pleasantly, for he was obviously indifferent to what I would later report. "I don't care what you say about me," he remarked with a smile, knowing that no comment I could make would shake his place in the world, which is president of the bank in Hazard. I left him with a certain admiration, in spite of myself.

Lee Crutchfield, befitting his station as president of the local Chamber of Commerce and Cadillac-Chevrolet dealer of Hazard, is a businessman more in the modern manner. Unlike Mr. Daniel, he was disturbed by the bad "image" Hazard had been getting in the press, and he assured me that the story had been blown up out of all proportion. Sitting in his office below a picture of President Kennedy, Crutchfield spoke with measured control and a fixed smile. "You can find anything here you look for, Mister Reporter—the worst squalor or the finest luxury." He insisted that not even the local "labor trouble" was unusual—his own sales, for instance, had been "about average." As for the shootings, burnings, and dynamitings: "Why, the same thing happens right off Broadway. Besides, these dynamitings haven't destroyed a single percentage point of productive capacity. It's pretty normal for the course." Smiling firmly, Mr. Crutchfield assured me that Hazard was "just an average American community." He may be right about that, more than most of us would like to think.

The epilogue to this story is set in Washington, that remote command post where our leaders deliberate upon the Big Picture. There the great international headquarters of the unions sit in grand testimony to the triumph of the working man, while inside, staffs of researchers produce statistics showing the benefits won in the years before the headquarters were built, and other researchers worry about such current problems as the use of leisure time. There seem to be no working men in Washington, only reporters, researchers, and congressmen—a circumstance which no doubt gives to the high-level work of the labor leaders a sense of reality that might otherwise be lacking.

At the offices of the United Mine Workers' *Journal* I was greeted by a man who did not wish to be identified by name but only as a "Union Spokesman." The Union Spokesman said that "under present conditions" he saw no way for the union to back the striking miners in Hazard. I asked if there was any way for the union to reconsider its decision to close the hospitals; after all, even though the UMW Fund was losing money in that particular area it was profiting in other places. (The UMW Welfare and Retirement Fund comes to more than $100 million, and the union has another $100 million in its own treasury.) "We are not," the Spokesman answered, "in the hospital business." I then asked him if the union had undertaken any kind of job retraining program for those of its members who had been put out of work by its own proud policy of bringing automation to the coal fields. "No," said the Spokesman, "we believe that is the function of the Federal Government."

Over at the "Federal Government," the replies were more elaborate. The Kennedy administration's answer to the problem represented by Hazard is a new branch of the Department of Commerce called the Area Redevelopment Administration. I met with two ARA spokesmen in an office decorated with a wall map of the nation on which the depressed areas were colored in red. The red part seemed to extend over what I would judge to be close to "a third of a nation," and of course took in all of Appalachia. I asked one of the spokesmen if he had ever been to Hazard. "God no," he replied, "those places depress me." However, a second spokesman said that he had recently been near Hazard along with the head of the agency on a visit to Paintsville, Kentucky— but first he sketched in the Big Picture.

The ARA, in the hope of creating new jobs, makes grants and loans to businesses in depressed areas, and also carries on a program of job retraining. As of last spring, a total of 18,000 men throughout the entire nation had been retrained under the program. An indication of the local impact can be seen from the fact that in Kentucky, where 65,800 were unemployed at the time, the ARA had spent $4.3 million in grants and loans to businesses which will create (eventually) an estimated 1,225 jobs, and had retrained 2,000 workers for new jobs. Of the 2,000 workers thus retrained in Kentucky, 1,000 had been unable to find the new jobs they had been retrained for. In Perry County, where 14.2 percent of the work force was unemployed that month—roughly two and one half times the national average—the ARA had created no new jobs and provided job retraining for exactly forty-five people. The ARA officials seemed pleased with their program, though as one of them noted, "I couldn't say in good conscience we have made a dent in the problem. The main effect so far has been psychological." A non-psychological estimate of the effects was made by Fred Luigart, who after spending several hours questioning the ARA officials in Paintsville, was entirely confirmed in his earlier judgment of their work: "You can quote me as saying that the Kennedy program in eastern Kentucky is a total failure."

The most interesting thing I learned on a visit to the ARA office was that the agency is very hopeful about the future of one of our fastest growing industries: tourism. One of the spokesmen told me that in five years, tourism would be a bigger industry in the U. S. than agriculture. "You see," he explained, "we really are an affluent society, and if only the affluent people will take their vacations in the depressed areas, things will get spread around." As it happens, several businessmen I had met in Hazard also had this idea, and in anticipation of the first modern highway that will soon be cut through the eastern Kentucky Mountains, they had already formed a corporation to build luxury motels and other such lures around the town. The corporation is called "The Magic Mountain."

You ought to see those old deserted coal mines in the Spring. . . .

THE LATEST REDISCOVERY OF APPALACHIA
Robert F. Munn

Most of us who dwell in Appalachia are by now aware of the widespread national interest in our region. This interest is all the more impressive because it is so sudden. Just a few years ago, the outside world could hardly have cared less. The average citizen barely knew we existed. Even the better educated viewed the region as little more than a setting for moonshining, feuds and Little Abner. The federal government was only dimly aware of the area, while the great private foundations never heard of it. Scholars ignored us and journalists found us dull.

How things have changed! Now the region's trials and tribulations are prime copy. Television producers vie with one another in ferreting out the most woebegotten of our citizens to place before their cameras. The *New York Times* and the *Wall Street Journal* publish "think" pieces about us, and there is no end to non-think pieces. Indeed, the region's more comfortable hotels now enjoy a brisk trade in earnest journalists.

Of course, this new-found interest in Appalachia is not confined to television and the popular press. Far from it. The world of learning has also discovered us, and the region has begun to attract the attention of

From *Mountain Life and Work*, Fall 1965. Used by permission of the author.

some of our most distinguished and heavily subsidized social scientists. Most amazing of all, people even want to give us money. The private foundations are spending very substantial sums in the area. And of course the federal government—for the first time in history—is favoring the region with an impressive flow of gifts, grants and other goodies.

All told, the level of interest and even activity has reached amazing proportions. There are now Commissions, Centers, Governors' Conferences, Seminars and Lord knows how many federal offices with the announced purpose of doing something for or to Appalachia.

It is certainly not our purpose to depreciate the importance and potential effectiveness of the plans and programs which are announced almost daily. However—just because all this sudden attention is so heady and exciting—it may be useful to point out that we are experiencing, not the first, but at least the fourth rediscovery of Appalachia by the American people.

The first major rediscovery of Appalachia was a literary one. In the post-Civil War period the reading public began to demonstrate an insatiable fondness for regional novels, especially those featuring quaint dialects and exotic customs. What better source for both than the coves and cabins of the Southern Mountains?

By 1870 there appeared the first tricklet of what was to become a mighty flood of mountain novels. By 1900 they were appearing at the rate of six or eight a year. These novels based on life in Appalachia were enormously popular; they sold by the million. The most successful author, John Fox, Jr., performed the remarkable feat of producing within five years two all-time best sellers: *The Little Shepherd of Kingdom Come* (1903) and *The Trail of the Lonesome Pine* (1908). However, this literary rediscovery was relatively short-lived and the popularity of the mountain novel waned as quickly as it had arisen.

The second rediscovery of Appalachia started shortly after the first and was to some extent stimulated by it. In 1895, Dr. William G. Frost, President of Berea College, announced his discovery of what he called "Appalachian America, the mountainous back yards of nine states . . . one of God's grand divisions." Unfortunately, the economic and social conditions in God's grand division were wretched, and Frost made it his mission to arouse the nation's conscience. In this he was remarkably successful. The major Protestant denominations began to take great interest in Appalachia and impressive sums were raised to finance the establishment of schools. Many idealistic young people came from comfortable New England homes to work as volunteers in the mountains (the VISTA workers of half a century ago). By 1920, there were over one hundred mission schools operating in Appalachia.

In more recent years, it has become fashionable to regard the mission schools with some disdain. This is both inaccurate and unfair. It is true that there was often more than a little denominational rivalry— although certainly no more rivalry than exists among the various public and private agencies who are now competing to do good in the area. Also, many of the workers were doubtless better intended than informed, and often fell victim to their own causes and panaceas. However, they were almost painfully idealistic and had no interest in either money or power. Indeed, the most serious weakness of the Mission School Movement was that there was not enough of it. It was never adequately supported and was in any case short-lived. For by 1930 the great days of the mission school were over—a victim of the Depression and a general loss of interest among the supporting groups.

The third rediscovery of Appalachia took place during the early 1930's. This one was confined largely to the coal-producing areas. During that period, the coal miners, especially those in Harlan and Bell counties, Kentucky, were discovered and "adopted" by many liberal groups. The National Committee for the Defense of Political Prisoners was formed by such luminaries as Theodore Dreiser and Anna Rochester. There were protest meetings, student marches and published articles without number. The movement attracted great attention and was widely reported in both newspapers and periodicals. However, once again, this interest waned almost as suddenly as it appeared, and the miners were left in substantially the same position as before.

These three major rediscoveries of Appalachia (and there have been at least a half dozen minor ones) all had one thing in common— they were short-lived. Also, only the Mission School Movement produced any significant results, and even it was often more warmhearted than effective. In short, the Nation's attitude toward Appalachia has been characterized by long periods of more or less complete indifference, broken by short-lived and generally abortive campaigns to "do something" about the region.

How does one explain this pattern? There appear to be four major reasons, plus a host of lesser ones. Let us note some of the more important factors.

Appalachia is, as Frost noted, made up of the back yards of nine states. With the exception of West Virginia, no single state has been primarily concerned with Appalachia. Back yards are often a nuisance, and the states preferred to use what political influence they had in Washington to improving their front yards. Because of this, there was never any sustained and powerful political pressure to improve conditions in Appalachia as a whole.

It is true that Appalachia has never been noted for the high quality of life it offered. However, until quite recently, it was not spectacularly behind the rest of the Nation. Coal, lumber and small farming provided an adequate livelihood—at least by local standards—for the majority. Those who wished to leave found ready employment in the assembly lines of Detroit or Cleveland. Thus conditions were difficult but not intolerable.

The third reason for the country's on-again-off-again interest in Appalachia appears to be rooted in one of our most basic national characteristics—impatience. As a people, we have a very short span of attention. We like, indeed we demand, quick and spectacular results. We grow bored or irritated with projects which do not seem to be paying off. Our political leaders are under enormous pressure to produce results quickly.

The fourth reason for the nation's attitude toward Appalachia follows from the third. Unfortunately, the problems of Appalachia are enormously complex and brutally difficult. Quick, spectacular, and permanent improvements are simply not possible. On the contrary, the very long term investment of enormous sums of money will be required. Results will be slow and in many cases probably disappointing. In short, the improvement of Appalachia is simply not the sort of project which has traditionally appealed to the American people.

Now what does this mean? Is the current rediscovery of Appalachia to be another "flash in the pan"? This is possible; the present enthusiasm may wilt before the hard facts. Political leaders may be unwilling to gamble our money and their prestige and careers on such a slow and unpromising investment. Then too, the American people—not for the first time—may simply grow bored with the whole matter.

All this is possible. However, there are several good reasons for thinking that the current interest in Appalachia may be both sustained and productive.

In the first place, some of the political and technical difficulties which used to inhibit effective action have now been solved or at least reduced. The states within the region have, for the first time, found it both possible and prudent to work together. Their combined political power can obviously accomplish—indeed has already accomplished—far more than any single state could hope to. Politics being what it is, there will doubtless be a certain amount of in-fighting among the states over who gets what. However, they all appear to recognize that without a joint effort nobody will get much of anything.

Certain technical problems also appear less difficult now. We have learned enough about the economics of depressed areas to know what are likely to be the best approaches, where we will get the best return for money spent and where the least.

And yet, paradoxically enough, by far the greatest cause for optimism is the very seriousness of the situation. Starting about 1950, mechanization and then automation of the coal industry reduced its labor requirements by over fifty percent. At approximately the same time, the great revolution in American agriculture began to take hold. Here again, mechanization and large-scale production units were the keys to survival. Even the well-managed one-family farm grew less and less viable. The traditional hill farm of Appalachia became an utterly hopeless proposition. Thus, in a few years, Appalachia's major fields of employment began to shrink.

At first, both the nation and the region reacted to the growing crisis in the usual manner: "Don't mention it and maybe it will go away." And for a while many of our problems did go away. They migrated. People left Appalachia by the hundreds of thousands, and the industrial cities of the Mid-West began (much to their dismay) to develop little Kentuckys and little West Virginias.

Exporting our surplus citizens was never a very happy solution; even worse, it may well prove a temporary one. For the other major industries are following the lead of coal. They are automating, and in the process thousands of workers are being displaced. Unfortunately, the very jobs which are the most easily automated are precisely those which the Appalachian migrants have filled—the routine, assembly-line jobs which demand no particular skill or education. The ability of the outside labor market to continue to absorb tens of thousands of Appalachia's unskilled, ill-educated, unemployed seems doubtful.

And why are our people ill-educated? Not, as is so often implied, because they were too stupid to see what was going on about them. But rather, because quite different things were going on. For several generations the increasingly complex industries of the North and Mid-West have demanded well-educated employees. Those regions responded to those demands. However, in Appalachia the two great industries were coal mining and lumbering and both were almost unique among major industries in that they did not require an educated work force. Boys could leave school at sixteen and enter the mines or go into the forests at wages greater than their teachers. Another few years of schooling offered no visible economic rewards. This was a fact of life in Appalachia and was well recognized as such. Here is but one example of the great chain reaction which is the curse of Appalachia. The new problems feed on the old, and the old make the solution of the new seem difficult indeed.

Thus, by the early 1960's much of Appalachia was in a state of crisis. The problems were clearly not going away; they were getting worse. National economic trends were not running in our direction. Appalachia and its people were in real danger of being by-passed.

The current national interest in helping Appalachia is obviously a reaction to this crisis. As is always the case in human affairs, motives are mixed. However, the two principal motives would appear to be (1) humanitarianism—the feeling that it is wrong for so many people to live so poorly within a rich society—and (2) the recognition that misery, ignorance and poverty are self-generating and in the long run produce a threat to the entire society.

It is obvious that this most recent rediscovery has already brought substantial benefits to Appalachia. There is good reason to be optimistic about the future. The one great danger is that genuine solutions will be too difficult, too time-consuming; that national political leaders will fear getting "bogged down" in Appalachia. If that happens, the temptation will be to buy us off and at the same time ease the national conscience by simply putting the entire area on a permanent dole. We would then indeed become in Harry Caudill's words "America's paleface reservation," with all that implies. Like most dangers, this is less likely to materialize if we are aware of the possibility.

Declarations of War
& Forecasts of Victory

NO MORE PORK BARREL:
THE APPALACHIA APPROACH
Jerald Ter Horst

If imitation is the sincerest form of flattery, then the Appalachia redevelopment program may indeed be the forerunner of a new era in
Federal public-works spending. Similar programs are already being
proposed for the Ozarks, the New England States, and the Upper Great
Lakes area, each fashioned in the belief that the gateway to the Great
Society is through regional concentration of Federal money instead of
scattershot spending in the fifty states.

In its purest form, the 1965 Appalachia proposal would mean that
the states and counties actually could tell Washington where and how
to spend Federal tax dollars to achieve the economic and social uplift
of a particular region. Ordinarily this alone would engender stiff opposition in Congress. But the eleven-state Appalachia concept dares
to go several steps further. Federal money would go primarily to a
region, not directly to impoverished people. It would not necessarily

From *The Reporter*, March 11, 1965. Used by permission of the author.

go to the neediest towns and counties, either, but to those with the greatest potential for economic growth. And the benefits, assuming that the program is successful, would not be immediately translatable into votes.

This tradition-shattering concept did not originate in Washington. It was the collective idea of a group of governors who began meeting periodically in the late 1950's in an effort to seek solutions to the common economic blight affecting many areas of their states. By May 20, 1960, the consultations had reached the point where the group, meeting in Annapolis, Maryland, formally created the Conference of Appalachian Governors. The following October, meeting in Lexington, Kentucky, the conference gave birth to "a special regional program of development" that envisaged a combined attack on their problems through the resources of the local, state, and Federal governments, and the assistance of private industry, civic groups, and philanthropic foundations. At the meeting were the governors of Alabama, Georgia, Kentucky, Maryland, North Carolina, Pennsylvania, Tennessee, Virginia, and West Virginia. Joined later by Ohio and South Carolina, the group represents that portion of the Appalachian Mountains ranging from northern Pennsylvania into southern Alabama, an area largely bypassed by the tremendous economic changes at work in the rest of the country since the Second World War.

In 1963, the Appalachia governors prevailed on President Kennedy to create the Appalachian Regional Commission to analyze the needs of the region and develop a co-ordinated plan for attempting some permanent cures of their chronic problems. Represented on the commission were the states and all the Federal agencies involved in such aid programs as highways, hospitals, public health, education, timber, crops, livestock, manpower retraining, mining, flood control and stream pollution, wildlife, and recreation. Under its chairman, Under Secretary of Commerce Franklin D. Roosevelt, Jr., the commission toured Appalachia twice and discussed the region's needs with public and private experts in the various states. Its report last spring to President Johnson set the stage for an unusual concerted program of economic-resource development by the cities, counties, and states and the Federal government.

The various subregions of Appalachia, the commission said, share this unhappy distinction: "Rural Appalachia lags behind rural America, urban Appalachia lags behind urban America, and metropolitan Appalachia lags behind metropolitan America." It found, for example, that one-third of Appalachia's families earn less than $3,000 annually; two-thirds of its people do not finish school; unemployment is half again the national average, and out-migration is at the high rate of 200,000 persons a year. "The most serious problems which beset Appalachia are low income, high unemployment, lack of urbanization, low educational achievement, and a comparatively low standard of living."

At first glance, the 1965 Appalachia program appears to be the usual grab bag of projects—new roads, soil improvement and erosion control, timber development, hospitals and treatment centers, vocational-education, sewage-treatment works, strip-mine reclamation, fish and wildlife projects—all intended to help Appalachia catch up with the rest of the nation.

But closer examination discloses that the Appalachia planners have broken new ground in the formulation and management of public-works spending. For the first time, the Federal government would delegate a major share of the decision-making to the participating states. The master plan for economic rehabilitation would be devised by the states or groups of counties in a multistate area with contiguous land and common problems.

While the actual operation of aid projects would be under the appropriate Federal agencies, the supervision and co-ordination of the whole Appalachia program would be vested in the Appalachian Regional Commission, to consist of the governor of each participating state, or his designee, and one Federal representative named by the President. Decisions would be made by a majority vote of the state members, plus the affirmative vote of the Federal representative, who would, in effect, have a veto over proposals by the state members of the commission. But the veto could be substantially limited, since a majority of state members could counter any move toward Federal "dictation" by withholding their votes.

This check-and-balance formula represents a major shift in bureaucratic thinking in Washington. It has inspired heated debate inside the administration and in Congress. Veteran agency heads still question the wisdom of letting states have such a large share of the decision-making process when most of the money comes from Federal revenue.

Congress has also been historically reluctant to appropriate money without a certain supervision over the decision-makers. This it can do most easily when funds are expended by Federal agencies—even to the extent of cranking into a program a few pet projects of a committee chairman and influential lawmakers. It is a precept of pork-barrel doctrine that a congressman and his constituents have a right to expect certain Federal benefits for their district to flow from his membership on key committees. Thus it comes as a minor miracle to find that both Federal bureaucrats and members of Congress seem willing to relinquish some of their authority in order to give the Appalachia program a trial.

One of the surprise converts is the Bureau of the Budget, known best as the "No" agency of government. "To be honest, this is a new venture," conceded Charles L. Schultze, until recently an assistant Budget Bureau director. "We are doing something different. While not saying it is experimental, we think it is an exceedingly interesting approach. We are going to have to work our way through this."

In his testimony before the House Public Works Committee, Schultze described the proposed Appalachia concept of multistate planning under Federal supervision as "a nice balance" of authority. Still to be tested, however, is just how the states will exercise their new license to tell Washington where to send Federal dollars. What's likely to happen, according to Senator Jennings Randolph, the West Virginia Democrat who steered the bill through the Senate, is that most of the hard bargaining will be done outside the commission's chambers. An Appalachia planner agreed. "We'll work it out informally before we take something in for a vote—just like they do in Congress."

The basis for this hope lies in the considerable give-and-take among the Appalachia governors and the Federal representatives in working out the terms of the legislation. For example, Georgia, North Carolina, and Maryland, because their needs are not so great, have consented to a smaller allocation of primary highway corridor mileage than is intended for West Virginia and Pennsylvania. Similarly, the governors of South Carolina and Alabama have agreed to take a smaller share of development highway money because their Appalachia counties will be adequately served by the Federal interstate highway program.

The spirit of compromise was equally apparent in Congress. The administration and Capitol Hill Democrats consented to a proposal by Senator Jacob K. Javits (R, New York) that no program for Appalachia should be implemented until the Appalachia commission had consulted with appropriate state officials and received their recommendations. The acid test, however, will come when individual lawmakers make their customary demands on Federal agencies for inclusion of projects dear to their constituents.

Another radical departure from tradition is the Appalachia concept of skipping the customary "means test" to determine which areas will be helped. The Area Redevelopment program, for example, uses specific criteria for establishing eligibility for Federal aid. A county must have a certain rate of unemployment in order to qualify for job-creating projects. But the Appalachia approach relies on "regional growth potential," a theory that economic uplift should be concentrated on certain cities or counties that have prospered in spite of Appalachia's general distress.

There is a hint of economic predestination here; the belief that many economically weak towns and counties do not have the potential to become thriving, prosperous centers of population. Instead, Appalachia planners believe that the economically strong places should be strengthened to support the weaker surrounding areas. One example is Huntsville, Alabama, with its space-industry complex and college environment in the midst of a depressed area. "Instead of trying to build up the area to compete with Huntsville, we should try to find ways of helping the rest of the region become auxiliary to Huntsville," one planner explained. "This could be done by improving the road network, providing sewer and water facilities for residential expansion, perhaps improving farm production and recreational opportunities in some sectors of the region."

Wilkes-Barre, Pennsylvania, is considered another center for regional growth potential that could attract more industries and commerce and provide new job opportunities through co-ordinated planning designed to increase the "social overhead capital" needed for area self-sufficiency. In all, there are probably fifty such core cities or counties in the 360 counties included in the Appalachia region.

One of the continuing controversies in the Appalachia program is its heavy emphasis on roadbuilding. About one thousand miles will be "local access" roads, intended primarily to link Appalachia's almost inaccessible valleys with nearby cities and towns. Another 2,350 miles would be designated as "development highways," linking core cities with each other and with areas outside Appalachia.

"There's been a sort of liberal versus pragmatist debate on this thing," said John L. Sweeney, the able young administrator the President chose as chairman of the Federal Development Planning Committee for Appalachia. "Most programs of economic help in the past have been based on the theory that a man has a right to a job where he lives and that government should help bring him that job. The Apppalachia approach is that a man has a right to a job, but it is reasonable to expect him to be willing to commute to it or move to it if necessary.

Using a mile-a-minute yardstick, Appalachia planners think it logical to expect people to travel forty minutes to reach their places of employment, a vocational school, or even a hospital. Thus a core-city plan will encompass an area extending as far as forty miles from the center, crossing county and state boundaries when necessary.

Not all economic and social planners agree, however, with the priority on roads. Doubts about its importance were heard at the American Institute of Planners conference in Newark, New Jersey, last year. One said he wished he could be "czar" of the Appalachia program just long enough to scrap the highway priority. An earlier Ford Foundation study concluded that the unemployed and unskilled coal and steel workers in Appalachia "must be written off so far as any major economic contribution is concerned." It advocated massive Federal aid to education, increased out-migration, and birth control.

The Appalachia rebuttal is both intriguing and indignant. "If we are going to be politically realistic about the Appalachia program, it is necessary to design a program that mirrors the political realities of the states involved," said Stuart F. Feldman, top staff aide for the Appalachia Development Committee. And the political realities are that the governors, senators, and representatives of the Appalachia states wanted a priority on roads—and so did the planning experts for the committee.

"From the point of view of public policy," Feldman told the planners' conference, "it is evident that Appalachia is an ongoing region whose 167,000 square miles, numerous metropolitan areas, and population of over sixteen million people represent a resource and an investment this nation cannot abandon through policies that encourage an out-migration of the able."

There is both historic and contemporary justification for the road priority. Appalachia once had been opened by the railroads, which came to fetch the coal for the steel mills and electric-power generation. But automation has hit each of the region's big three—coal, steel, and the railroads—throwing thousands upon thousands of men and their sons out of manual-labor jobs. Oil and natural gas became victorious competitors of coal for the fuel market; even the coal-burning loco-motives gave way to diesels. In the old days, rail spurs ran back into almost every Appalachia hollow to reach the mines; because they were not built for private gain, roads seldom followed. There are still hamlets whose only connection with the outside world is over the abandoned railbeds.

The Federal interstate highway system has helped to open Appa-lachia. But states and communities with a low tax base haven't been able to raise extra funds for the auxiliary highways and local access roads. In mountainous areas of West Virginia, for example, Appalachia planners note that it costs $2 million a mile to construct a two-lane paved highway. Moreover, Appalachia needs road money not so much to accommodate existing traffic as to stimulate new traffic.

Surprisingly, the press has been rather uncritical in reporting that seventy-six percent, or $840 million, of the Appalachia program's $1.1 billion price tag is for roadbuilding. The road money actually is a five-year authorization; the rest of the money for other Appalachian needs covers the first two years only. Seen in perspective, then, the road ratio is not so lopsided as it appears.

The debate will be more intense over another aspect of the Appa-lachia program—namely, its assumption that there should be preferen-tial treatment for an eleven-state area, as well as internal discrimination inherent in selecting one town as a growth center while bypassing an-other. One of Appalachia's problems is the inability of counties and cities to raise the usual local share necessary to obtain Federal matching funds for such things as airports, hospitals, vocational education fa-cilities, libraries, and flood control. The Appalachia bill will make it possible for the Federal government to pay up to eighty percent of the total cost in such instances, even if other regions of the country would get only fifty percent Federal aid. Additionally, there are special sup-plemental funds to cover actual operating costs of hospitals for up to two years, plus a $36.5 million fund to alleviate land damage wrought by collapsed coal mines, underground fires, and acid seepage into streams. And Republicans charge gross discrimination in that the road program "is almost as large as the annual program for construction of Federal-aid primary and secondary highways" for the entire country.

There has been, inevitably, some compromise. The bill's current dollar total is about one-third of the $3 billion in Federal money originally sought. A proposed public development corporation, to be financed by bond sales and Federal funds, had to be scrapped when it appeared to be just another back-door raid on the Treasury. Western cattle interests knocked out a $17 million program for pastureland improvement. And administration lobbyists have had to tell envious lawmakers from other areas that if they will go along with the Appalachian plan, the White House will entertain similar regional development programs for other parts of the country.

Behind it all lies a growing conviction in Congress and in the councils of a Democratic administration that pork-barreling, accelerated public-works spending, and such things as the Area Redevelopment program—generally classed as economic pump priming—have missed the mark. The past, however, has not been a complete loss, at least not in the view of the President's Council of Economic Advisers. The Council has analyzed the weaknesses of these earlier programs, and all of its conclusions point toward more Appalachia-type solutions. Add a pinch of Johnsonian consensus, and the rationale is simply that states and local communities cannot do the job alone—and that the Federal government should not.

HOW MUCH BETTER WILL
THE BETTER WORLD BE?
Rupert B. Vance

The word is out: There is money in the budget for the Appalachians. This article offers no recipe on how to get it, but it will speculate on what ought to be done with available funds and what may come of the various programs. At last the country is seriously concerned with persistent problems of poverty in the Southern mountains, notably the coal mining areas hard hit by unemployment. Here, at last, is the op-

From *Mountain Life and Work*, Fall 1965. Used by permission of the author.

portunity for which many of the leaders in the Appalachians have hoped.

No one at this date is able to tell us for sure how much better the better world will be in Appalachia. Nevertheless it is well that we develop a sense of urgency about the poverty problems of the Appalachian area. We need, as it were, to set up a statute of limitations as to what these new programs may do and how their degree of success may be measured. Elsewhere I have addressed myself to this question somewhat as follows:

The Appalachian problem has been with us this long, we believe, because it was self-renewing. To be explicit, population growth has proceeded at a more rapid rate than new employment opportunities have been provided and migration has been able to drain off the surplus. The institutions of the region, geared to an economy of poverty, not only have failed to solve the problems of poverty, but have often contributed to their perpetuation. The schools, for example, have failed to provide outcoming youth with the knowledge and skills required for high income employment, thus severely restricting the development of an economy that could support better schools. Local government agencies, operating in an atmosphere of poverty in which any expenditures beyond the bare functional minimum are regarded as luxuries, are unable or unwilling to make the capital investments needed for economic growth. How long a period should be allotted to carry through the new programs and when should we be able to determine that the Appalachian problem is no longer self-generating?

The answer suggested is one generation. This is implicit in the provision of the Area Redevelopment Act that no industrial or commercial development loan, including extensions and renewals, shall exceed twenty-five years. Certainly this seems long enough to separate the industries that will prosper from those that will fail. In thirty years the "lost generation of mountaineers," those too old to adjust and too set in their ways to change, will be over seventy and passing off the stage. Realistically, most of this group must be written off at forty to fifty years of age so far as any major economic contribution is concerned and special provision as necessary should be made for their welfare in the form of public assistance. But public assistance must not be perpetuated as a way of life in the areas where dependence upon it has become so widespread.

For the oncoming youth, a period of thirty years will be required to realize the full benefits of efforts devoted to the improvement of education, the provision of vocational training, and guided migration. Because of the slow pace at which our institutions change, three decades of concerted effort will probably be needed to bring about substantial reforms in the methods of community organization and action to deal with social and economic problems. Particularly is this likely to be the case where current constitutional and legislative provisions perpetuate obsolescent structures and practices of local government units. During this period systematic retirement of submarginal land should be effected through public purchase of subsistence farms to which families in the area cling to their own detriment.

A final ten-year period, 1990–2000, should be devoted to a "mopping-up" operation that will consist of concentrated attacks on remaining problems and the determination that conditions leading to the regeneration of poverty have been eliminated. The mountains have suffered from a kind of fatalism in the past; they must not become victims of overoptimism in the future.

Research furnishes the scientific basis for planning and development. Accordingly, one value of the suggested priority schedule is that we will have three census periods in which to measure the progress of the new program. Analyses of the 1970 censuses of agriculture, business, and manufactures should enable us to set a bench mark from which to measure population movement out of low-level agriculture and the success of manufacturing and commercial enterprises in areas expected to benefit from the Area Redevelopment Act. Data from the population censuses of 1980 and 1990 should be analyzed to determine the progress of out-migration and fertility control, changes in the employment structure, and the extent to which the gaps between regional and national levels of education and income have been closed. Examination at these checkpoints of other pertinent statistics such as school consolidation and enrollments, local government finances, number of public relief beneficiaries, and the like should serve to identify remaining problems and problem areas. On the basis of these findings, programs should be revised as necessary to focus on the most critical problems, and efforts should be redoubled to eliminate self-renewing problem conditions where they will persist. Where spot areas of poverty are disclosed in 1990, intensive campaigns should be organized as part of the mopping-up operation to eliminate them before the program is closed out by the year 2000. Little of this program will be accomplished unless vigorous state and local leadership is tied in with the new Federal Programs.

In the new attack on the problems of the Appalachians, it is safe to say that we will soon be faced with an embarrassment of riches. Those who work in the undeveloped areas of the world are appalled at the lack of social facilities and agencies to help with the problems they face. Here in the Appalachians we are likely to be appalled by the number of agencies that must be co-ordinated, placated, worked into the program and given credit for anything that is done or likely to be done. Consider the list: welfare, extension programs, vocational education, agricultural, highway, recreation, water programs, etc., already exist. They now have been joined by the Area Redevelopment Agency whose administration was placed in the Department of Commerce, and the administrative arm of the Economic Opportunity Act of 1964, which will administer the attack on poverty set up under President Johnson. Throughout, the attack will be firmed up under the Appalachian Act. In addition, we have various voluntary and state programs. In West Virginia a group of core counties, organized under the combined Extension Services of the State University, have embarked on a program of development proposed and guided by core county committees. Under a grant from the Kellogg Foundation, the University of Kentucky is carrying integrated extension services to the thirty counties of the Cumberland in an attempt to hasten redevelopment. The idea is to stimulate key communities by these services, to encourage them to inventory their needs and work toward alleviation. The Governor of North Carolina and his advisors organized a program entitled, "End the Cycle of Poverty in North Carolina," secured the support of the Ford Foundation and other groups and established the North Carolina Fund, an agency devoted to "ending the cycle" of poverty in the state. The Council of the Southern Mountains with offices in Berea, Kentucky, is active in a broad range of programs financed by both private and federal funds.

With administrative machinery at hand, with seed capital in sight, with favorable climate of public opinion, we come to a most important question: What alternatives should be set up and what choices will have to be made in the attempt to develop physical and human resources in a program of induced social change in the Southern Appalachians? The

Appalachians and the nation have come to a point where they must ponder policy. Do we have any guide lines in such a program of deliberately breaking the trend line of continuity with the past and embarking on a program of hastening social change?

Certainly, if this region or any other is to be more fully developed, it must be agreed that the program for its development will take place in the context of national growth and development. Not all areas in need of advance are equally capable of it. What America wants is the equitable and desirable development of physical and human resources. It appears, however, that inevitably a Spartan decision may have to be made. When the potential physical resources of a given area do not furnish a basis for further development, the resources to be conserved are the people themselves and their development must be put foremost. This conclusion means that for certain areas, the conservation and development of the human resources of the Appalachians must proceed elsewhere. Parents in the region should no longer rear their children to go into subsistence agriculture. And if less than one-tenth of the males growing to adulthood in the mining camps can expect to find employment in the mines, these facts must be faced in the necessity for outward movement. Large contingents of mountain youth must be prepared to migrate to strange cities, to engage in new trades and crafts. The institutional agencies of the region must give them all the aid they can in this difficult adventure.

If migration is one of the major solutions, what shall we tell people who seek to better themselves? A major dilemma in any program devoted to clearing out "pockets of poverty" is the lack of information about the number of persons with particular skills needed in particular places. Marshall R. Colberg points out that the United States Department of Labor has done very little to secure such information. There exists a very real reason for this deficiency. The best measure of relative shortage in occupations is found in wage rates that are out of line with wages in similar occupations in regard to training, hardships, regularity of employment, etc. Such favorable conditions are the goal of every well-organized trade union, and a true "undersupply" of labor is difficult to detect and to demonstrate. Training programs are simply one approach. Widely disseminated information about these opportunities in so-called "understaffed trades" is another. When no protection is available, shortages in labor by areas and by trade tend to disappear and wage rates to fall. If the mobility of labor is blocked, the conventional remedy taken by management will likely prevail. Rather than employ more labor in these situations, management has had increasing recourse to automation and the more complex forms of mechanization. The mountain people are not only up against the barrier of improved skills, they are also up against the barriers of a protected undersupply of labor power.

It now seems likely that the Appalachian program has almost as much to fear from its friends as from its foes. Its friends include those politicians who realized the need for action in poverty stricken areas and got behind the cause and pushed. It is natural to assume that some of these leaders are now prepared to reap certain of the benefits. Here I think that the contrast with what the Peace Corps has been able to do abroad should be pointed out. The Peace Corps was not designed as a great corps of "experts" to be paid high level salaries for their skills. It was seen rather as a place where voluntary workers could go into the kind of service that appealed to them most. Working at home, in something of the same kind of problems, we have already abandoned the spirit of the missionaries who, first in this field, hitherto have done the most to advance the cause of the mountain people. Instead we now demand "expertise," bureaucracy, and we are likely to get in return those politically-minded administrators who come high in any market. This program, let us emphasize, is going to be judged on the basis of its failures and its successes. This means that it will be examined for cases of the padded budget and it could well be found wanting. To attack the problem of poverty, we need budgets and we need ideas that work. We have now come to the point where we are better supplied with money than with plans to use this money.

Let us close with a warning that I hope will be taken very seriously. "Hope deferred," we are told, "maketh the heart sick." Hopes almost realized and then blasted drive men mad. To ask how much better will the better world be is also to ask in reverse: How much worse will it be if it fails? If I were called upon to issue a warning against cynicism it might come close to a note of ingratitude. It is my sincere feeling that the success of these programs has the most to fear from its friends. To come to the aid of the Appalachians was a political decision firmed up by practicing politicians—which is as it should be in the democratic process. In the Peace Corps as set up, the politicians showed no interest in the positions they had helped to create. There are no voters to be wooed in the middle of Africa and living conditions are not too comfortable. As one result the program is in the hands of glorified amateurs, the one American export that almost everybody likes—even more than they like foreign aid with its tremendous budget. At home, as Mr. Sargent Shriver finds, things seem to be somewhat different. Everybody gets into the act and this includes the politicians, those good men who came to the aid of the party and supported the war on poverty. If there are good jobs to be had there are also criteria of achievement to be met. This is no time to abandon the program to its new-found friends. Bureaucracy is all right in its place. So are political appointees. I suggest that in the Appalachian program each be put in its place.

Finally, I wish to ask in all seriousness, "Do we really have the courage required, the hard-headed realism, and the sense of responsibility to set up a region-wide program of family planning?"

If people can no longer rear their children to go into subsistence farming; if less than one-tenth of the males growing to adulthood in mining camps can expect to find employment in the mines; if large contingents of mountain youth must migrate to strange cities to engage in new trades and crafts; if those who remain must face difficult periods of adjustment in relation to new industries which may or may not survive; if the rate at which the regional labor force replaces itself or is disemployed exceeds the rate at which its members are re-employed or migrate outward; if the region's problem is thus self-renewing—a certain drastic conclusion is inevitable. It may be that the people of depressed areas can no longer allow themselves the luxury that the American people are now enjoying in the midst of the new prosperity—that is, the enjoyment of the "baby boom." In a comparable, though more perilous situation, the Irish population responded to famine by postponing marriage, by sharply reducing their birth rate, and by migrating to America.

Family limitation is not sufficient by itself to enable such regions to attain economic equality with the nation. Used in conjunction with redevelopment and migration, however, an effective program would enable young couples to marry at a normal age and to postpone having their families until they are established. Population growth thus checked is not likely to outrun economic growth and thus endanger the whole range of redevelopment plans. The Appalachian problem no longer need be self-renewing.

Part Two

Between a Rock &
a Hard Place

The Quality of Life:
Hard Times in God's Country

LIFE IN APPALACHIA—
THE CASE OF HUGH McCASLIN
Robert Coles

Hugh McCaslin is unforgettable. He has red hair and, at 43, freckles. He stands six feet four. As he talked to me about his work in the coal mines, I kept wondering what he did with his height down inside the earth.

Once he must have been an unusually powerful man; even today his arms and legs are solid muscle. The fat he has added in recent years has collected in only one place, his waist, both front and back.

"I need some padding around my back; it's hurt, and I don't think it'll ever get back right. I broke it bad working, and they told me at first they'd have it fixed in no time flat, but they were wrong. I don't know if they were fooling themselves, or out to fool me in the bargain. It's hard to know what's going on around here—that's what I've discovered these last few years.

From *Trans-Action*, June 1968. Used by permission of publisher. © June 1968 by Trans-Action, Inc., New Brunswick, N.J.

"I'll tell you, a man like me, he has a lot of time to think. He'll sit around here, day upon day, and what else does he have to keep his mind on but his thoughts? I can't work, and even if I could, there's no work to do, not around here, no sir. They told me I'm 'totally incapacitated,' that's the words they used. They said my spine was hurt, and the nerves, and I can't walk and move about the way I should. As if I needed them to tell me!

"Then they gave me exercises and all, and tole me I was lucky, because even though I wasn't in shape to go in the mines, I could do anything else, anything that's not too heavy. Sometimes I wonder what goes on in the heads of those doctors. They look you right in the eye, and they're wearing a straight face on, and they tell you you're sick, you've been hurt digging out coal, and you'll never be the same, but you're really not so bad off, because your back isn't so bad you can't be a judge, or a professor, or the president of the coal company or something like that, you know."

Once Hugh McCaslin (not his real name) asked me to look at an X-ray taken of his back and his shoulders—his vertebral column. He persuaded the company doctor to give him the X-ray, or so he said. (His wife told me that he had, in fact, persuaded the doctor's secretary to hand it over, and tell her boss—if he ever asked—that somehow the patient's "file" had been lost.) He was convinced that the doctor was a "company doctor"—which he assuredly was—and a "rotten, dishonest one." Anyway, what did I see in that X-ray? I told him that I saw very little. I am no radiologist, and whatever it was that ailed him could not be dramatically pointed out on an X-ray, or if it could I was not the man to do it. Well, yes he did know that, as a matter of fact:

"I got my nerves smashed down there in an accident. I don't know about the bones. I think there was a lot of pressure, huge pressure on the nerves, and it affected the way I walk. The doctor said it wasn't a fracture on a big bone, just one near the spine. He said it wasn't too serious, that I'd be O.K., just not able to go back to work, at least down there.

"Then, you see, they closed down the mine itself. That shows you I wasn't very lucky. My friends kept telling me I was lucky to be alive, and lucky to be through with it, being a miner. You know, we don't scare very easy. Together, we never would talk about getting hurt. I suppose it was somewhere in us, the worry; but the first time I heard my friends say anything like that was to me, not to themselves. They'd come by here when I was sick, and they'd tell me I sure was a fortunate guy, and God was smiling that day, and now He'd be smiling forever on me, because I was spared a real disaster, and it was bound to come, one day or another. It kind of got me feeling funny, hearing them talk like that around my bed, and then seeing them walk off real fast, with nothing to make them watch their step and take a pain pill every few hours.

"But after a while I thought maybe they did have something; and if I could just recover me a good pension from the company, and get my medical expenses all covered—well, then, I'd get better, as much as possible, and go fetch me a real honest-to-goodness job, where I could see the sun all day, and the sky outside, and breathe our air here, as much of it as I pleased, without a worry in the world.

"But that wasn't to be. I was dumb, real dumb, and hopeful. I saw them treating me in the hospital, and when they told me to go home I thought I was better, or soon would be. Instead, I had to get all kinds of treatments, and they said I'd have to pay for them, out of my savings or somewhere. And the pension I thought I was supposed to get, that was all in my mind, they said. They said the coal industry was going through a lot of changes, and you couldn't expect them to keep people going indefinitely, even if they weren't in the best of shape, even if it did happen down in the mines.

"Well, that's it, to make it short. I can't do hard work, and I have a lot of pain, every day of my life. I might be able to do light work, desk work, but hell, I'm not fit for anything like that; and even if I could, where's the work to be found? Around here? Never in a million years. We're doomed here, to sitting and growing the food we can and sharing our misery with one another.

"My brother, he helps; and my four sisters, they help; and my daddy, he's still alive and he can't help except to sympathize, and tell me it's a good thing I didn't get killed in that landslide and can see my boys grow up. He'll come over here and we start drinking. You bet, he's near 80, and we start drinking, and remembering. My daddy will ask if I can recollect the time I said I'd save a thousand dollars for myself by getting a job in the mines and I say I sure can, and can he recollect the time he said I'd better not get too greedy, because there's bad that comes with good in this world, and especially way down there inside the earth."

He will take a beer or two and then get increasingly angry. His hair seems to look wilder, perhaps because he puts his hands through it as he talks. His wife becomes nervous and tries to give him some bread or crackers, and he becomes sullen or embarrassingly direct with her. She is trying to "soak up" his beer. She won't even let it hit his stomach and stay there a while. She wants it back. He tells her, "Why don't you keep your beer, if you won't let it do a thing for me?"

They have five sons, all born within nine years. The oldest is in high school and dreams of the day he will join the army. He says he will be "taken" in, say, in Charleston or Beckley—in his mind, any "big city" will do. He will be sent off to California or Florida or "maybe New York" for basic training; eventually he will "land himself an assignment—anywhere that's good, and it'll be far away from here, I do believe that." Hugh McCaslin becomes enraged when he hears his son talk like that; with a few beers in him he becomes especially enraged:

"That's the way it is around here. That's what's happened to us. That's what they did to us. They made us lose any honor we had. They turned us idle. They turned us into a lot of grazing sheep, lucky to find a bit of pasture here and there. We don't do anything here anymore; and so my boys, they'll all want to leave, and they will. But they'll want to come back, too—because this land, it's in their bones going way back, and you don't shake off your ancestors that easy, no sir.

"My daddy, he was born right up the road in this here hollow, and his daddy, and back to a long time ago. There isn't anyone around here we're not kin to somehow, near or far. My daddy was the one supposed to leave for the mines. He figured he could make more money than he could dream about, and it wasn't too far to go. He went for a while, but some years later he quit. He couldn't take it. I grew up in a camp near the mine, and I'd still be there if it wasn't that I got hurt and moved back here to the hollow. Even while we were at the camp we used to come back here on Sundays, I re-member, just like now they come here on weekends from Cincinnati and Dayton and those places, and even from way off in Chicago. I can recall the car we got; everybody talked about it, and when we'd drive as near here as we could—well, the people would come, my grandparents and all my uncles and aunts and cousins, and they'd look and look at that Ford, before they'd see if it was us, and say hello to us. I can recollect in my mind being shamed and wanting to disappear in one of those pockets, where my daddy would keep his pipes. My mother would say it wasn't they didn't want to see us, but the Ford, it was real special to them, and could you blame them for not look-ing at us?

"That was when things were really good. Except that even then I don't think we were all that contented. My mother always worried. Every day, come 3 or so in the afternoon, I could tell she was starting to worry. Will anything happen? Will he get hurt? Will they be coming over soon, to give me some bad news? (No, we had no telephone, and neither did the neigh-bors.) It got so we'd come home from school around 2 or so, and just sit there with her, pretending—pretending to do things, and say things. And then he'd come in, every time. We could hear his voice coming, or his steps, or the door, and we'd all loosen up—and pretend again, that there was noth-ing we'd worry about, because there wasn't nothing to worry about.

"One day—I think I was seven or eight, because I was in school, I know that—we had a bad scare. Someone came to the school and told the teacher something, whispered it in her ear. She turned into a sheet, and she looked as though she'd start crying. The older kids knew what had happened, just from her looks. (Yes, it was a one-room schoolhouse, just like the one we have here, only a little bigger.) They ran out, and she almost took off after them, except for the fact that she remembered us. So she turned around and told us there that something bad had happened down in the mines, an explosion, and we should go home and wait there, and if our mothers weren't there—well, wait until they got home.

"But we wanted to go with her. Looking back at it, I think she worried us. So she decided to take us, the little ones. And I'll tell you, I can remember that walk with her like it was just today. I can see it, and I can tell you what she said, and what we did, and all. We walked and walked, and then we came through the woods and there they were, all of a sudden before our eyes. The people there, just standing around and almost nothing being said between them. It was so silent I thought they'd all turn around and see us, making noise. But, you see, we must have stopped talking, too, because for a while they didn't even give us a look over their shoulders. Then we come closer, and I could hear there was noise after all: The women were crying, and there'd be a cough or something from some of the miners.

"That's what sticks with you, the miners wondering if their buddies were dead or alive down there. Suddenly I saw my father, and my mother. They were with their arms about one another—real unusual—and they were waiting, like the rest.

"Oh, we got home that night, yes, and my daddy said they were gone— they were dead and we were going away. And we did. The next week we drove here in our Ford, and I can hear my daddy saying it wasn't worth it, money and a car, if you die young, or you live but your lungs get poisoned, and all that, and you never see the sun except on Sundays.

"But what choice did he have? I thought I might want to do some farming, like my grandfather, but there's no need for me, and my grandfather couldn't really keep more than himself going, I mean with some food and all. Then I thought it'd be nice to finish school, and maybe get a job someplace near, in a town not a big city. But everything was collapsing all over the country then, and you'd be crazy to think you were going to get anything by leaving here and going out there, with the lines standing for soup— oh yes, we heard on the radio what it was like all over.

"It could be worse, you say to yourself, and you resolve to follow your daddy and be a miner. That's what I did. He said we had a lousy day's work, but we got good pay, and we could buy things. My daddy had been the richest man in his family for a while. In fact, he was the only man in his family who had any money at all. After the family looked over our Ford, they'd give us that real tired and sorry look, as though they needed some help real bad, and that's when my daddy would hand out the dollar bills, one after the other. I can picture it right now. You feel rich, and you feel real kind."

Hugh McCaslin's life wouldn't be that much better even if he had not been seriously hurt in a mine accident. The miners who were his closest friends are now unemployed, almost every one of them. They do not feel cheated out of a disability pension, but for all practical purposes he and they are equally idle, equally bitter, equally sad. With no prompting from my psychiatric mind he once put it this way:

"They talk about depressions in this country. I used to hear my daddy talk about them all the time, depressions. It wasn't so bad for my daddy and and me in the thirties, when the Big One, the Big Depression, was knocking everyone down, left and right. He had a job, and I knew I was going to have one as soon as I was ready, and I did. Then when the war come, they even kept me home. They said we were keeping everything going over here in West Virginia. You can't run factories without coal. I felt I wouldn't mind going, and getting a look at things out there, but I was just as glad to stay here, I guess. I was married, and we were starting with the kids, so it would have been hard. My young brother, he went. He wasn't yet a miner, and they just took him when he was 18, I think. He come back here and decided to stay out of the mines, but it didn't make much difference in the end, anyway. We're all out of the mines now around here.

"So, you see it's now that we're in a depression. They say things are pretty good in most parts of the country, from what you see on TV, but not so here. We're in the biggest depression ever here: We have no money, and no welfare payments, and we're expected to scrape by like dogs. It gets to your mind after a while. You feel as low as can be, and nervous about everything. That's what a depression does, makes you dead broke, with a lot of bills and the lowest spirits you can ever picture a man having. Sometimes I get up and I'm ready to go over to an undertaker and tell him to do something with me real fast."

I have spent days and nights with the McCaslin family, and Hugh McCaslin doesn't always feel that "low," that depressed, that finished with life. I suppose it can be said that he has "adapted" to the hard, miserable life he faces. At times he shouts and screams about "things," and perhaps in that way keeps himself explicitly angry rather than sullen and brooding. His friends call him a "firebrand," and blame his temper on his red hair. In fact, he says what they are thinking, and need to hear said by someone. They come to see him, and in Mrs. McCaslin's words, "get him going." They bring him home-made liquor to help matters along.

The McCaslins are early risers, but no one gets up earlier than the father. He suffers pain at night; his back and his legs hurt. He has been told that a new hard mattress would help, and hot baths, and aspirin. He spends a good part of the night awake—"thinking and dozing off and then coming to, real sudden-like, with a pain here or there."

For a while he thought of sleeping on the floor, or trying to get another bed but he could not bear the prospect of being alone:

"My wife, Margaret, has kept me alive. She has some of God's patience in her, that's the only way I figure she's been able to last it. She smiles when things are so dark you'd think the end has come. She soothes me, and tells me it'll get better, and even though I know it won't I believe her for a few minutes, and that helps."

So he tosses and turns in their bed, and his wife has learned to sleep soundly but to wake up promptly when her husband is in real pain. They have aspirin and treat it as something special—and expensive. I think Hugh McCaslin realizes that he suffers from many different kinds of pain; perhaps if he had more money he might have been addicted to all sorts of pain-killers long ago. Certainly when I worked in a hospital I saw patients like him—hurt and in pain, but not "sick" enough to require hospitalization, and in fact "chronically semi-invalids." On the other hand, such patients had tried and failed at any number of jobs. We will never know how Hugh McCaslin might have felt today if he had found suitable work after his accident, or had received further medical care. Work is something a patient needs as he starts getting better, as anyone who works in a "rehabilitation unit" of a hospital well knows. Hugh McCaslin lacked medical care when he needed it, lacks it today, and in his own words needs a "time-killer" as much as a pain-killer. His friends despair, drink, "loaf about," pick up a thing here and there to do, and "waste time real efficiently." So does he—among other things, by dwelling on his injured body.

He dwells on his children, too. There are five of them to leave West Virginia. Sometimes in the early morning, before his wife is up, he leaves bed to look at them sleeping:

"I need some hope, and they have it, in their young age and the future they have, if they only get the hell out of here before it's too late. Oh, I like it here, too. It's pretty, and all that. It's peaceful. I'm proud of us people. We've been here a long time, and we needed real guts to stay and last. And who wants to live in a big city? I've been in some of our cities, here in West Virginia, and they're no big value, from what I can see, not so far as bringing up a family. You have no land, no privacy, a lot of noise, and all that. But if it's between living and dying, I'll take living; and right here, right now, I think we're dying—dying away, slow but sure, every year more and more so."

He worries about his children in front of them. When they get up they see him sitting and drinking coffee in the kitchen. He is wide-awake, and hungrier for company than he knows. He wants to learn what they'll be doing that day. He wants to talk about things, about the day's events and inevitably a longer span of time, the future: "Take each day like your life hangs on it. That's being young, when you can do that, when you're not trapped and have some choice on things." The children are drowsy, but respectful. They go about dressing and taking coffee and doughnuts with him. They are as solicitous as he is. Can they make more coffee? They ask if they can bring him anything—even though they know full well his answer: "No, just yourselves."

Mrs. McCaslin may run the house, but she makes a point of checking every decision with her husband. He "passes on" even small matters—something connected with one of the children's schoolwork, or a neighbor's coming visit, or a project for the church. She is not sly and devious; not clever at appearing weak but "manipulating" all the while. She genuinely defers to her husband, and his weakness, his illness, his inability to find work—and none of those new medical, social, or psychological "developments" have made her see fit to change her ways. Nor is he inclined to sit back and let the world take everything out of his hands. As a matter of fact, it is interesting to see how assertive a man and a father he still is, no matter how awful his fate continues to be. He is there, and always there—in spirit as well as in body. I have to compare him not only with certain Negro fathers I know, who hide from welfare workers and flee their wives and children in fear and shame and anger, but also with a wide range of white middle-class fathers who maintain a round-the-clock absence from home (for business reasons, for "social" reasons), or else demonstrate a much-advertised "passivity" while there. Hugh McCaslin, as poor as one can be in America, not at all well-educated, nevertheless exerts a strong and continuing influence upon everyone in his family. He is, again, there—not just at home, but very much involved in almost everything his wife and children do. He talks a lot. He has strong ideas, and he has a temper. He takes an interest in all sorts of problems—not only in those that plague Road's Bend Hollow:

"My daddy was a great talker. He wasn't taken in by the big people who run this country. He didn't read much, even then when he was young, but he had his beliefs. He said we don't give everyone a break here, and that's against the whole purpose of the country, when it was first settled. You know, there are plenty of people like him. They know how hard it is for a working man to get his share—to get anything. Let me tell you, if we had a chance, men like me, we'd vote for a different way of doing things. It just isn't right to use people like they're so much dirt, hire them and fire them and give them no respect and no real security. A few make fortunes and, the rest of us, we're lucky to have our meals from day to day. That's not right; it just isn't.

"I tell you boys not to be fooled. It's tough out there in the world, and it's tough here, too. We've got little here except ourselves. They came in here, the big companies, and bled us dry. They took everything, our coal, our land, our trees, our health. We died like we were in a war, fighting for those companies—and we were lucky to get enough money to bury our kin. They tell me sometimes I'm bitter, my brothers do, but they're just as bitter as I am—they don't talk as much, that's the only difference. Of course it got better here with unions and with some protection the workers got through the government. But you can't protect a man when the company decides to pull out; when it says it's got all it can get, so goodbye folks, and take care of yourselves, because we're moving on to some other place, and we just can't do much more than tell you it was great while it lasted, and you helped us out a lot, yes sir you did."

He does not always talk like that. He can be quiet for long stretches of time, obviously and moodily quiet. His wife finds his silences hard to bear. She doesn't know what they will "lead to." Every day she asks her husband whether there is anything "special" he wants to eat—even though they both know there isn't much they can afford but the daily mainstays—bread, coffee, doughnuts, crackers, some thin stew, potatoes, homemade jam, biscuits. Mrs. McCaslin defers to her husband, though; one way is to pay him the courtesy of asking him what he wants. I have often heard them go back and forth about food, and as if for all the world they were far better off, with more choices before them:

"Anything special you want for supper?"
"No. Anything suits me fine. I'm not too hungry."
"Well, if that's it then I'd better make you hungry with something special."
"What can do that?"
"I thought I'd fry up the potatoes real good tonight and cut in some onions. It's better than boiling, and I've got some good pork to throw in. You wait and see."
"I will. It sounds good."

He hurts and she aches for him. His back has its "bad spells," and she claims her own back can "feel the pain that goes through his." They don't touch each other very much in a stranger's presence, or even, I gather, before their children, but they give each other long looks of recognition, sympathy, affection, and sometimes anger or worse. They understand each other in that silent, real, lasting way that defies the gross labels that I and my kind call upon. It is hard to convey in words—theirs or mine—the subtle, delicate, largely unspoken, and continual sense of each other (that is the best that I can do) that they have. In a gesture, a glance, a frown, a smile, they talk and agree and disagree:

> "I can tell what the day will be like for Hugh when he first gets up. It's all in how he gets out of bed, slow or with a jump to it. You might say we all have our good days and bad ones, but Hugh has a lot of time to give over to his moods, and around here I guess we're emotional, you might say."

I told her that I thought an outsider like me might not see it that way. She wanted to know what I meant, and I told her: "They call people up in the hollow 'quiet,' and they say they don't show their feelings too much, to each other, let alone in front of someone like me."

"Well, I don't know about that," she answered quickly, a bit piqued. "I don't know what reason they have for that. Maybe they don't have good ears. We don't talk loud around here, but we say what's on our mind, straightaway, I believe. I never was one for mincing on words, and I'll tell anyone what's on my mind, be he from around here or way over on the other side of the world. I do believe we're cautious here, and we give a man every break we can, because you don't have it easy around here, no matter who you are; so maybe that's why they think we're not given to getting excited and such. But we do."

I went back to Hugh. Did she think he was more "emotional" than others living nearby?

"Well, I'd say it's hard to say. He has a temper, but I think that goes for all his friends. I think he's about ordinary, only because of his sickness he's likely to feel bad more than some, and it comes out in his moods. You know, when we were married he was the most cheerful man I'd ever met. I mean he smiled all the time, not just because someone said something funny. His daddy told me I was getting the happiest of his kids, and I told him I believed he was right, because I'd already seen it for myself. Today he's his old self sometimes, and I almost don't want to see it, because it makes me think back and remember the good times we had.

"Oh, we have good times now, too; don't mistake me. They just come rare, compared to when times were good. And always it's his pain that hangs over us; we never know when he'll be feeling right, from day to day.

"But when he's got his strength and there's nothing ailing him, he's all set to work, and it gets bad trying to figure what he might do. We talk of moving, but we ask ourselves where we'd go to. We don't want to travel a thousand miles only to be lost in some big city and not have even what we've got. Here there's a neighbor, and our kin, always. We have the house, and we manage to scrape things together, and no one of my kids has ever starved to death. They don't get the food they should, sometimes, but they eat, and they like what I do with food. In fact they complain at church. They say others don't brown the potatoes enough, or the biscuits. And they like a good chocolate cake, and I have that as often as I can.

"When Hugh is low-down he doesn't want to get out of bed, but I make him. He'll sit around and not do much. Every few minutes he'll call my name, but then he won't really have much to say. I have those aspirin, but you can't really afford to use them all the time.

"When he feels good, though, he'll go do chores. He'll make sure we have plenty of water, and he'll cut away some wood and lay it up nearby. He'll walk up the road and see people. He has friends, you know, who aren't sick like him, but it doesn't do them much good around here to be healthy. They can't work any more than Hugh can. It's bad, all the time bad.

"We find our own work, though, and we get paid in the satisfaction you get. We try to keep the house in good shape, and we keep the road clear all year around. That can be a job come winter.

"A lot of the time Hugh says he wished he could read better. He'll get an old magazine—the *Reader's Digest*, or the paper from Charleston—and he'll stay with it for hours. I can see he's having a tough time, but it keeps him busy. He tells the kids to remember his mistakes and not to make them all over again. Then they want to know why he made them. And we're off again. He talks about the coal companies and how they bribed us out of our 'souls,' and how he was a fool, and how it's different now. When they ask what they'll be doing with their reading and writing, it's hard to give them an answer without telling them to move. You don't want to do that, but maybe you do, too. I don't know.

"Hugh fought the television. He said it was not good, and we surely didn't have the money to get one. You can get them real cheap, though, secondhand, and there's a chance to learn how to fix it yourself, because some of the men who come back from the army, they've learned how and they'll teach you and do it for you if you ask them. We had to get one, finally. The kids, they said everyone else didn't have the money, any more than we did, but somehow they got the sets, so why couldn't we? That started something, all right. Hugh wanted to know if they thought we could manufacture money. So they wanted to know how the others got their sets. And Hugh said he didn't know, but if they would go find out, and come tell him, why then he'd show them that each family is different, and you

can't compare people like that. Well, then they mentioned it to their uncle—
he works down there in the school, keeping it in order, and he's on a regular
salary, you know, and lives as good as anyone around here, all things told,
I'd say. So he came and told us he'd do it, get a set for us, because the kids
really need them. They feel left out without TV.

"That got Hugh going real bad. He didn't see why the radio wasn't
enough, and he wasn't going to take and take and take. He wanted help, but
not for a TV set. And then he'd get going on the coal companies, and how we
got that radio for cash, and it was brand-new and expensive, but he was making plenty of money then. And he didn't want to go begging, even from kin.
And we could just do without, so long as we eat and have a place to sleep
and no one's at our door trying to drive us away or take us to jail.

"Finally I had to say something. I had to. It was one of the hardest things
I've ever had to do. He was getting worse and worse, and the kids they began
to think he was wrong in the head over a thing like TV, and they didn't
know why; they couldn't figure it out. He said they wouldn't see anything
but a lot of trash, and why should we let it all come in here like that? And
he said they'd lose interest in school, and become hypnotized or something,
and he'd read someplace it happens. And he said gadgets and machines,
they came cheap, but you end up losing a lot more than you get, and that
was what's happening in America today.

"Now, the kids could listen for so long, and they're respectful to him,
to both of us, I think you'll agree. They'd try to answer him, real quiet,
and say it wasn't so important, TV wasn't, it was just there to look at, and
we could all do it and have a good time. And everyone was having it, but
that didn't mean that the world was changing, or that you'd lose anything
just because you looked at a picture every once in a while.

"And finally, as I say, I joined in. I had to—and I sided with them. I said
they weren't going to spend their lives looking at TV, no sir, but it would
be O.K. with me if we had it in the house, that I could live with it, and I
think we could all live with it. And Hugh, he just looked at me and didn't
say another word, not that day or any other afterwards until much later on,
when he had the set already, and he would look at the news and listen real
careful to what they tell you might be happening. He told me one day, it was
a foolish fight we all had, and television wasn't any better or worse than a
lot of other things. But he wished the country would make more than cheap
TVs. 'We could all live without TV if we had something more to look forward to,' he said. I couldn't say anything back. He just wasn't feeling good
that day, and to tell the truth TV is good for him when he's like that,
regardless of what he says. He watches it like he used to listen to his radio,
and he likes it better than he'd ever admit to himself, I'm sure."

On Sundays they go to church. Hugh says he doesn't much believe
in "anything," but he goes; he stays home only when he doesn't feel
good, not out of any objection to prayer. They all have their Sunday

clothes, and they all enjoy getting into them. They become new and different people. They walk together down the hollow and along the road that takes them to a Baptist church. They worship vigorously and sincerely, and with a mixture of awe, bravado, passion, and restraint that leaves an outside observer feeling, well—skeptical, envious, surprised, mystified, admiring, and vaguely nostalgic. I think they emerge much stronger and more united for the experience, and with as much "perspective," I suppose, as others get from different forms of contemplation, submission, and joint participation. Hugh can be as stoical as anyone else, and in church his stoicism can simply pour out. The world is confusing, you see. People have always suffered, good people. Somewhere, somehow, it is not all for naught—but that doesn't mean one should raise one's hopes too high, not on this earth.

After church there is "socializing," and its importance need not be stressed in our self-conscious age of "groups" that solve "problems" or merely facilitate "interaction." When I have asked myself what "goes on" in those "coffee periods," I remind myself that I heard a lot of people laughing, exchanging news, offering greetings, expressing wishes, fears, congratulations and condolences. I think there is a particular warmth and intensity to some of the meetings because, after all, people do not see much of one another during the week. Yet how many residents of our cities or our suburbs see one another as regularly as these "isolated" people do? Hugh McCaslin put it quite forcefully: "We may not see much of anyone for a few days, but Sunday will come and we see everyone we want to see, and by the time we go home we know everything there is to know." As some of us say, they "communicate efficiently."

There is, I think, a certain hunger for companionship that builds up even among people who do not feel as "solitary" as some of their observers have considered them. Particularly at night one feels the woods and the hills close in on "the world." The McCaslins live high up in a hollow, but they don't have a "view." Trees tower over their cabin, and the smoke rising from their chimney has no space at all to dominate. When dusk comes there are no lights to be seen, only their lights to turn on. In winter they eat at about 5 and they are in bed about 7:30 or 8. The last hour before bed is an almost formal time. Every evening Mr. McCaslin smokes his pipe and either reads or carves wood. Mrs. McCaslin has finished putting things away after supper and sits sewing—"mending things and fixing things; there isn't a day goes by that something doesn't tear." The children watch television. They have done what homework they have (or are willing to do) before supper. I have never heard them reprimanded for failing to study. Their parents tell them to go to school; to stay in school; to do well in school—but they aren't exactly sure it makes much difference. They ask the young to study, but I believe it is against their "beliefs" to say one thing and mean another, to children or anyone else.

In a sense, then, they are blunt and truthful with each other. They say what they think, but worry about how to say what they think so that the listener remains a friend or—rather often—a friendly relative. Before going to bed they say good-night, and one can almost feel the reassurance that goes with the greeting. It is very silent "out there" or "outside."

"Yes, I think we have good manners," Hugh McCaslin once told me. "It's a tradition, I guess, and goes back to Scotland, or so my daddy told me. I tell the kids that they'll know a lot more than I do when they grow up, or I hope they will; but I don't believe they'll have more consideration for people—no sir. We teach them to say hello in the morning, to say good morning, like you said. I know it may not be necessary, but it's good for people living real close to be respectful of one another. And the same goes for the evening.

"Now, there'll be fights. You've seen us take after one another. That's O.K. But we settle things on the same day, and we try not to carry grudges. How can you carry a grudge when you're just this one family here, and miles away from the next one? Oh, I know it's natural to be spiteful and carry a grudge. But you can only carry it so far, that's what I say. Carry it until the sun goes down, then wipe the slate clean and get ready for another day. I say that a lot to the kids."

Once I went with the McCaslins to a funeral. A great-uncle of Mrs. McCaslin had died at 72. He happened to be a favorite of hers and of her mother. They lived much nearer to a town than the McCaslins do, and were rather well-to-do. He had worked for the county government all his life—in the Appalachian region, no small position. The body lay at rest in a small church, with hand-picked flowers in bunches around it. A real clan had gathered from all over, as well as friends. Of course it was a sad occasion, despite the man's advanced age; yet even so I was struck by the restraint of the people, their politeness to one another, no matter how close or "near kin" they were.

For a moment I watched them move about and tried to block off their subdued talk from my brain. It occurred to me that, were they dressed differently and in a large manor home, they might very much resemble English gentry at a reception. They were courtly people; they looked it and acted it. Many were tall, thin, and close-mouthed. A few were potbellied, as indeed befits a good lusty duke or duchess. They could smile and even break out into a laugh, but it was always noticeable when it happened. In general they were not exactly demonstrative or talkative, yet they were clearly interested in one another and had very definite and strong sentiments, feelings, emotions, whatever. In other words, as befits the gentry, they had feelings but had them under "appropriate" control. They also seemed suitably resigned, or philosophical—as the circumstances warranted. What crying there was, had already been done. There were no outbursts of any kind, and no joviality either. It was not a wake.

A few days later Hugh McCaslin of Road's Bend Hollow talked about the funeral and life and death:

"He probably went too early, from what I hear. He was in good health, and around here you either die very young—for lack of a doctor—or you really last long. That's the rule, though I admit we have people live to all ages, like anywhere I guess. No, I don't think much of death, even being sick as I am. It happens to you, and you know it, but that's O.K. When I was a boy I recall my people burying their old people, right near where we lived. We had a little graveyard, and we used to know all our dead people pretty well. You know, we'd play near their graves, and go ask our mother or daddy about who this one was and what he did, and like that. The other way was through the Bible: Everything was written down on pieces of paper inside the family Bible. There'd be births and marriages and deaths, going way back, I guess as far back as the beginning of the country. I'm not sure of the exact time, but a couple of hundred years, easy.

"We don't do that now—it's probably one of the biggest changes, maybe. I mean apart from television and things like that. We're still religious, but we don't keep the records, and we don't bury our dead nearby. It's just not that much of a home here, a place that you have and your kin always had and your children and theirs will have, until the end of time, when God calls us all to account. This here place—it's a good house, mind you—but it's just a place I got. A neighbor of my daddy's had it, and he left it, and my daddy heard and I came and fixed it up and we have it for nothing. We worked hard and put a lot into it, and we treasure it, but it never was a home, not the kind I knew, and my wife did. We came back to the hollow, but it wasn't like it used to be when we were kids and you felt you were living in the same place all your ancestors did. We're part of this land, we were here to start and we'll probably see it die, me or my kids will, the way things are going. There will be no one left here and the stripminers will kill every good acre we have. I thought of that at the funeral. I thought maybe it's just as well to die now, if everything's headed in that direction. I guess that's what happens at a funeral. You get to thinking."

KENNEDY HEARS OF NEED
T. N. Bethell, Pat Gish, & Tom Gish

Sen. Robert F. Kennedy came to Eastern Kentucky this week for a first-hand look at some of the poorest counties in all of Appalachia. After two days of touring and talking with residents, he termed many conditions in the Kentucky mountains "intolerable," "unacceptable," and "unsatisfactory." Kennedy looked at poor housing, strip-mined areas, outmoded school buildings and traveled over dusty rutted roads to the heads of hollows to talk with several mountain families who are suffering because they have no jobs and little or no income.

He talked with poor people at a one-room school at Vortex, Wolf county, looked over an urban renewal area at Hazard, drove through strip-mined hills in Knott county, spoke to students at Alice Lloyd College, held an open hearing at the gymnasium at Fleming-Neon High School in Letcher county and spoke to students at the University of Kentucky Community College in Prestonburg. All along the tour route, he stopped occasionally for visits with poor families typical of the many mountain residents who are in economic trouble.

Throughout his trip, Kennedy heard tales of too little money, too little food, too few jobs, too much exploitation of the mountains' natural wealth by outside firms, too little government aid to solve the massive problems of a jobless society. He commented that there was plenty of wealth in America and plenty that needs to be done in Eastern Kentucky "and it seems to me we should bring them all together and get on with the job."

He said he did not think it made sense to move people out of Eastern Kentucky into crowded cities where there is already unemployment.

From *The Mountain Eagle*, February 15, 1968. Used by permission of the publisher.

"If we can't bring industry in, then it seems to me the government should provide jobs," Kennedy said. "Whether we will do it is a different question, but that's what we should do." Both Kennedy and Rep. Carl D. Perkins of Hindman, who accompanied him on the tour, said they felt some of the inequities in federal programs which the tour revealed would be corrected.

The hearing at Fleming-Neon was an official proceeding of the Senate Subcommittee on Employment, Manpower and Poverty. For more than four hours, Kennedy, Perkins and an audience of some 500 Eastern Kentucky residents heard witness after witness tell of manpower programs that don't provide enough work, welfare programs that don't provide enough help, food programs that don't provide enough food. Throughout it all, the plea of both poor mountaineers and professional anti-poverty workers was for programs that would provide jobs with adequate incomes and restore dignity to the lives of mountain families.

Disillusionment and dissatisfaction with current efforts to cure poverty were evident. The head of the Leslie, Knott, Letcher, Perry Community Action Council, E. J. Safford, pointed out that anti-poverty programs so far "have only made the state of poverty more livable." He called for the replacement of welfare checks with paychecks, which in turn would lead to needed public facilities in the mountains. Anti-poverty efforts should concentrate, he said, "on creating jobs that are jobs even though they are paid for by the federal government" and proposed that the poor be hired to build roads, houses, bridges, parks, schools and other public buildings.

Safford said his own agency had run up "against a stone wall because of what seem to be conflicting strategies among federal and state agencies." Programs are "arbitrarily dictated" from Washington, he said, and the agency is seldom permitted to apply the benefit of its own learning, many local talents and several years of experience. Safford said the government has been playing a cat-and-mouse game with Eastern Kentucky people, cutting them off programs, promising them, picking them up again. Eastern Kentucky men need to be assured that they can have work, he said.

Both Kennedy and Perkins indicated they favor the government as an "employer of last resort" in areas such as Eastern Kentucky where the traditional American economic patterns are not providing enough jobs. Rep. Perkins already has made several speeches on the floor of the House of Representatives calling for a WPA-type program which would hire the unemployed for public works projects. Kennedy said the federal government aids private industry which goes into urban ghettos and said he saw no reason why this could not be extended to rural areas.

Judge George Wooton of Leslie county called for programs to put people to work. He is the chairman of the board of directors of the LKLP Council. Hobart Maggard of Perry county said it doesn't quite make sense to have a federal program training people for jobs that don't exist. Frank Collins of Eolia said that he had to quit a training program because his wife got sick, but even if he had completed it, there is nothing around here he could work at. Clay Collins of Yerkes said that after his training ended he received no help from any agency in finding a job but was told he was on his own. Several men said they knew of others who had been trained and sent to Detroit with the promise of jobs, but when they got there, they found no jobs and eventually had to come back home.

Cliston Johnson of Partridge, father of nine school-age children, said "You have to be hungry or see children go to bed hungry to know how a poor man lives." "Did you ever see fifteen kids in three beds?" Johnson asked Kennedy. "I'm moving in that direction," quipped the Senator, who is the father of 10 children.

Johnson said his family pays $26 a month for $112 worth of food stamps. The amount of food which the stamps will buy lasts only two weeks, he said, and during the last two weeks of a month, it's "beans and bread one week, and the next week bread and beans." Johnson gave the Senator some additional advice: "The more children you've got, just add a little more water to the gravy." Johnson also asked for manpower programs which would provide training leading to better jobs. He said he was on one program in which he was taught to write checks—but "who in the hell can write checks" with no money?

Robert Messer of Clay county said Eastern Kentucky needs jobs so people don't have to leave, better schools, hot lunches, water systems, and more anti-poverty money in the hands of the poor people. A Pike county mother of nine said she believes school lunches should be free for everyone. Sie Hamilton, a retired Floyd county miner, said he knew of a man who had been ill for five years and was cut off the work experience and training program, a federal program which provides jobs for fathers of dependent children. After the cutoff, it was a year before the man could get on welfare, Hamilton said. He said he thought all government programs should work together.

John Tiller of Dickenson county, Virginia, said a lot of people have come to the point of being without hope. He predicted a "lot of us in the Appalachian South" will be attracted to new political parties. He suggested that Kennedy turn the hearing over "to the people" and "really hear what bugs us." He said local officials are "great on saying 'help yourself before you ask the government'—try it!"

Tommy Duff, a student at Evarts High School in Harlan county, said he had been expelled because he had taken pictures of conditions in the school restrooms and had them printed in a community newsletter. He and a large number of students asked for better schools, and for better distribution of jobs in the Neighborhood Youth Corps. They suggested that some agency outside the school system determine which students are in NYC. Many of the group wore paper bags over their heads—this, they said, was to show that they were faceless people in the eyes of the school board—and carried signs reading "we can't eat your fancy promises."

Dr. Doan Fisher, a Harlan pediatrician who has worked in Appalachia for twelve years, reported on a survey of preschool children which showed that 30 percent of the low-income children surveyed were below normal height, 17½ percent were below normal weight. Fifty percent were infested with one or more intestinal parasites, 60 percent have rampant dental caries. He said the survey showed no anemia and no vitamin deficiencies. A survey of infants, however, showed anemia was frequently severe, and one-fourth of the babies in health department clinics are below accepted norms for babies their age.

Mrs. James Frazier, a public health nurse from Letcher county, said she thinks school children should be required to attend classes in nutrition. She said many families do not know what foods are best for them. Low protein diets create a high incidence of children who appear dull, listless and undernourished, she said. Wincel Raborn, a social worker for the LKLP Council, said he would like to see food stamps given free to people with no income and would like to see the process of issuing food stamps made less involved for the recipients.

Mrs. Tom Gish, also an LKLP employee, said she had taken a Department of Agriculture list of what a family of eight would need for a month and shopped for the recommended items at a local supermarket. The total cost was $155, she said, yet a family of eight with no income would receive only $82 worth of stamps, or only half what the Department of Agriculture said is needed. The department also supervises the food stamp program. Mrs. Gish said many children would be unable to eat free lunches at school except for extra aid from the Title I program of the Elementary and Secondary Education Act. Title I puts more than $10,000 a year into the school lunch program in Letcher county, she said. If the lunch program had sufficient financing by the federal government, the Title I money could be spent for classroom instruction improvements, she added.

Arthur Dobson, an official of the food stamp program, said the program was not designed to provide a complete diet, but to supplement. He said he did not believe the government should give poor families enough food unless it also can provide them adequate clothing and housing. Otherwise, he said, an imbalance occurs. He said many food stamp families don't have enough to eat, but what they do have is much better than they had before. Senator Kennedy asked him if he could feed his family for a month on $112 worth of food stamps. Dobson replied that he "couldn't possibly get by." "I'm accustomed to a different level," he added. He pointed out that one man who complained about the food stamp program had been smoking a cigarette. "He has to make a choice," he said. Dobson said the food stamp program "works very satisfactorily as a normal thing." Kennedy commented that "it works better for you than it does for the people receiving it."

Eastern Kentucky's coal mining economy, its problems and virtues, came in for considerable comment during the visit of Sen. Kennedy. Harry Caudill testified at the Senate hearing that he believes the federal government should pass a severance tax on minerals in an effort to put some of the wealth of the mountains back into improving the lot of the people who live here.

After a tour of strip-mined areas in Knott county, Kennedy told students at Alice Lloyd College that he would support a severance tax in Congress and would work for it. Sen. Lee Metcalf from Montana already has introduced a severance tax bill, which reportedly would return $25 million a year to Kentucky if it is enacted into law.

Kennedy spoke frequently during his tour of the wealth of Appalachia and its removal from the mountains. "Riches still flow from these hills," he said, "but they do not benefit the vast majority of those who live here . . . and I think that situation is intolerable."

Caudill's statement at the hearing detailed the history of coalmining in Appalachia and accused coal and land companies of draining off the area's natural wealth without leaving anything in return. At the end of the hearing, D. A. Zegeer of Beth-Elkhorn Corp., a subsidiary of Bethlehem Steel, asked to speak in rebuttal to Caudill's testimony. Zegeer said he agreed with Caudill that the area's main problem is a lack of good roads to attract industry. But, he said, much of the testimony at the hearing seemed to indicate that industry is bad.

He recalled that Bethlehem had bought the Jenkins properties of Consolidation Coal Co. twelve years ago and said that "Bethlehem coming here was one of the finest things that could have happened in this area." He said that last year the firm paid $200,000 in property taxes and $500,000 in all taxes. It put $950,000 into the United Mine Workers Welfare and Retirement Fund and donated $50,000 to Appalachian Regional Hospitals. Its 850 employees had earnings of $6,887,693 and average incomes of $8,000. The firm owns 7 percent of the surface land in Letcher county and pays 20 percent of the property taxes, he said. "This is a side of the coin you rarely see," Zegeer said.

In answers to questions from Kennedy, Zegeer said he did not know the assessment rate on Beth-Elkhorn properties but promised to furnish them for the committee's records. He could not recall how much the firm paid for its Letcher county holdings but said he would obtain that information also. He said the company made a profit of 20 cents a ton of coal mined last year. He pointed out that on ten tracts of land bought in 1905 when the coal fields were opened, the mineral owner made a profit of more than 373 percent. (Low prices paid for mineral rights in the early part of the century are a frequent topic of critics of the coal industry.)

Zegeer said his firm does not strip mine now, but has in the past and will in the future if there is an economic need for it. Zegeer said there is a lot of talk about out-of-state ownership of coal mines. But, he said, Bethlehem has 800 stockholders in Kentucky. Persistent questioning from Kennedy produced the fact that the total number of stockholders in the firm is about 50,000 to 75,000. "I would hardly say that is a Kentucky-owned company," Kennedy said.

The senator said he would like to see more industry, not less, "but we have to reach the conclusion from history" that outsiders came in, taking the coal out of the ground and replacing it with money, "and obviously there hasn't been a distribution of that wealth to the people of Eastern Kentucky." Zegeer said he knew when he appeared at the hearing that he was "walking into a lions' den" but he wanted to present a "side of the coin you rarely see." He said Beth-Elkhorn is proud of its operations in Eastern Kentucky and wants to remain here.

On the tour of strip mines in Knott county, Kennedy's party was confronted by no-trespassing signs and guards in automobiles. At one point when Kennedy started onto a strip-mine bench, he was stopped by Roy Mullins, an employee of coal operator William Sturgill, who agreed to let Kennedy and his party and a few reporters enter the strip-mine area but declined to allow "all those curiosity seekers" to go along. To this Kennedy rejoined, "Well, all right, all you curiosity seekers stay behind, and the rest of us, let's get in our cars and go." No curiosity seekers stayed behind.

At Alice Lloyd College Tuesday night, Kennedy urged students to remain in Eastern Kentucky and help others. "You are the most exclusive minority in the world. Very, very few citizens of the world have a college education. And with training comes responsibility to help others. . . . You can make a difference. One person fighting for his people, his community, his state, his cause can make a difference."

The Politics of Coal

EAST KENTUCKY COAL MAKES PROFITS FOR OWNERS, NOT REGION

James C. Millstone

King Coal is back on the throne. Across the coal-rich mountains of eastern Kentucky, the black diamonds are pouring from the earth at a staggering rate. The narrow, snaking highways are clogged with trucks piled high with coal, and with empties returning for another load. The hills rattle with the grinding of the great earth-moving machines stripping away the land to rip out the riches beneath the surface.

Ever-increasing numbers of mammoth railroad gondolas are hauling away eastern Kentucky's wealth faster than ever before, more than 1,000,000 tons of coal a week worth more than $4,000,000, most of it headed from the remote mountain fastnesses to the teeming manufacturing centers of the nation.

Coal is the single most important industry in the impoverished mountains, yet a reporter searches in vain for signs that the smashing new coal comeback is denting the poverty that has gripped, crushed and depopulated this most backward corner of Appalachia.

From the *St. Louis Post-Dispatch*, November 18 and 20, 1967. Used by permission of the author.

Unemployment still runs far above the national average, for the mining industry now works largely with machines, not men. Even as coal productivity has soared by 203 percent in the past twenty years, employment has fallen 65 percent. There are now only 25,000 fulltime mining jobs in all of Kentucky.

The standard scene in Harlan, Hazard, Whitesburg and Pikeville the first week of every month is the food stamp lineup—men, women and children stretching for blocks before the grocery stores.

The dregs of earlier boom and bust days in the coal industry still contaminate the once magnificent countryside. In the hidden hollows of Pike, Floyd, Letcher, Perry, Leslie, Knott, Bell and Harlan counties— the heart of the eastern Kentucky coal field—the joyless coal camps still stand, gray and rotting, occupied by gray and rotting people. The gnarled old women still sit rocking on the tilted porches. The rusted, wheelless automobile hulks still litter the hillsides, backyards and creekbanks. Nearly anywhere in eastern Kentucky where a road may be found it will lead to a ghost town where the ghosts still live.

The coal boom has accentuated the startling contrast between the wealth of this land and the poverty of the people. For the fact of the matter is that some of the poorest, saddest, most despairing people in the nation live on some of the richest land and have as their next door neighbors some of the most profitable corporations in America.

If the coal surge has brought no comfort to those who stand in the food lines and rock on the creaking porches, it must be a source of deep satisfaction in far-off board rooms in Philadelphia, New York, Pittsburgh, Detroit and Baltimore. These figures tell why: production of bituminous coal has risen spectacularly in Kentucky, from a low point of 62,800,000 tons in 1959 to a record high of 93,100,000 tons last year, a 50 percent increase. Production last year went up 8 percent over 1965 and the state's coal output was valued at $345,000,000. The surge was most noticeable in eastern Kentucky which produced nearly 51 million tons in 1966, close to 10 percent above the 1965 totals.

Among the states, Kentucky ranks second to West Virginia in total coal production, turning out 17 percent of the nation's coal last year and its experience mirrors the national trend. American coal production has soared from a low mark of 403,000,000 tons five years ago to a record 533,000,000 tons last year.

Consumption of coal has risen steadily since 1961 after a long slump that began in 1920. Coal is slowly reclaiming from oil and gas its share of the nation's energy market and has gained on its competitors every year since 1963.

The future for coal could hardly be brighter. The Federal Power Commission estimates that the needs of the electric utility industry, which now consumes half the coal produced in the nation, will increase two-and-one-half times by 1980. Exciting new uses for coal appear to be within reach. There is talk of a process for converting coal to gasoline, of utilizing coal in desalting sea water.

The industry in Kentucky has even more reason for optimism. Much of the 33 billion tons still buried in the splendid mountains and along the winding streams of eastern Kentucky is the finest grade in America, low in sulfur content and thus increasingly desirable as a protection against air pollution.

Confirmation of the bountiful times in the coal business can be found in the annual and financial reports of three of the oldest coal companies operating in Kentucky. All three are land-owning companies which mine no coal but own mineral rights over vast expanses of land which they lease to coal operators. As a rule, they receive 25 cents for each ton of coal removed from their property.

The Penn Virginia Corp. of Philadelphia, which until last April did business under the name of the Virginia Iron and Coal Company, started buying up coal lands in eastern Kentucky and elsewhere in 1882, paying as little as 50 cents an acre for mineral rights to land fairly crammed with black gold. It now owns 105,000 acres in eastern Kentucky, Virginia and West Virginia, and its properties produced 7,974,785 tons of coal last year.

Two years ago, a business publication called *Dun's Review and Modern Industry* referred to coal-leasing as "one of the most lucrative investments in America" and cited the Virginia Coal and Iron Co. as "what may well be the most profitable company in all of American industry." The assessment of the company was based on the fact that its net earnings came to 61 percent of its revenues in 1964.

If Penn Virginia was, indeed, the most profitable company in the nation in 1964, it is moreso now because it is making more money now than ever. The 1966 annual report, under the heading, "another record year," told stockholders: "Once again improved demand for bituminous coal, reflected in higher royalty income, was the principal area of growth. A continuing trend in this direction, multiplied by higher per-ton royalty rates, will create an even greater gain in net income for 1967 . . . prices for low sulfur fuel are on the way up and will be re-flected in your company's earnings."

The company reported revenues of $2,700,000 and $2,900,000 in 1965 and 1966, respectively, and net earnings of $1,800,000 and $1,900,000. The consistent 60 percent plus margin would make the mightiest corporations envious. General Motors, for example, nets about 10 percent on its sales, and United States Steel Corp. had a 5.6 percent return last year.

Reflecting Penn Virginia's healthy profits, the company distributed to its stockholders dividends totaling $1,100,000 in 1965 and $1,200,000 last year. By contrast, local governments in the land that produced much of this wealth—Harlan and Letcher counties in Kentucky and five Virginia and West Virginia counties—received a combined total of $75,000 in 1965 and $65,000 last year in property taxes from Penn Virginia.

The company's income taxes were nearly as negligible because of massive tax breaks for coal royalties. Thanks to depletion allowances and capital gains benefits, Penn Virginia paid only $163,584 in federal income taxes in 1965 and $317,000 last year. The result of low taxes and few other expenses provided every Penn Virginia stockholder with net earnings of $4.08 for every share of stock last year.

Penn Virginia has been increasing its coal-based profits in recent years by wheeling and dealing astutely, having bought heavily into the Southern Railway Co., Westmoreland Coal Co., a coking operation in Brazil and a Canadian mining firm.

Equally astonishing profits have accrued to the Kentucky River Coal Corp., Inc., founded in Virginia in 1915 and owner of 190,000 acres of coal lands in eastern Kentucky, principally in Perry, Knott, Letcher, and Leslie counties. In 1964, the 258 stockholders of Kentucky River Coal received $8.76 in earnings for each share of stock and in 1965 earnings per share jumped to $11.17.

With nearly all its income coming from coal royalties, Kentucky River took in $1,500,000 in 1964 and $1,870,0000 in 1965. The combination of low overhead (chiefly salaries of 17 employees) and low taxes left the firm with net profits of $874,500 in 1964 and $1,110,155 in 1965, just under 60 percent of sales each year. Kentucky River paid out much of its profits in dividends, distributing $723,949 in 1964 and $871,710 in 1965.

Visits to county courthouses where Kentucky River holds land and mineral rights accentuated the niggardly return to local governments from these vast holdings. The tax books in Hazard for 1966 showed that in Perry county, the company owns 30,933 acres of surface lands and 75,200 acres of mineral rights. Tax Commissioner (assessor) Roy Johnson valued the property at $2,864,500 altogether but on appeal ("I always have to fight with them, year after year," Johnson said) the company had $400,000 knocked from its valuation. It's final tax bill: $19,017.

In Leslie county, which Harry Caudill has called, "probably the most primitive political entity in the nation," Kentucky River was assessed for 1967, $7,850 for its 17,715 acres of coal land. Tax Commissioner John D. Muncy tried to get a few more pennies from the company with a $908,000 valuation, but Kentucky River's appeal resulted in a final valuation of $782,895.

"It's politics," Muncy said, in the squalid and littered courthouse in Hyden, a cluster of dark and dirty buildings that serves as the Leslie county seat. "They have lawyers and engineers. We don't have enough information to challenge them."

The Virginia Iron, Coal and Coke Co. began purchasing coal lands in 1899 and prospered during the earlier coal booms. Among the legacies it left eastern Kentucky is the town of Vicco, built in the boom days on the road from Whitesburg to Hazard, and which still stands today in its dreary, disheveled ugliness, unaffected by the soaring fortunes of the company whose initials it bears.

Included in Virginia Iron, Coal and Coke's wide holdings are 253,000 acres of land and mineral rights in five states with the largest single amount in eastern Kentucky. This includes 73,000 acres in Floyd, Knott, Leslie, Letcher, Perry, and Pike counties.

In the doldrums as recently as 1958, the company now is boasting its highest profits ever. Its 1966 annual report said, "revenues and earnings generated were the highest in our history. Net earnings amounted to $1.09 a share of common stock as compared with $1.03 in 1965. The coal industry enjoyed a profitable year and your company enjoyed its proportionate position in this healthy economic market."

With $23,000,000 in sales in each of the past two years, VICCO had net incomes of $1,390,000 and $1,470,000 respectively and paid dividends each year totaling $678,876. Compare these figures with the local taxes paid. According to its own figures, VICCO had property in five states last year valued at $13,100,000 for which the tax bill came to $42,390.

In Perry county—an area so poor that last year 2681 of its 6090 families had sub-poverty incomes, according to Office of Economic Opportunity figures—the company owns 6600 acres of land and 27,500 acres of mineral rights. County tax records show that the tax bill for 1966, VICCO's record earnings year, came to $4,653.

In Knott county last year, 1665 of the 2900 families—more than 57 percent—had income under the poverty level. That meant that they were in the lower 1 percent of all American counties in the magnitude of poverty. From a population of 20,320 in 1950, the county has dropped to 16,200 and expects to have no more than 13,600 residents by 1970.

Out-of-state coal companies own an extensive portion of Knott county land. One is the Elkhorn Coal Corp., with headquarters at Charleston, W. Va. For the mineral rights to 15,107 acres of Knott county coal property this year, Elkhorn was charged $2750 in taxes. The company leases coal lands and reported a gross income of close to $1,000,000,000. It netted $506,367 on that amount and paid its stockholders $424,840 in dividends.

Other owners of Knott county coal lands include Kentucky River Coal Corp. and Virginia Iron, Coal and Coke Co., two of the most profitable operations in the coal business today. They paid the county $1985 and $306 respectively in taxes on their properties for 1966.

"The coal companies pretty much set their own assessments," Knott county tax commissioner Delmar Draughn confided. "We pretty much have to work with them. We have no system for finding out what they own. Like they may tell us they own 50 acres at a certain place when actually they own 500 acres. As far as mineral rights are concerned, we can't tell what's under the ground. If a company says an area is barren or mined out, we have to accept it." The valuation on land that is barren or mined out, of course, will be far less than that known to possess fuel coal seams. Draughn said that in his ten years as tax commissioner he has become more convinced that "most of these companies come in here with a straight and honest list."

His confidence in the companies was not shared by some Kentuckians. A study by the *Louisville Courier-Journal* in 1965 concluded that "coal has been a reluctant taxpayer." The newspaper said that "the industry has been able to get rockpile assessments on land loaded with black wealth." "Thousands of acres of coal worth $200 to $300 an acre get on the assessment books at $2 an acre," the newspaper said. "Over thousands of acres are literally hidden from the assessor."

In Leslie county's courthouse at tiny Hyden, Tax Commissioner John D. Muncy described his yearly bouts with the Fordson Coal Co. Fordson has held mineral rights to large areas in Leslie county for years. Consistently, Muncy said, the company submits valuation figures that are inaccurate and just as consistently he places a higher assessment. On appeal Fordson invariably wins.

Last year, for example, Fordson managed to lower Muncy's valuation by 25 percent from $880,000 to $660,000. This year the company tax bill totaled $5189. Just for the record, Leslie county is the most impoverished county of the eastern Kentucky coal producers with two-thirds of its families having incomes below the poverty line. Ford Motor Co., on the other hand, reported record sales of $12.2 billion last year and net income of $621,000,000.

If any further evidence is needed that something is wrong with the Kentucky taxing system, consider Pike county, long the major producer of coal in eastern Kentucky. Pike in 1965 accounted for more than 15,000,000 tons valued at almost $61,000,000. Last year its production went up to 16,300,000 tons worth more than $65,000,000. But although it is one of the nation's richest coal counties, Pike could raise only 18.3 percent of the $4,100,000 needed to operate its schools last year. Also 45.3 percent of its people subsisted on incomes below the poverty level.

To a few Kentuckians, notably Harry M. Caudill, the exploitation of the state's resources by outside investors and the traditionally inadequate local tax rates have been galling for years. Caudill is particularly impatient when local or state officials defend the coal interests as paying their proportionate share of taxes.

Caudill, who fought a lonely fight against the coal exploitation for years, is beginning to attract a few allies among elements opposed to the rising amount of strip mining that is further scarring and gouging the mountains. The Kentucky League of Women Voters, whose project for the year is natural resources, has taken a critical look at the relationship between coal wealth and eastern Kentucky poverty. A study by the League's Lexington chapter found that the coal industry had been "very successful at avoiding taxation of their properties and their operations." One subject that the League is looking into is the possibility of a severance tax. As Caudill sees it, under the longstanding system, Kentucky receives nothing in return for the wealth drained from her hills. A tax of 10 cents a ton, for instance, on each ton of coal mined would have raised $9,000,000 for the state last year.

Calling Appalachia "the last bastion of colonialism," Caudill said, "we think the great wealth that was pilfered from our ancestors by shrewd and unprincipled men should be returned to the people of the mountains. It is certain that Appalachian fossil fuels will power much of the nation in the future. The coal and water will be turned into electricity and will be sold at a profit. Whether these profits will go out as dividends to distant stockholders or stay behind to finance the institutions our people need so desperately and have been promised so long is the question that we in the mountains must answer."

CONSPIRACY IN COAL
T. N. Bethell

To most Americans, Consolidation Coal Company is hardly a household word, even though 78 miners lost their lives three months ago in the company's Mountaineer No. 9 mine in Mannington, West Virginia.

True, its name did appear in newspaper and television accounts of the explosion, along with the information that Consol (as the company is familiarly known to the industry) is one of the two largest coal companies in the world; that its No. 9 mine was removing 10,000 tons of coal a day; and that the company sold more than 52 million tons of coal in 1967, giving it roughly 10 percent of the total U.S. market. But little else was heard about the company at the time.

By way of contrast, the United Mine Workers of America has retained its status as a household word since John L. Lewis made it one,

From *The Washington Monthly*, March 1969. Used by permission of the author.

though its currency had faded in the months and years prior to last November's disaster. The UMW's familiar name reappeared in newspapers around the country at the time of the disaster. Its president, W. A. (Tony) Boyle, visited Mannington soon after the mine explosion and was widely quoted in his praise of Consol as a "cooperative" and safety-minded company. "I know what it's like to be in an explosion," Boyle said philosophically. "I've gone through several of them." There is always, he said, "this inherent danger connected with mining coal," and he emphasized that Consol is "one of the better companies to work with."

A day or two later the U. S. Bureau of Mines admitted that its inspectors had found this same exemplary company in violation of federal rock-dusting regulations in all two dozen inspections of the No. 9 mine since 1963 and had cited the mine for 25 other safety violations since December 1966. No. 9 had already weathered an explosion that took 16 lives in 1954—a few months after Consol bought the mine from another company—and it was widely recognized as an unusually dangerous mine because of the high concentration of volatile methane gas in its coal seams. Yet no action had ever been taken by Bureau of Mines inspectors to enforce regulations or to close the mine. "Close a Consol mine? You must be kidding," one Bureau official said recently when asked why the government had been so tolerant. "Any inspector who closed a Consol mine would be looking for another job the next day."

Competent mining engineers have privately criticized the design of the Consol mine for reasons much more basic than questions of adequate rock-dusting and other "housekeeping" details. The mine is located in the same gassy seam of coal in which the worst mining disaster in American history took place—10 miles away at Monongah, West Virginia, where 361 men were killed in 1907—and has operated under conditions similar to those at a mine in West Frankfort, Illinois, which blew up in 1951 and killed 119 men. "When you go in with a mine like No. 9, you know in advance that you're in potential trouble," one engineer explained not long ago—off-the-record, because he has had connections with Consol. "The company could have taken any one of three steps to minimize the possibility of an explosion. It could have mined coal in well-separated blocks so that build-ups of gas in one area wouldn't penetrate to another; it could have drilled gas-ventilation bore holes from the ground above down to the mine; or it could have mined coal only when conditions were safe, when gas was at acceptable levels."

Mining conditions, the engineer explained, are at their most dangerous during weather changes, when low barometric pressures allow gas to escape from coal seams in greater quantities than normal. The Monongah, West Frankfort, and Mountaineer No. 9 disasters all took place, he said, during or immediately after snowfalls, when the barometer had fallen abruptly. "To the extent that you can predict any disaster," he said, "you could have predicted this one." Why hadn't Consol taken any of the three basic precautions? "They would all have cost the company money," he said simply.

None of this was reported from the scene of the disaster, yet it must have been common knowledge among mining engineers—and presumably among the top officials of the UMW, who consider themselves well informed on safety. But there was no protest from the union —nothing, in fact, except praise for Consol. Why?

What no newspaper or television account of the disaster had mentioned was that only three weeks earlier a federal jury in Lexington, Kentucky, had rendered a verdict against Consolidation Coal Company and the United Mine Workers of America for conspiring since 1950 to create a monopoly of the soft-coal industry, in direct violation of the Sherman Antitrust Act.

This virtually unreported case, formally known as South-East Coal Company vs. United Mine Workers of America and Consolidation Coal Company, marked the first time that a jury has ever found the highest levels of big labor and big business guilty of a conspiracy to dominate a major American industry. Despite the trial's economic and historic significance, the jury's findings received negligible and incomplete mention: a brief account in *The Wall Street Journal*, a few paragraphs on the Associated Press wire, a single story in the *Louisville Courier-Journal*.

After hearing a month of testimony in the United States District Court, the jury concluded that such a conspiracy had existed since 1950 and that the plaintiff, a marginal operator in eastern Kentucky called South-East Coal Company, had been victimized by the Consol-UMW conspiracy and was entitled to collect $7,300,000 in compensatory damages—half from Consol, half from the union.

For people who have tried to solve the puzzle of union-industry cordiality, the trial provided some key pieces—pieces that help tie together an array of activities on the part of labor, management, and government that had been fragmentary and baffling before.

The camaraderie reflected in testimony at the trial, and in Boyle's statements at Mannington, have not always been characteristic of union-management relationships in the coal industry, as anyone over 40 is no doubt aware.

For a period of 60 years after the United Mine Workers of America came into being in 1890, and particularly after John L. Lewis became president of the union in 1920, the coal business was a saga of hostility between labor and management, with almost a dozen years of uninterrupted warfare in the period immediately before 1950. But with the signing of the National Bituminous Coal Wage Agreement in 1950, all that changed—abruptly, permanently, and somewhat mysteriously. Reminiscing later about the 1950 contract negotiations, George Love— then president of Consol and now chairman of its board of directors— would observe happily that "we haven't had any major strikes or labor trouble in coal" since then. And John L. Lewis would say that "George Love is an industrial statesman. Our nation would fare well had we more of his breed."

Harry Moses, who was head of U. S. Steel's mining division during the stormiest years of union-management warfare, would say of the UMW after 1950 that "they have joined us without reservation in all our efforts to combat the influences of competitive fuels, government interference, and unreasonable safety regulations."

By 1959, moreover, Lewis and Love were getting together to form the National Coal Policy Conference, an unprecedented lobbying operation in which coal operators and union leaders, like lions and lambs lying down together, joined forces to assault the halls of Congress. A year later, when Lewis retired, labor writer Paul Jacobs noted that "he was heaped with lavish praise by the mine owners."

But this was the very same John L. Lewis who had vilified management for 30 years in some of the most splendidly rococo oratory ever heard in America: who had condemned two Democratic Presidents without mercy; who had once ironically compared George Love to Samson by saying that Love was "so successful in putting his shoulders to the columns and supports of the temple [of industry] that he pulled it down about his ears." This was the same Lewis who, just a few months before an apparently permanent peace came to the industry, described the corporations which Love represented as "a tremendous group of immense power who have apparently decided to make this struggle . . . final and significant in American economic history." The turnabout after 1950, seen with the benefit of hindsight, was startling and complete. That it didn't simply happen by accident was the verdict of the jury in the South-East Coal Company trial late last year. The jury saw the signing of the 1950 wage agreement as the beginning of an intricate collaboration between labor and management.

The National Bituminous Coal Wage Agreement of 1950 was significant not only because it marked the end of large-scale labor warfare in the coal industry but also because it was the first industry-wide contract in the history of the coal business. One of the principal questions argued in South-East vs. UMWA and Consol was whether there was more than a coincidental connection between these two facts.

Until 1950 the UMW had been in the habit of negotiating contracts separately with three different groups of coal operators: the Northern Coal Operators Association, which represented companies mining principally in Pennsylvania, northern West Virginia, Ohio, Illinois, and western Kentucky; the Southern Coal Producers Association, representing companies in southern West Virginia, Virginia, eastern Kentucky, Tennessee, and Alabama; and the so-called "captive" mines, which were owned outright by steel-producing companies and did not sell coal commercially (except at times when steel required less than their total production).

Contract negotiations were invariably long drawn-out affairs featuring heavily publicized theatrical performances by both sides. Originally the UMW spokesmen had enjoyed the public spectacle hugely; even if most of the newspapers in the country took sides with the operators, the publicity did wonders for organizing efforts among the rank and file and created a solidarity within the union that might never have been possible otherwise. Over the years, however, Lewis and his two principal UMW lieutenants, vice-president Thomas Kennedy and secretary-treasurer John Owens, found themselves arguing more and enjoying it less. Owens, who went to work in the mines when he was 10 years old and is still handling the union's finances at the age of 78, admits to having felt considerable awe when he faced the coal operators: "It was rather embarrassing sometimes to Lewis and Tom Kennedy and myself," he once said, "not being able to cope with the intelligence and leadership that the coal industry provided when they met us." Lewis would never have admitted that, but Owens wasn't Lewis; there was only one Lewis.

The Northern operators produced more coal than the other two groups, and their negotiations with the union were invariably the noisiest and the most heavily reported—partly because Lewis himself represented the union (Kennedy was generally assigned to bargain with the captive mines, Owens with the Southern operators) and partly because the Northern operators were represented for nearly 20 years by Charles O'Neill, a blusteringly intractable man almost as fond as Lewis of melodramatic speech-making. Whenever the two men met, the resulting furor resembled a supremacy battle between bull walruses in mating season. Negotiations between O'Neill and Lewis were generally attended by scores of reporters who reacted much like fight fans at Madison Square Garden, scribbling happily while Lewis elaborately castigated the coal operators for endless perfidies and O'Neill predicted economic disaster for the entire world if American coal companies were forced to pay their miners a penny more. O'Neill backed himself up with a portable squad of statisticians who attended the negotiations with him and supplied impressive data to support his claims. "Ringling Brothers," one reporter remembers fondly now, "had nothing on Charlie O'Neill."

But by 1950 Charlie O'Neill was dead and the Northern operators were represented by George Love of Consolidation Coal Company. Negotiating was something new for him; he claims now that he didn't enjoy it. After all, Love said, Lewis "was an old hand at negotiating and it was something new for me . . . that was sort of like matching an elephant and a mouse."

George Love's self-description is appealing, but wide of the mark. By 1950 George Love was the largest mouse in the coal business. He knew his way around. He had been a coal operator since 1926—after Princeton, the Harvard Business School, and two years as a stockbroker—and had moved into the Consolidation Coal Company in 1943. Consol was a shaky giant then, not yet fully recovered from bankruptcy during the Depression. Love proceeded to take control of Consol by merging it with his old company, Union Collieries, and acquiring the majority of the new corporation's stock—a project in which he had the powerful financial help of George Humphrey, then president of the M.A. Hanna Company and later to become President Eisenhower's Secretary of the Treasury and principal guru for domestic affairs.

Once Love and Humphrey had taken control of Consol, they merged it with Pittsburgh Coal Company, and in 1945 Love became president, at the age of 44, of the largest coal company in the United States (Humphrey chose to stay in the background, merely holding 25 percent—the largest single block—of Consol's stock). If the 1950 negotiations pitted an elephant against a mouse, it was a battered 70-year-old elephant going into combat against an aggressive mouse 21 years younger.

Love remembers the negotiations as a "long, bitter struggle." The presence of so many reporters "forced both . . . the union and the operators to take a public position," and he was opposed to that. He was not accustomed to involving the public in his work. He was also profoundly opposed to government intervention in the coal industry, and when Mr. Truman finally went to Congress to ask for enabling legislation to seize the mines, Love caved in immediately and signed with Lewis. The Southern operators and the captive mines followed suit the same day.

The signing of the contract under such unfavorable circumstances left Love determined not to repeat the experience. The 1950 agreement went into effect in March; by July, after a number of private meetings with Harry Moses of U. S. Steel, Love succeeded, without any publicity at all, in engineering an alliance between the Northern operators and the captive mines. A new organization, the Bituminous Coal Operators Association, came into being for the purpose of representing both groups in future negotiations with the United Mine Workers. Love chaired the first meeting of the new BCOA and arranged the election of Moses as its president.

There was nothing innocuous about the BCOA. Its members outproduced the Southern operators more than two to one. They mined approximately half of all the coal in the United States. This gave them far more than domination of the industry, since much of the remaining production came from small mines, many of which belonged to no association and were too busy struggling for survival to participate in national contract negotiations.

Just as George Humphrey had stayed behind the scenes during George Love's campaign to make Consol the biggest company in the industry, so now did Love stay behind the scenes in the development of the BCOA. As usual, he is beguilingly modest about his role in the organization. In the course of the conspiracy trial, John Rowntree asked him whether he had what might be described as a special relationship with the BCOA. "None," Love said firmly. "Somebody from Consol was a director, along with 23 or 24 others, but we had no particular arrangement with anybody. We were one member out of a great number."

Humility is George Love's long suit. However, BCOA's bylaws clearly provided that voting was to be carried out in accordance with the tonnage produced by each member—one vote per million tons. Consol accounted for 15.5 million tons, but Love also served as representative of other companies with 37.5 million tons. The total tonnage of the BCOA's members was 110.5 million; at each BCOA meeting, therefore, Love controlled 52 votes out of 110. If by some exceedingly remote chance that had not been enough to give him control of the organization, he had only to join forces with his friend Harry Moses, who represented the 19.2 million tons produced by U. S. Steel and therefore had 19 votes. By no possible combination could the other members of the BCOA defeat Love's aggregate 71 votes with their 39; voting was by a simple majority, not by two-thirds. "Very democratic organization," Rowntree's co-counsel, Gibson Downing, remarked drily at one point during the trial—a private joke that amused the 12 jurors.

The public and the press were not aware in 1950 of the means by which a single company had come to hold a commanding position in one of the nation's largest industries. John L. Lewis must have been very much aware of it, and he may also have been impressed by the speed and sophistication with which George Love had engineered such a coup. At any rate Lewis wasted no time in dealing with the new Bituminous Coal Operators Association. Less than six months after the formation of the BCOA, Lewis approached Harry Moses about renegotiating the 1950 contract—although it still had nearly a year to run.

Moses was ready and willing to meet with Lewis. They conferred in complete secrecy—the first time since 1890 that labor negotiations in the coal industry had been closed to the press, public, and the union membership. Reporters could get nothing out of either one of them during the negotiations, except that there was no hint of a strike. The agreement, when they reached it, was immediately ratified by the BCOA and by the membership of the UMW. Lewis came out of the negotiations sounding like a new man. "The country," he said, "is now freed from any thought of a so-called coal crisis for an indefinite period of time."

The change was dramatic. The threat of a paralyzing national strike had always been Lewis's principal weapon against the coal operators and he had always held it over them like a Damoclean sword. He removed that sword in 1950 by stating publicly that there would be no further crises in the coal industry. It was not the kind of thing anyone expected, and it was inconsistent with historical patterns.

The pattern in Lewis's case was particularly clear. Since 1920 he had been hammering away without variation on three principal themes: employment for the maximum possible number of men; pay at the highest possible levels; work in the best possible conditions. He was basically opposed to socialism, but he favored government regulation of the industry whenever it would advance his goals. The coal industry had a tendency to overproduce, resulting in unpredictable layoffs of large numbers of men and temporary closing of mines. Lewis wanted the government to help with the problem. At the union's 1936 convention, for example, he called on President Roosevelt to set up "a system of proper federal regulation which will encompass a synchronized system of price-fixing and allocation of tonnage on a basis equitably fair to mine workers and operators alike." Two years later he was demanding "a parity in competitive conditions which will as nearly as practicable allow each of the operators in the several [union] districts an opportunity to secure their fair share of the markets, and, at the same time, provide as equitably as possible equal work opportunities for all the mine workers employed in various districts."

Ten years later, in 1948, he was battling the post-war overproduction that was creating new turmoil in the industry. "If the operators of this country can't give any leadership on the commercial side of this industry," he thundered, "the United Mine Workers can and will . . . if there are only three days' work in this industry, we will all have the three days' work." It was no idle threat; the three-day week that Lewis imposed in 1949 was his method of imposing a production control on the industry.

Production control, whether imposed by Lewis or by the government, was anathema to free-enterprise boosters like George Love. "We complained bitterly," he testified, "about trying to operate our mines one day, three days, any number of days that we didn't decide." Love thrived in the chaos of the coal industry. In a well-regulated industry untroubled by overproduction, he might never have built the colossus of Consol. Nor could he have so shrewdly maneuvered half the industry into an association that he controlled. Conditions in the coal industry were allowing him to build an unprecedented economic empire with unprecedented speed; by his own admission, he was not about to let Lewis or anyone else take that away from him.

Through this concentration of power a peace descended on the coal industry that was awesome to behold. Successive contracts were negotiated and signed, without publicity, in 1952, 1955, 1956, and 1958. There were no alterations in the arrangements except for the succession of Edward J. Fox, president of the Philadelphia and Reading Coal and Iron Company, to the job of BCOA negotiator after Harry Moses died. Lewis continued to do the negotiating on behalf of the union, and even his own men generally didn't know the terms of the new contracts until they were read aloud at the union conventions.

The men were not supposed to worry, however. "These things don't come by accident or coincidence," union vice-president Tom Kennedy reassured them at the 1956 convention. "They are all very carefully planned out. Our strategies and our policies are worked out in detail. And it is remarkable how these strategies and policies have worked. . . ."

It is also remarkable, and especially so in retrospect, that the rank and file sat back in silence and took Kennedy's word without argument or challenge. By 1956 automation was creating great gaping holes in the UMW's membership figures, and yet there was hardly any objection to Lewis's assumption of negotiating powers that made it unnecessary for him to go to his membership at any time for approval. When Lewis retired in 1960, Paul Jacobs observed that none of the mine owners paying fulsome tribute to him mentioned his dictatorial control over the UMW. "There was good reason for the silence," Jacobs concluded, "for it was Lewis's autocratic domination of the union . . . that permitted the coal industry to automate without resistance from its workers. It was because Lewis was not responsive to his membership—indeed, because he was protected from them—that the price of coal to the consumer was kept down and the mine owners were enabled to make profits at the cost of permanent unemployment for many mine workers."

In 1958, while Lewis was still experimenting with the management side of coal mining and Love was leading Consol to the highest profits in its history, the BCOA and the UMW sat down together once again to negotiate a contract. This time the secrecy surrounding the meetings was so total that few people outside the industry even knew they were taking place. Lewis represented the union and Fox the BCOA.

Aside from the normal wage increases, the agreement included a "Protective Wage Clause." This clause did three things: (a) it specifically prohibited the UMW from negotiating any contract with any individual company or group; (b) it prohibited members of the BCOA from sub-contracting with nonunion companies; and (c) it created a "Joint Industry Contract Committee" with powers to enforce the Protective Wage Clause.

The JICC was to be composed of six members—three from the union, two from BCOA, one from the Southern operators—and it was charged with obtaining certificates of compliance on the Protective Wage Clause provisions from every union mine operator. Operators who failed to sign, or who signed but were later found to be violating the subcontracting provision, could expect their coal to be boycotted. Within six months the JICC had obtained compliance certificates from more than 2,000 coal operators and was taking action against another 1,344 who had either refused to sign or had not gotten around to it. Almost all of the nonsigners were relatively small operators.

Let us now return to the federal trial and to South-East Coal Company's allegations that union and management had conspired to restrain trade.

The 1958 recession hit eastern Kentucky harder than it did the rest of the country, and lasted longer. Coal production dropped 18 percent nationally between 1958 and 1961; the drop was 30 percent in eastern Kentucky. The result was runaway unemployment. With no other industries to turn to, eastern Kentucky found itself in desperate economic straits. Even before the end of the Eisenhower Administration, federal agencies began to look with dismay at the mushrooming poverty in the coal towns scattered through the mountains.

For South-East Coal Company the general problems of the recession were complicated by some peculiarities of the company's own operation. South-East's two mines were nearing the end of their coal reserves, and the company's president, Harry LaViers, faced a major business decision whether to develop new mines at considerable expense in a declining market, or divide the company's profits among the stockholders and quit the business. After much agonizing, the company reinvested its money in the construction of a new mine and a modern cleaning-and-preparation plant. The expenses involved in both projects turned out to be much higher than the company had calculated, and by 1959 South-East was in serious financial trouble.

The company's sales continued to decline as the recession deepened. LaViers went to George Love to ask Consol to act as sales agent for South-East's coal; Consol had effectively monopolized South-East's principal markets by that time, and LaViers hoped to ease his problems by joining Love instead of competing with him. Consol signed on as sales agent, and the company's sales improved—but not fast enough. South-East's expenses continued to run ahead of its income. By the end of 1961 the company was on the edge of bankruptcy.

In January 1962, Harry LaViers went to Washington to visit Thomas Kennedy, who had become president of the United Mine Workers after Lewis's retirement two years earlier. LaViers had decided that South-East could not remain in business unless he could find a way to cut production costs. As with most mines, South-East's highest production costs were for labor. LaViers went to Washington hoping to negotiate a new contract with the union—a contract that would give him temporary relief.

LaViers must have felt a little quixotic as he sat down with 74-year-old Tom Kennedy to discuss a new contract. Kennedy, a former Lieutenant Governor of Pennsylvania who had served as Lewis's faithful sidekick for 33 years, was not about to deal. "You know we have a national agreement," he allegedly told LaViers. "I can't modify that agreement." LaViers pointed out that in 1961, while South-East was losing $250,000, it was simultaneously paying $215,000 into the Welfare Fund. The Fund might have gotten by on a little less, he thought, in view of its $106 million surplus. Kennedy was not impressed. LaViers complained that South-East could not compete against the smaller eastern Kentucky mines, many of which were not keeping up their royalty payments but were being left alone by the UMW. LaViers asked for a new contract which would grant relief from the welfare payments and would pay the company's union men for eight hours at the job site, rather than portal-to-portal. "If you can't do it for an indefinite period of time," he asked Kennedy, "do it temporarily." Kennedy wouldn't do it, period. "We have a national agreement, and I can't modify it," he said, and that was that.

LaViers returned to Kentucky in a low state of mind. After long discussions with his son, Harry LaViers, Jr., who had become general manager of the company, he decided to take a gamble: break the contract with the union. He wrote a letter to each of his employees, advising them that as of March 1, 1962, South-East no longer would be a signatory to the national wage agreement, and asking them to continue work.

No sooner had South-East gone non-union than Consolidation Coal Company stopped selling South-East coal. LaViers testified at the trial that Consol officials told him they would boycott his coal, under the Protective Wage Clause, if he broke the contract. George Love testified that that just wasn't so. He said LaViers had told him South-East could do better if it handled its own sales, "and I had no objection." He could hardly have believed that South-East would in fact be able to do better; South-East, with no sales organization of any kind at that time, would be in direct competition for the Great Lakes market with Consol, which had sales offices in Cincinnati, Pittsburgh, Cleveland, Chicago, and other cities—a sales operation that would, in Love's typically modest words, "compare favorably with that of any other producer."

In 1960 Consol sold 270,000 tons of South-East coal; the following year Consol's sales on behalf of South-East were 133,000 tons. In the first part of 1962, when Consol knew South-East was preparing to go non-union, sales fell to 443 tons. After March 1, 1962, while South-East coped with a strike at its mines and struggled to set up its own sales force, Consol sold not a gram of LaVier's coal.

Testimony in the trial of South-East Coal Company vs. United Mine Workers of America and Consolidation Coal Company lasted four weeks; the jury reached its verdict in four hours. "I thought things would turn out all right when the foreman came back and asked for an adding machine," Harry LaViers, Jr., said later. With the help of the machine, the jurors concluded that the company was entitled to collect more than $7 million in damages from the defendants.

But the ultimate outcome of the case is uncertain. A previous conspiracy suit against the United Mine Workers was remanded by the Supreme Court to a lower court, which ruled in favor of the union; the Supreme Court last month refused to re-hear the case. South-East vs. UMW and Consol is being appealed by both defendants and will be argued next in the Sixth U. S. Circuit Court of Appeals in Cincinnati—but it will take at least 14 or 15 months because of the court's crowded calendar. Meanwhile, South-East Coal Company will be unable to collect a dime and vital questions of future action against this and other monopolies will remain unanswered.

The defendants, however, are likely to continue to prosper no matter what the outcome of the South-East case may be. The United Mine Workers, despite continuing problems of declining membership in a heavily automated industry (fewer than 128,000 members now, compared to about 350,000 in 1948) has net assets of more than $100 million, most of which comes not from membership dues but from investments—principal among them the highly profitable National Bank of Washington and the C&O Railroad. Annual returns on its investments alone run into millions of dollars and increase steadily while membership declines. UMW President Boyle, a former assistant to Lewis who took over after Tom Kennedy's death in 1963, is highly irritable about people who criticize his organization. "These individuals," he has said, "are castigating and berating the greatest Welfare and Retirement Fund and the greatest union in America because the union didn't give them all jobs. We don't have that many jobs to go around."

True enough, as thousands of unemployed miners can testify. But Boyle's job is secure at a salary of $50,000 per year, and when he retires he will continue to get his full salary. The union's 27 district presidents are secure in their jobs, too, at up to $30,000; they will retire at half pay.

Rank-and-file members of the union, on the other hand, draw only $1,380 per year now from the Welfare and Retirement Fund when they retire—if they can qualify. Twice in recent years the Fund has tightened its eligibility requirements. When a miner retires, he must be able to prove that his last job was in a union mine, and he is likely to be disqualified if he worked at any time in a supervisory job or for a non-union mine (the old UMW men who went back to work for South-East after the company's 1962 strike, for example, will never be eligible for retirement benefits even though some of them had been union men since the Depression). Applicants for pensions may request a hearing if they are turned down, but the Fund can refuse such requests and generally does.

The Fund has no financial problems and its trustees are well taken care of. The "neutral" trustee, Miss Josephine Roche, is drawing a salary of $60,000. She is 82. The industry trustee, Henry G. Schmidt, chairman of North American Coal Company, is 68. He receives $35,000 a year from the Fund in addition to the $75,000 salary he gets from his company. The union trustee until his death was John L. Lewis himself, who was paid $35,000 a year—which, when added to his retirement pay of $50,000 a year from the union, provided a comfortable income indeed.

Miss Roche, like Mr. Boyle, is sensitive to criticism. "We do not pass a week without saying, is there any possibility of this sort of thing or that sort of thing happening which may jeopardize some of our benefit payments," she told the union's convention last year. "We try to be on the alert constantly." No doubt. On the other hand, one can only wonder why the Fund keeps more than $67 million in a general checking account at the union's National Bank of Washington, where the money collects no interest. At current rates the interest might be as much as $3 million. While $3 million might be small potatoes compared to the Fund's current cash surplus of $180 million, it would cover more than 2,000 men per year at current pension levels; or, seen from another viewpoint, it would go far toward covering the Fund's $4 million annual staff payroll. In effect, the Fund is giving the National Bank a gift of $3 million—which of course, is a gift to the union, since the union controls the bank. Boyle and his lieutenants are not about to find themselves short of cash when they retire.

Despite these questionable uses and non-uses of Fund money, Miss Roche was quick to warn the union convention: "We cannot promise you definitely that any Fund benefit increases can be authorized in the near future. We can assure you, however, that your comments and viewpoints will be given the fullest consideration." This must have been most reassuring.

For his part, George Love has long since moved on to bigger things than the mining of coal. In 1961 he took over the Chrysler Corporation when it was on the decline, pouring Consol's money into it and attempting a merger with Mack Trucks, Inc.; the merger was blocked by the Justice Department, thwarting Love for perhaps the first and only time in his career. Through the 1960's, however, he guided Consol's absorption of a number of smaller companies and led the company to constantly higher annual profits—from $12 million in 1954, for example, to more than $45 million in 1966. In 1967, he merged the company with Continental Oil Company, creating a colossal combine that deals in all the major sources of energy—oil, gas, coal, and the atom.

The merger is part of an awesome trend that is building up speed while the South-East case waits its turn on appeal in the courts. Within a few months after the Consol-Continental merger, Peabody Coal Company was absorbed by the Kennecott Corporation, and Island Creek Coal Company was absorbed by Occidental Oil. These three coal companies, with a handful of other giants, had already spearheaded the drive that gave 15 companies control of more than half of all American coal production by 1967 (18 years earlier, before the creation of the BCOA and the unpublicized labor-management alliance, the top 15 companies controlled only 26 percent of production). Their absorption by giant oil companies has created super-giant corporations whose full strength is just beginning to be felt by the American public.

This may, of course, be an unnecessarily dour view of the world. George Love is not admitting that he ever conspired with anybody to monopolize anything. For him the question of his relationship with John L. Lewis is a more personal thing. "Mr. Lewis claims he made a man out of me," Love said recently, "and I claim I made an enlightened labor leader out of him. I don't know who won."

The question is interesting. With the unemployed miners of Appalachia and the dead miners of Mountaineer No. 9 in mind, however, it may be more relevant to ask, "Who lost?" Or perhaps, with the future activities of the oil-coal combines in mind, "Who's next?"

THE SCANDAL OF DEATH &
INJURY IN THE MINES
Ben A. Franklin

"Of the 54 men in the mine, only two who happened to be in some crevices near the mouth of the shaft escaped with life. Nearly all the internal works of the mine were blown to atoms. Such was the force of the explosion that a basket then descending, containing three men, was blown nearly 100 feet into the air. Two fell out and were crushed to death, and a third remained in, and with the basket, was thrown some 70 to 80 feet from the shaft, breaking both his legs and arms."

These sentences matter-of-factly describing the pulverization of a shift of coal miners, including the three men grotesquely orbited out of the mine shaft as if launched from a missile silo, are from the first detailed record of an American mine disaster. Antiquity probably explains the nursery rhyme quality—"two fell down and broke their crowns. . . ." For this earliest remembered mine catastrophe, in the Black Heath pit near Richmond, Va., occurred March 18, 1839.

A primitive time, no doubt. The nation was then so new that Martin Van Buren, warming his feet at the coal-burning grates in the White House, was the first President to have been born a United States citizen. The daguerreotype was introduced here that year by Samuel F. B. Morse, while awaiting the issuance of a patent on his telegraph. Half the coal-producing states were not yet in the Union.

The coal mines, on the threshold of fueling a manufacturing explosion that was to make this country an unmatched industrial power, produced barely one million tons in 1839, less than 1/500th of the output today. In the absence of all but the crudest technology, men relying on the death flutterings of caged canaries to warn them of imminent suffocation obviously would die in the mines. Some mines employed suicidal specialists known as "cannoneers," whose mission was to crawl along the tunnel floors under a wet canvas before a shift, igniting "puffs" of mine gas near the roof with an upraised candle.

From *The New York Times*, March 30, 1969. © 1969 by The New York Times Company. Reprinted by permission.

Dead miners were not even counted. Their enormous casualty rate was not archived until less than 100 years ago.

A glimpse into this dim crevice of American industrial history is necessary to put into perspective the myths and realities of the men who work in the mines today. For the real story of coal is not its multiplying inanimate statistics—tons and carloadings and days lost in strikes. It is the agony of those men—a tale as old as Black Heath and one that is so full of extravagantly evil personalities and atrocious acts that Charles Dickens would have loved to tell it. For behind and beneath the mountains of the Appalachian coalfield, miners have remained since Black Heath the most systematically exploited and expendable class of citizens (with the possible exception of the American Indian and the Negro) in this country.

The story at last may have an unDickensian ending. For now, coal miners can see light at the end of the tunnel. In this 1969 spring, 130 years after the Black Heath disaster, the mining industry may finally agree to pay the modest cost of keeping its work force alive, of abandoning the embedded idea that men are cheaper than coal. And—small pittance—we may all be involved in helping pay what it costs to write this long delayed postscript to the industrial revolution; the price of bringing miners into the 20th century probably will appear, as we shall see, as pennies on our electric bill.

In the context of technological advancement in nearly every other area of human enterprise, very little has changed for men who go down to the mines in shafts. Only four months ago, 78 coal miners were trapped and killed below ground in West Virginia in one of the most volcanic eruptions of explosion and fire in the memory of Federal mine inspectors. As at Black Heath, the explosion at the Consolidation Coal Company's 27-square-mile No. 9 mine at Farmington, W. Va., almost certainly was caused by an ignition of methane gas, a volatile, highly flammable, usually odorless and invisible hydrocarbon gas liberated from virgin coal.

At Consol No. 9, a modern, "safe" mine operated by one of the wealthy giants of the industry, the daily methane emission was 8 million cubic feet, enough to supply the heating and cooking needs of a small city if it were captured and sold. The explosion hazard was dealt with there as it is generally in mining today, by only modestly more sophisticated methods than those at Black Heath.

Fresh air is drawn into the mines by giant fans and circulated and directed constantly through the honey-comb of tunnels by means of doors, ducts or sometimes by curtains called brattices (miners call them "braddishes"). The intake air is supposed to dilute and, by law, "render harmless or carry away" the methane and hold the mine atmosphere to less than the legal limit of 1 percent gas. Unless coal dust is mixed with it—in which case the explosion threshold drops significantly—methane will not ignite or explode in concentrations of less than 5 percent. Miners live and die today on a margin of 4 percentage points—or less if coal dust is suspended in the air.

It is known that the giant electric mining machines in use for the last 20 years—machines that chew up and claw coal from the face with rotary bits the size of railroad wheels—churn up an immense amount of dust. The machines have water sprays to settle the dust. But the machines' rapid rate of advance through the seam also liberates much methane.

The first explosion at Consol No. 9 came at 5:25 A.M., Nov. 20, during the cateye shift. It was a day after the passage over northern West Virginia of a cold front accompanied by an abrupt drop in barometric pressure. In the primitive mythology of mine safety, these natural events—the arrival of cold, dry air and a barometric low, which increases the methane liberation in a mine—have been associated for years with disasters. The legendary great mine explosions, from Monongah and Darr in 1907, Rachel & Agnes in 1908 and on up to Orient No. 2 in 1951, have occurred in November and December and in cold, dry weather. The dry air dehumidifies a mine and sets coal dust in motion.

Every fall through 1967, the *United Mine Workers Journal* had published a fraternal warning to union brothers to observe special precautions in "the explosion season." But, no research having been done in a century of such meteorological coincidences, the industry can and does take no account of what it, therefore, regards as a folklore factor—which might interfere with production. The *U.M.W. Journal* had not got around to running the 1968 warning when Consol No. 9 blew up. "We figured afterward it would be no use," a *Journal* editor said later.

No one yet knows what death befell the 78 men in No. 9. Miners who survive the shock wave, heat and afterdamp (carbon monoxide) of an underground explosion are instructed to barricade themselves in good air, if any, and await rescue. But during the nine days and nights that rescue teams stood by helplessly on the surface at Farmington, there were at least 16 further explosions in the mine. The first blast had burst up 600 feet through the portals and ventilation shafts, blowing the internal works of the mine to atoms and knocking out ventilation circuits. At the top, the main shaft became the muzzle of a mammoth subterranean cannon. The massive headframe, a trestled structure of bridge-size steel I-beams that supported the main hoist, was blown apart. For days, a boiling plume of poisonous black smoke alternately belched from the shaft and then unaccountably reversed its flow and inhaled, bursting forth again with renewed detonations below.

Finally, on Nov. 29, all five shafts and portals at the mine were sealed—capped and made airtight with tons of rock, steel and concrete. Not for months, until engineers are certain that restoring ventilation will not reignite coked embers and trigger the millions of cubic feet of methane collecting in the primordial atmosphere below, will Farmington's dead be disinterred from their gassy grave. The same mine was sealed for more than a year following a less violent explosion in 1954 that killed 16 men (including one, Black Heath-style, topside near the mine mouth), and fires continued to burn in sealed sections of the mine even after production was resumed.

If entombing a mine fire to control it seems primitive in this day of chemical fire fighting agents and automatic deluge sprinkler systems, it is futuristic, compared with the industry's performance in disaster prevention. There have been profitable technological advances in the extraction of coal from the seam, and today the industry is on the brink of such a long, secure production boom that big oil companies, with some of the sharpest eyes for markets and profits in the business world, are buying up and merging with coal companies at a rapid rate. But production economies in the past have more often than not been at the expense of human economies, and Big Oil may be surprised to find itself saddled with coal's amazing insensitivity to mayhem and death. It was the fatalistic acceptance of Farmington more than the disaster itself (President Nixon has since criticized this acceptance of death as "as much a part of their job as the tools and the tunnels") that finally started the mine-safety revolution.

At first, at the daily post-explosion news conferences in Consol's cinder-block company store near Farmington (many miners are still today in debt to their employers' merchandising subsidiaries for nearly a full paycheck before they are paid), William Poundstone, Consol's executive vice president for mining operations, insisted that the mine was "only technically gassy." W. R. Park, a senior Federal mine inspector familiar for years with the mine, insisted it was "extremely gassy," and John Roberts, a Consol public relations man, called it "excessively gassy." Roberts, a master of malapropism who greeted the news corps before one vigil news conference by asking cheerily, "Are all the bodies here?" also described the No. 9 explosion hazard as "something that we have to live with."

Then came the parade of V.I.P.'s. U.M.W. president W. A. (Tony) Boyle came to the mine head not only to congratulate Consol on being "one of the better companies as far as cooperation and safety are concerned," but to add that if this "safe" mine blew up, "you can imagine what the rest are like." "As long as we mine coal," said Boyle, the philosophical miners' ombudsman, "there is always this inherent danger of explosion." The then assistant Secretary of the Interior, J. Cordell Moore, the department's top minerals man, flew up from Washington to add that "unfortunately—we don't understand why these things happen—but they do happen," and to venture that "the company here has done all in its power to make this a safe mine." (In fact, Moore's own Bureau of Mines had reported substandard rock dusting at Consol No. 9—the most basic of explosion-prevention measures involves rendering coal dust inert with 65 percent crushed limestone—in all 24 of its inspections there since 1963. The bureau had cited No. 9 for 25 other safety violations since December 1966. Moore probably saw nothing unusual in that because violations are the norm in most mines.)

Hulett C. Smith, then the Governor of West Virginia, also stood before the television cameras and observed more in sadness than in anger that "we must recognize that this is a hazardous business and what has occurred here is one of the hazards of being a miner."

With that, the fuse, delayed so long, finally blew in Washington. The then Secretary of the Interior, Stewart L. Udall, after eight years of more concern for California redwoods than for miners, denounced the whole system of coal mining—the technological and moral systems— as "unacceptable." As an astonished layman, Udall noted that Consol was mining "in an area that really is a low-grade gas field" and that "obviously it is not a solution that is completely adequate to dilute the gas by pumping in air." Within three weeks, Udall summoned a national coal-safety conference which turned out to be one of the most amazing gatherings in bureaucratic history. In a Soviet-style mood of confession, Udall publicly admitted that "we have accepted, even condoned, an attitude of fatalism that belongs to an age darker than the deepest recess of any coal mine. At every level of responsibility, from the individual miner to the highest councils of Government, we have looked with horror on the specters of death and disease that haunt our mines. Then we have shrugged our shoulders and said to ourselves, 'Well, coal mining is an inherently hazardous business' or 'It's too bad, of course, but as long as coal is mined men inevitably will die underground.' These easy rationalizations are no longer acceptable in this time in history."

The stubborn Black Heath syndrome—so costly in human life and so profitable to the industry—finally was broken. Within a week, Bureau of Mines Director John F. O'Leary, on the job one month, issued orders to his inspectors. They were to cease immediately giving prior notification of impending inspections to the operators, a practice known for years to encourage a sudden, temporary kind of mine housecleaning for the benefit of the inspector—"baking a cake," one inspector called it. They were to cease reviewing mine violation reports with owners. Where violations occurred involving imminent danger of explosion, they were no longer merely to write them down as before, they were to close the mine. The list was startling for what it said about past practices.

It is hard to tell which is more gripping—the penny-pinching, corner-cutting and profiteering waste of human life in mines still operated today—Black Heath-style—with bland abandon of what the U. S. Bureau of Mines calls "ordinary regard for safety," or the callous result, the history of human carnage in the mines. The record to date, even the most contemporary chapters of it, is appalling. In the 100 years that partial records of fatal mine accidents have been kept (the early figures are incomplete) more than 120,000 men have died violently in coal mines, an average of 100 every month for a century. The total does not include those who died of what passes for "natural causes" in work that is as notoriously hazardous to health as it is to life and limb. Today, among men aged 60 to 64, the "natural" death rate of miners is eight times that of workers in any other industrial occupation. Chronic lung disease may, in fact, turn out to be a far worse killer of miners than accidents. The U. S. Public Health Service, in unfinished research that is 25 years behind completed medical findings in British mines, has recently documented that coal dust—not the rock dust associated for decades with miners' silicosis—has become perhaps the pre-eminent threat to survival in the mines.

A prevalence study completed in 1964 found that, conservatively, 100,000 active and retired American coal miners suffered from the progressive, gasping breathlessness associated with prolonged inhalation of fine coal dust, a condition known (from autopsy observation) as "black lung" or pneumoconiosis. The U.M.W. estimates that in the 20 years that electric mining machines have been churning up greater and greater clouds of dust at least one million men have been exposed to an occupational disease whose ravages do not stop with removal to a dust-free environment.

The black-lung hazard—as the coal industry and physicians in its employ constantly point out—is as yet a qualitatively and quantitatively uncertain threat to life. It is real enough, however, to have caused more than 30,000 West Virginia miners, normally among the last in the industry to engage in wildcat strikes, to walk off their jobs for three weeks in February of this year to demand that the State Legislature include black lung in the list of injuries and diseases for which disabled miners are eligible to collect workmen's compensation benefits. Until then, only three coal-producing states—Alabama, Virginia and Pennsylvania—authorized workmen's compensation payments (generally financed by the industry) to black-lung victims, and only Pennsylvania has paid any claims. (In Pennsylvania, the benefits are paid for by the taxpayers, not the industry, which may explain how the legislation survived there. Coal has a history of very aggressive lobbying to protect its economic interest.)

In West Virginia's Statehouse last month, a doctor testifying in support of the industry's proposal of further medical studies of black lung before changing the compensation law "in haste," charged that Drs. I. E. Buff, Donald L. Rasmussen and Hawey Wells, the three crusading physicians in that state who had galvanized the miners to strike for health reform, had done more damage as "alarmists" than the disease itself. There was nothing more pathetic, the lachrymose industry witness testified, than a coal miner told to quit the only work he knows just because he is a little breathless. It was a Dickensian performance.

The coal operators, or some of them, have taken the position that pneumoconiosis does not exist. But sudden violence in the mines has been documented monotonously since Black Heath. Last year, alone, 309 miners died in accidents—"needlessly," according to John O'Leary, the new and aggressively safety-conscious director of the Bureau of Mines—and the miners' death and injury rates, already the highest of any industry, are on the rise this year.

The injury severity rate in mines, also the highest, is two and a half times that of lumbering, nearly four times that of trucking. Since records of nonfatal accidents began to be archived in 1930, the number of men temporarily or permanently disabled digging coal has risen to 1.5 million. Today, a miner surviving a lifetime in coal (and there is one chance in 12 that he will not) can expect three or four lost-time injuries, not counting one chance in 5 or 10 of serious and eventually fatal lung disease.

Mining, like prostitution, is one of the oldest occupations in the world and is probably as impossible to stop. From the beginning, coal has been a curse on the land from whence it came, blighting the landscape with strip mines and culm banks and polluted streams, extracting for absentee owners vast fortunes from Appalachian states that are today synonymous with poverty, and plunging generations into despair.

But the scandal of gratuitous death and injury in the mines—almost all of it recognized, as the Interior Department report put it recently, as the result of the operators' "tendency to cut safety corners when profits are low and ignore good safety practices when profits are high" —has finally reached the point at which a Republican Administration in Washington is talking about limiting coal production to save lives.

In testimony this month supporting the sudden rush of mine-safety bills in Congress following the explosion at Farmington, this radical notion was put forth by none other than Secretary of the Interior Walter J. Hickel. "It is clear that our society can no longer tolerate the cost in human life and human misery that is exacted in the mining of this essential fuel," Hickel said. "Unless we find ways to eliminate that intolerable cost, we must inevitably limit our mining of coal, which has an almost inexhaustible potential for industrial, economic and social good."

Republican coal barons must have rolled in their graves. Even from Democratic Administrations, this most destructive of industries had never received such a radical warning. In fact, Democrats in Congress have been the protectors of the industry's economic interests over the survival interests of its workers.

In 1941, at the end of three decades during which miners died at an average rate of better than 2,000 a year, a series of terrible disasters which had killed 276 men during the closing months of 1940 finally forced passage of the so-called Coal Mine Inspection and Investigation Act. It was conceded, as the Bureau of Mines timidly put it then, that "speed of operation and demand for maximum tonnage at a minimum cost resulted in a neglect of ordinary safety measures."

In 1941, when technology in the United States had advanced to the threshold of the atomic era, the gross and calculated neglect of ordinary prudence in the powder-house atmosphere of coal mines was evidenced by the fact that barely half the underground coal miners had been equipped with battery-powered electric cap lamps, approved by the Bureau of Mines for the absence of spark hazards. Incredibly, the rest still wore carbide lamps, which gave their light by generating acetylene gas and emitting an open, two-inch jet of flame.

In 1941, half the mines still used unstable black powder for blasting rather than the safer "permissible" explosives recommended for 30 years by the bureau. The carbide lamps were handy for lighting fuses. Some mines had advanced to the employment of "shot firers," solitary men whose job was to shoot down the drilled coal after everyone else had left the mine. It was a concession to modernity. If the mine blew up, only one man was lost.

Everyone knew that disasters could be stopped. "In view of the present knowledge of preventing explosions, disasters are inexcusable and discredit the mining industry," the Bureau of Mines said in 1940. Everyone knew that more improvements in the feeble state mining laws were being blocked than passed. But Congress heeded the industry's states' rights argument. The 1941 act gave the Bureau of Mines for the first time authority to enter and inspect mines and write reports containing noncompulsory safety recommendations, but no powers of enforcement. The states would take care of that.

Since 1910, when the Bureau of Mines was established, its engineers have been testing and recommending to the industry as approved or disapproved—as "permissible" or "nonpermissible" (words that convey more authority than the bureau had then or has today to require their use)—a whole range of mining equipment, including explosives and electric wiring, lights, drills, cutting machines and haulage devices. Such safety-designed machinery is obviously the key to disaster prevention in mines full of a mixture of inflammable methane gas and explosive coal dust.

Yet, nearly half the explosions—835 miners dead—between May 1941, when the bureau got its authority to inspect and recommend, and July 1952, when Congress next amended the mine-safety law, were caused by electric arcs from nonpermissible mine machinery. Most of the rest involved nonpermissible—but still not illegal—use of explosives.

Unbelievably, when the misnamed Federal Coal Mine Safety Act of 1952 finally emerged from the coal lobby's permissible cutting machine, it contained a "grandfather clause" which allowed the indefinitely continued use of knowingly dangerous nonpermissible electrical machinery "if, before the effective date of this section . . . the operator of such mine owned such equipment . . . or had ordered such equipment." The law also set up two clasees of mines—gassy and nongassy —and it stretched the loophole for nonpermissible equipment even further for the 85 percent of mine owners lucky enough to meet the nongassy standard.

In effect, Congress told the mine operators that "if you were creating an avoidable explosion hazard before we passed this law, it's all right to go on doing so until the dangerous machinery wears out." Today, this means that spark-hazard machines—some of them rebuilt twice and three times over under the same serial numbers—are still in use in some mines 17 years after the law was passed. A count by the Bureau of Mines in 1967, when the law had been on the books 15 years, showed 1,117 pieces of nonpermissible electrical equipment in use in 159 mines.

The 1952 mine-safety act may have been one of the great legislative mirages of all time. It specifically exempted small mines, those with fewer than 15 employees. Although the small mines were depicted in the industry's testimony as too inefficient and limited in capital resources to bear the cost of retooling for the most basic disaster prevention, their number immediately doubled after the law was passed. Large mines were simply separated into smaller units to evade the law. (In 1966, the small mines were finally brought in—with all "grandfather clauses" still intact.)

Moreover, the law was deliberately written to apply to, and to give Federal mine inspectors jurisdiction over, only certain kinds of "major disasters"—defined by Congress as those killing five or more miners in one stroke. More than 90 percent of mine deaths then occurred in lonely ones, twos and threes. Far more than half were caused by rock falls from the mine roof, largely at the working face. The 1952 law established roof-control standards, but only for established tunnels used as haul-aways where such accidents were least common.

Having extended Federal safety jurisdiction to the kinds of "major disasters" that made the news wires and brought discrediting publicity, Congress emphasized that the new law was not to protect the miners from "the lack of, or inadequacy of, guards or protective devices." It was totally silent on hazards to health.

In signing the act into law, former President Truman obviously did not overstate the facts in observing that "I consider it my duty to point out its defects so that the public will not be misled into believing that this is a broad-gauge accident-prevention measure . . . I am advised that loopholes in the law were provided to avoid any economic impact on the coal-mining industry."

Congress has considered mine-safety legislation only three times in the last three decades. But in the years between enactments, there was activity. In 1962, after explosions in the Robena and Compass mines had killed 59 men, President Kennedy commissioned a task force to review the situation. Its report concluded that the industry's continuing disregard of the most basic hazards to life and limb deserved Congressional attention. For one thing, the task force proposed to put a deadline—one year after enactment of an implementing amendment by Congress—on the nonpermissible machinery "grandfather clause." It also noted that Britain, producing only a fraction of the coal output of the United States, was spending more than twice as much on mine health research.

But then in a series of private conferences with Bureau of Mines and Interior Department officials, the Bituminous Coal Operators Association, the union-negotiating arm of the coal industry, persuaded them to recommend to Congress a "grandfather clause" deadline of five years. Since Congress took no action on it, the B.C.O.A. had another opportunity last year to persuade the Bureau of Mines to propose an even further extension to ten years. The capitulation was so flagrant that the White House, overseeing the draftsmanship of the 1968 mine-safety bill, demanded its exclusion from the bill, which went up to Congress in September. It died without hearings.

Other capitulations to the industry have perpetuated the Bureau of Mines's reputation as the submissive captive of the industry it is supposed to police. As recently as a year ago, a long-proposed revision of the 1952 law specifically requiring diversion of a minimum flow of dust-and-gas-diluting forced air ventilation to the working face of coal mines—a point beyond the last moving air current in the established workings—was dropped by the bureau upon the B.C.O.A.'s complaint that it would be too costly.

It has been known for years that progressive contamination of mine ventilation air—a pickup of dangerous amounts of methane or coal dust, or both—results from coursing air from one working section of a mine to another before routing it to the surface. The practice is known to have caused explosions and deaths. Yet a year ago the B.C.O.A. was still dickering privately with the bureau, demanding language in the bureau's proposals for tougher mine ventilation standards which would say that if it cost too much to provide a separate "split" of air to each active working place it would not be required until after "a reasonable time"—not, of course, defined.

It is not that any of these proposals were new. The industry could claim no element of surprise—except at the idea of being compelled to adopt them after so long a history of lethal laissez-faire. Mine technology has been equal to all of these proposed measures for at least all of this century—for 101,000 mine deaths.

The inclusive almanac of mine disasters published by the Bureau of Mines in 1960 (it is now out of print) says that the violently explosive and unpredictable characteristics of suspended coal dust in mines were known as long ago as 1886. A team of mining engineers which visited all the major coalfields in 1908, a year after the worst mine explosion in American history had killed 362 men at Monongah, W. Va., published a detailed report identifying every source of all the subsequent mine disasters (72,501 deaths—1909 through 1968) and recommending disaster-prevention standards which are still not observed.

While lobbying privately against safety, the industry has publicly promoted the idea that the death and mutilation of its workers was a cost of doing business. It got a depletion allowance on its taxes. Its workers got none for their depletion. The industry reaction to disaster was in the brave tradition of "what can you expect in an inherently risky business"—and with some of the most effective lobbying in legislative history to perpetuate the trade-off of cheap life for cheap coal. And it has not been alone.

Even on the left in this medieval atmosphere, the miners' union, the United Mine Workers of America, has been so concerned with helping the industry survive its postwar slump and with preserving coal's low-cost competitive advantage over other basic fuels—oil, natural gas and nuclear energy—that it long ago sacrificed what could have been the leadership of a mine-safety crusade for high wages, mechanized high production, and the highest accident rate of any industry.

Some of the accidents were no accident. In 1947, the U.M.W. in Illinois was found to have voluntarily signed a labor contract with coal operators in that state whose terms forbade the union from seeking improvements in Illinois' mine-safety law, upon which the industry placed such store in opposing greater Federal control. The Federal law of 1941, then in effect, was no threat to the cheapest production economies; the 1941 act had been so considerate of the industry's faith in state regulation that Federal mine inspectors were denied enforcement powers.

Since 1946, moreover, the U.M.W. had become locked in an embrace with the operators nationally. Through the 1946 coal labor contract, which set up the U.M.W. Welfare and Retirement Fund and financed it by an industry royalty—now 40 cents a ton for all coal taken out of union mines—the U.M.W. also acquired an immense interest in production. The Welfare and Retirement Fund collects income from operating mines, not from those harried by mine inspectors or closed down for safety violations.

The U.M.W.'s obvious conflicts of interest are a legacy of John L. Lewis, the 89-year-old former president. Lewis's postwar decision to help the coal industry survive by sacrificing 400,000 miners' jobs to mechanization in return for the company royalties was regarded then as a modernizing act of industrial statesmanship. But it established alliances that obviously are not in the best interests—on mine safety, if nothing else—of the rank-and-file membership. For example, under Lewis the U.M.W. bought control of the National Bank of Washington, a profitable sideline that has furthered the appearance, if not the fact, of shared interests by making loans to coal companies.

Since Congress was no help, in 1946 the Interior Department, which was then operating the mines under President Truman's strike-induced Federal seizure order, negotiated with the unions (as a condition in the contract) safety standards unobtainable by other means. Compliance with the contract's so-called Mine Safety Code, which incorporates many of the reforms talked about since the early nineteen-hundreds, is monitored by Federal mine inspectors. But its enforcement depends on the union, through its contractual right to withdraw men from mines in violation of the code.

Compliance, according to Bureau of Mines Director O'Leary, "leaves much to be desired." The compliance average in 20 of the largest mines is 65 percent, O'Leary has told Congressional committees, but in some states (depending on coal operator attitudes and union militance) it is as low as 30 percent and in one state as low as 7 percent. The U.M.W.'s "safety division" at its headquarters in Washington consists of one man.

The Welfare and Retirement Fund is not the only loser when the men walk out of an unsafe mine. The miners lose wages. When I asked him several months ago whether the U.M.W. had considered negotiating with the companies a requirement that they pay regular wages to men who left a shift while demonstrable code violations were corrected, the U.M.W.'s Boyle, a slight, normally combative Irishman from Montana, told me that that would be impossible because even among miners there were "lazy men"; there would be abuses to get pay for no work. Later, in a safety proposal prepared by the U.M.W., the union finally supported the idea that miners should be paid for time off the job if a Federal inspector closed a mine.

But more than any other witnesses on this year's crop of catch-up mine-safety bills, Boyle has agreed with the industry's position. On the proposed revision that Secretary Hickel and O'Leary have called the reform of "paramount importance," Boyle's stand is significantly less reformist than the industry's. In view of the miserable record of Congressional inaction and protection of the industry, the Administration this year is asking Congress to give the Secretary of the Interior the flexibility of administrative rule-making authority. After hearings, he would establish the safety standards. There would be the right of appeal. It is the system in use since 1938 in nearly every other area of Federal regulatory activity, and the coal industry now says it will go along with it if the Secretary's authority is suitably circumscribed to prevent "arbitrary" decisions. Boyle, however, has said he "would rather take our chances with Congress."

Those chances this year are very good indeed, partly because Boyle himself has underlined the unequal forces working for mine safety in the private sector. The U.M.W. is clearly embarrassed by the reformist zeal of what it calls "Johnny-come-lately experts" since Farmington, like Udall, Ralph Nader and Representative Ken Hechler of West Virginia. For suggesting that the union bears some responsibility and that it has compromised and "snuggled up to" management on safety issues, the U.M.W. Journal recently labeled Nader and Hechler as "finks" in a front-page editorial. And the union magazine has engaged in such a Mao Tse-tung glorification of Boyle and his record as a "union chieftain"—that the U.M.W. has become an embarrassment to its friends in Congress.

Moreover the coal industry can hardly cry poor this year. Because of its secure grip on a growing share—now more than half—of the fuel market in the surging electric utility business, even the National Coal Association is calling the future "glittering." It turns out that local boosters who, through depression, have been calling the state of West Virginia "The Billion Dollar Coal Field" were not far from wrong.

As Senator Harrison A. Williams, Jr., of New Jersey noted in starting mine-safety hearings, coal has become so profitable that since 1966 the three largest coal producers have been taken over by other giant mineral corporations—Peabody Coal Company by Kennecott Copper, Consolidation by Continental Oil Company, and Island Creek Coal Company by Occidental Oil. According to the National Coal Association, the list of oil corporations that have acquired coal-mining companies now includes at least 20 of the major petroleum producers— Gulf, Shell, Humble, Standard Oil, Atlantic-Richfield, Sun, Ashland and Kerr-McGee among them. It was a relief to know, Senator Williams noted, that the safety hearings would not be "complicated" by the usual coal claims of imminent bankruptcy. To the oil owners of coal, Williams pointedly observed that the spectacle of oil-well pollution of the Pacific Ocean off Santa Barbara, Calif., and new evidence of "lung pollution" in the mines "may be trying to tell us something." "In both cases," he said, "we find at the top of the ownership structure big oil companies."

Whether or not by corporate edict from these powerful new coal owners, the fact is that the National Coal Association, the largest industry group, is taking a remarkably calm and even welcoming view of the strenuous safety legislation before Congress this year. By enacting the Nixon Administration bill, which is among the strongest of the lot, Congress could close all the old loopholes at once and take—for coal—a daring new step into industrial human ecology. The Nixon bill would require mine operators to attack the black-lung epidemic among miners by reducing coal dust contamination in mine air to 4.5 milligrams of respirable dust per cubic meter of air, as a starter. The standard is a compromise of the U. S. Public Health Service's 1968 recommendation—3 milligrams. It would become effective six months after passage of the law and could be lowered later by decision of the Secretary of the Interior. The dust-control problem is publicly pictured as a cost nightmare by the industry. The Bureau of Mines estimates that the cost will be only pennies per ton.

The economics of mine safety are the one great unknown in this year's reform spree. No one knows what the cost of a century of neglect has been. Lee White, the chairman of the Federal Power Commission, which regulates wholesale electric power rates, opened the door a crack during Secretary Udall's post-Farmington mea culpa last December by observing that, as a nation, we have lost money as well as life in the mines, "and we must pay." The F.P.C. is anxious to pass on to consumers "all savings in costs that are properly made," White said. But if it takes an increase in the cost of electricity to indemnify the miners who dig the coal for steam-electric power, "I believe the American people are willing and should be willing to pay that extra cost. . . . For all I know, we are not talking about increased rates but only a smaller decrease in rates."

It may be significant that John Corcoran, the president of Consol— a moderate man to start with, by coal industry standards, and one who has been deeply affected by the Farmington disaster—also is chairman of the National Coal Association and a director of the American Mining Association and the Bituminous Coal Association. The industry does seem to be speaking with a new voice. But the coal industry is still a very loose coalition of new humanists and old buccaneers. And as one of its publicists put it recently, "We are like any association—we reflect the lowest common denominator. We have a few members who think the world is flat, so we have not publicly endorsed the use of globes."

[*Editors' note*: Even before the death of thirty-eight miners in the December 30, 1970, disaster near Hyden, Kentucky, the 1970 coal mine fatality toll exceeded that of 1969. During 1970, the year in which the 1969 Federal Coal Mine Health and Safety Act took effect, 254 persons died, compared with 203 in 1969, according to data from the Bureau of Mines.]

Environmental Pillage

THE LOGICAL THING, COSTWISE
Calvin Trillin

Once Bethlehem Steel had decided to begin large-scale strip-mining for coal in the mountains of eastern Kentucky, its public-relations men might have been expected to advise picking a spot as far away from Whitesburg as possible. The *Mountain Eagle*, one of the few county weeklies in the United States that ever print anything that might cause discomfort to anyone with any economic power, is published in Whitesburg; it could be counted on to discuss Bethlehem's plans editorially in terms of mountains scarred, streams polluted, timber destroyed, and houses being endangered by floods and mud slides. Also, Whitesburg's best-known citizen is a lawyer named Harry Caudill, the author of a classic study of Appalachia called "Night Comes to the Cumberlands," and there is no subject that inspires Caudill to greater heights of acid eloquence than the subject of strip-mining—except, perhaps, the subject of out-of-state corporations that have managed to extract extraordinary riches from eastern Kentucky while the mountaineers who live there remain the poorest white people in the

From *The New Yorker*, December 27, 1969. Reprinted by permission. ©1969 The New Yorker Magazine, Inc.

United States. More than any other man in Appalachia, Caudill can bring a controversy to the attention of the outside press and can muster the support of national conservation groups. He also happens to have the old-fashioned habit of assigning responsibility for a corporation's actions to the families that are said to own large chunks of its stock. "This may be the oldest forest of its kind on the planet," he says. "This forest was here when the Rockies rose up and when they went down and when they rose up again. It has withstood two great sieges by glaciers. But it couldn't withstand a single assault by the Mellons."

Bethlehem, through a subsidiary called Beth-Elkhorn, owns the mineral rights to about forty thousand acres of land in eastern Kentucky, but it happened to be convenient to start strip-mining at Millstone, in the southern end of Letcher county—not far from Whitesburg. The work, subcontracted to a local firm, began last summer. The letters from Caudill and his allies—to the governor ("I urge you to call upon Bethlehem to abstain from this act of greed"), to the president of Bethlehem Steel, to the New York *Times* and Charles Lindbergh and Arthur Godfrey and just about anyone else who had ever indicated an interest in conservation—began even earlier than that. Before long, the Louisville *Courier-Journal* ran an item pointing out that the Millstone operation appeared to be in violation of several provisions of a law Kentucky passed in 1966 to minimize the damage caused by stripmining. Then the Division of Reclamation, the state agency responsible for enforcing the law, suspended the permit to mine at Millstone. The president of the state's Izaak Walton League—a young lawyer who had helped write the strip-mine legislation while working for the state—visited the site and eventually filed a two-million-dollar damages suit on behalf of one of the local landowners.

But in a few days Bethlehem's subcontractors had corrected the violations to the satisfaction of the Division of Reclamation—which, the *Courier-Journal* wrote, had come to be so easily satisfied that its behavior "raised suspicions of political interference." Bethlehem took full-page ads in the *Mountain Eagle* and some other papers in the area listing its accomplishments in reclamation and beautification throughout the country. Thanks to Bethlehem's restoration programs, the ad said, "hundreds of acres of previously ugly terrain in various locations have been transformed into flowering fields and verdant slopes, pulsing with game and other wildlife." At Millstone, the strip-mining continued.

The question that occurs to someone seeing Hellier for the first time is what damage a strip-mine could do to it that hasn't already been done. Hellier and Lookout and Henry Clay and Allegheny are what remain of an isolated cluster of camps that various coal companies built in Pike county for their workers earlier in the century. The roads are accompanied by streams the color and consistency of old gravy, and dotted with the hardy roadside blossom of eastern Kentucky— abandoned automobile hulks. The creeks are spanned by decaying bridges leading to dilapidated old coal-camp houses, many of them now occupied by retired or disabled miners. The lines of houses are broken occasionally by abandoned slag heaps—known locally as "red dogs"—which sometimes catch fire from spontaneous combustion and burn for years, giving off a putrid smoke. The second site scheduled for strip-mining by Beth-Elkhorn is not far from the old camps, and one of the protest letters sent to the president of Bethlehem came from the Pike County Citizens Association, a poor people's organization that has its headquarters in an old company store in Hellier.

The mineral rights to the land that many poor mountain people live on were sold to coal companies for practically nothing at the turn of the century under the terms of what is known as a "broad-form deed"—giving the coal company the rights to do any damage to the land it considers necessary for the extraction of the coal. Strip-mining happens to be the cheapest way of getting coal. In the dense mountains that cover eastern Kentucky, it amounts to cutting out a wedge all the way around a mountain, as if for building a very wide road—the purpose usually being to remove the outer edge of a seam of coal whose center has already been extracted by underground mining. If the dirt and rock that covered the coal are merely pushed off the cut into a pile on the mountainside, they can, with the addition of some moisture, slide down into the valley below, burying a road or a corn- field, blocking a creek, or destroying a house. The sediments can pollute rivers and alter the channels of creeks enough to cause flash floods. If the coal mined has a high sulphur content—which a small percentage of coal in eastern Kentucky does—the "acid mine water" formed from its exposure can get into a stream and kill every living thing. In eastern Kentucky, there are fifty-five thousand acres of "orphan mines"—land that, having been reached before strip-mining regulations were established, was mined with no consideration whatever for the reclamation of the mountain or the life of the people below. "Right when they do it, it's not so awful bad," Edith Easterling, a local woman who runs the Marrowbone Folk School, in Lookout, has said. "But when it rains, it's terrible. And after they've ruined your land, you still pay taxes on it. You can go to town, but you can't get a lawyer to represent you." In an eastern Kentucky county, most of the "town people"—particularly the public officials—have some financial interest in the coal industry, and it is sometimes said of the local lawyers, "If there's one who's not on a monthly retainer to a coal company, it's an oversight." The Appalachian Volunteers and other poverty workers who came to eastern Kentucky at the beginning of the War on Poverty inevitably found strip-mining the most compelling issue among the poor—and the issue that brought the greatest hostility from the people in political and economic control.

In Pike county, opposition to strip-mining reached a climax in the summer of 1967. In a quiet place called Island Creek, a retired miner named Jink Ray told the Puritan Coal Company that its bulldozer was not going to come on the steep mountainside that rises in back of his house. Ray was supported not only by poverty workers but by a number of his neighbors, two of whom stood in front of Puritan's bulldozer when an attempt was made to come onto the property. After some arguing in court and a lot of arguing in the newspapers, the governor himself withdrew Puritan's permit. The incident is regarded by some local historians as the only victory for poor people in the history of Pike county, but the coal operators also seem to have profited from the experience. Landowners are ordinarily given a small royalty on the coal removed from their land, even if payment is not legally required, and if a man appears to be as stubborn as Jink Ray even after money is offered, coal operators skip his land rather than start a controversy that could stir up pressure for stricter regulations or could get somebody shot. The policy doesn't involve passing over much land. Although poor people in Pike county might point to Jink Ray as an example of how a mountaineer ought to act when his land is threatened, years of being poor and helpless have left many of them afraid to act that way.

"Fear in poor people is one of the awfulest things," Edith Easterling says.

An organized effort of poor people against strip-mining in eastern Kentucky is hampered by the fact that there are practically no organizers left. Ten days after Jink Ray's victory, three poverty workers were arrested for sedition—attempting to overthrow the government of Pike county. Not long after that, the Appalachian Volunteers lost the grant from the Office of Economic Opportunity they were operating under. Eventually, the Kentucky Un-American Activities Committee—widely known as QUACK—came to hold hearings at the Pike county courthouse in order to ascertain how far Communists had gone in subverting established authority. When Edith Easterling was subpoenaed, she used the occasion to make known her opinion of the county's officials. "I went down to the courthouse," she recalls. "I told them, 'I've not done but one thing I'm ashamed of, and that's to vote for these dirty birds.'" About the only outside organizer left in Pike county is the director of the Pike County Citizens Association, and he and Edith Easterling don't get along—so the remnant of an organization is split into two remnants.

There are some people who believe that Bethlehem might run into violence in Pike county; strip-mining equipment has been blown up in the past. But anger in the past has usually been related to strip-mining that occurs right above people's houses, and the proposed Bethlehem site is rather remote. It's a section called Flatwoods, back in the mountains, where the auto bodies and the slag heaps and the grim, gray houses of Hellier can't be seen. It's so removed from Hellier, in fact, that it's still beautiful.

David Zegeer, the division superintendent of Beth-Elkhorn's operations in eastern Kentucky, talks a lot about blackberries. A visitor to Zegeer's office in Jenkins is almost certain to leave with a tiny jar of pure blackberry jelly—made, the label says, from blackberries "picked from the fruitful vines of Marshall's Branch surface mine." Beth-Elkhorn had never done any extensive strip-mining in eastern Kentucky, but several years ago, at a place near Jenkins called Marshall's Branch, it did do some surface mining, mainly by augering—a method that is similar to stripping, although somewhat less severe. According to Zegeer, the results of Beth-Elkhorn's reclamation work at Marshall's Branch demonstrate that surface mining actually improves the land. For one thing, he says, the mining cut creates a flat area encircling the mountain (known in the trade as a "bench"), and "except for aesthetically, there is no commercial value to steep land." ("Dave told me the bench would be good for cattle grazing," Harry Caudill likes to say, "and I told him when Bethlehem finished stripping all that land they will have created the longest, narrowest cow pasture in the history of agriculture—fifty feet wide and five thousand miles long.") Zegeer enjoys taking visitors around the mountain at Marshall's Branch, remarking on what a nice access road the flat bench makes, describing the *Sericea lespedeza* and crown vetch and Chinese chestnuts Beth-Elkhorn has planted, and, most enthusiastically of all, pointing out the blackberries. Because of Zegeer's enthusiasm, the Jenkins Kiwanis Club plans to dispense jelly jars to the women living near Marshall's Branch, buy the jelly they produce for a fair market price, and sell it at stores in state parks—after affixing a label that points out its origin. "Not to fight back, exactly," Zegeer says, "but just to show what people can do." Although Zegeer says he is proud to have a hand in improving the land of eastern Kentucky and helping the economy of Jenkins, he emphasizes that the decision to begin strip-mining was made because it was "the logical thing, costwise." An area northwest of Jenkins that has been almost mined out by Bethlehem through one of its underground mines, for instance, still has about ten million tons of outcrop coal that can be reached through strip-mining, and Zegeer says that the time to mine it is obviously when it can be used to keep the underground mine's preparation plant operating. Zegeer points out that Bethlehem paid good money for the mineral rights to the land, and obviously has the right to get its money's worth by recovering all the coal in it. (It is common in the coal industry to talk about "recovering" coal, as if the mountain snatched the coal away from Bethlehem sometime in the past, and Bethlehem is obligated to get it back; a pro-strip-mining letter to the *Mountain Eagle* said, "I don't believe God would have put all this coal here if he hadn't intended for it to be taken out.") In an interview in the *Mountain Eagle* just after Bethlehem announced its strip-mining plans, Zegeer was quoted as saying, "If there's something wrong with my company, there's something wrong with the country."

There are, of course, disagreements between Zegeer and his opponents about the facts of strip-mining. According to Zegeer, for instance, the idea that strip-mining causes sedimentation in the streams is one of the many myths concocted by the conservationists; according to the conservationists, the idea that strip-mining is vital to the eastern Kentucky economy is one of the many myths invented by the coal operators. But Zegeer and the conservationists would disagree even if they agreed on the facts. The reclamation job that Zegeer proudly displays at Marshall's Branch—where the vertical side of the cut still forms a naked bluff that is thirty feet high in places—would strike most conservationists as a horror. And when Zegeer is told of some conservationists believing that Bethlehem ought to be satisfied with the millions of tons of coal it has already deep-mined from the area northwest of Jenkins, he shakes his head in amazement and says, "You can't just walk away from ten million tons of high-grade metallurgical coal."

The decision of Bethlehem to join the local firms that have been strip-mining in eastern Kentucky was bound to revitalize the anti-strip-mining efforts of Kentucky conservationists—partly because Bethlehem could be expected to be more sensitive to criticism than local coal operators. There is obviously an increasing national concern about problems of the environment, and Bethlehem, having been accused of doing more than its share to create the problems, has been active lately in trying to patch up its reputation. It is widely believed that public-relations considerations might lead a corporation such as Bethlehem to stop doing anything that offended any vocal segment of the population —although in this case public-relations considerations have so far merely led it to run full-page newspaper ads about good works and to give away jars of blackberry jelly while continuing to do whatever is logical costwise.

Not long after strip-mining was begun by Beth-Elkhorn at Millstone, the Kentucky Conservation Council passed a resolution calling for the prohibiting of strip-mining in eastern Kentucky—the feeling of many conservationists being that the steep terrain and heavy rainfall of that part of the state make reclamation impossible. When the council called a meeting in Lexington for people who were interested in lobbying to turn the resolution into law, those who attended did not appear to be particularly optimistic about their chances for success. From past battles, they are aware that the defenders of strip-mining have formidable economic and political resources. It is also possible that the most effective weapon conservationists had in the past—public opinion—may have been weakened by their own efforts. Even without strict enforcement, the 1966 law makes it much less likely that a poor mountaineer will lose his house to a strip-mining landslide, and the general policy of avoiding people like Jink Ray makes it much less likely that strip-miners will become involved in an embarrassing confrontation. The conservationists are left in the position of talking less about living, identifiable people and more about sedimentation and ecological balance and the obligation of the society toward generations unborn. "People!" Caudill said at the Lexington meeting when somebody mentioned to him that the human element in the controversy might have diminished. "We've already fought this on the people issue, and nobody cared. They said, 'They're just a bunch of paupers—let it go.' Nobody cares about people in this country. I think we're better off talking about the environment."

HOT TIME AHEAD
T. N. Bethell

Sie Saylor of Cowfork, Kentucky, makes his living as night watchman for the Round Mountain Coal Company. One Saturday night last fall he was parked as usual in his jeep on the access road to the company's Leslie county strip mine when four men suddenly appeared out of the darkness. Before he could get a good look at them, they flashed a spotlight in his eyes, grabbed him, tied him up and blindfolded him.

For nearly four hours, while Sie Saylor sat captive in his own jeep, the men drove it around, stopping frequently, and it wasn't long before he realized they were setting explosive charges. The men worked quietly and professionally. They seemed to be familiar with Round Mountain's operations—they were, in fact, using the company's own explosives, liberated from a supply shed.

In due course the saboteurs removed Sie Saylor to a safe place and then detonated their charges. By the time the watchman had worked

From *Mountain Life and Work*, April 1969. Used by permission of the author.

himself free of his blindfold, the four men were gone. Gone too—totally demolished or badly damaged—was nearly $750,000 worth of the company's equipment, including a giant diesel shovel, a D-9 bulldozer (largest model that Caterpillar makes), an auger, a conveyor belt, three hi-lifts (rubber-tired bulldozers used to move loose coal), a truck, three generators and Saylor's jeep.

Next morning, Detective J. E. Cromer of the Kentucky State Police described the destruction as the most extensive he had seen in eleven years of investigating sabotage. Round Mountain announced that it wouldn't be able to mine coal at capacity for a matter of weeks or months, and a company vice-president, Bill Arnold, allowed that he couldn't understand what might have motivated the saboteurs. "There are no problems up there," he said. "No problems at all."

In fact, however, strip mining is nothing but problems, as most eastern Kentuckians could have told Arnold. The technique itself, of course, is not a problem; there's nothing much simpler or more economical than blasting away mountain tops, breaking up the seams of exposed coal and hauling it away in trucks.

Gravity, however, is definitely a problem because it brings the blasted rocks and earth and acid wastes down into the hollows where people live, uprooting their trees, burying their fields and sometimes their homes, and polluting their streams.

During the ten years or so that strip mining has been carried out on a large scale in eastern Kentucky, there has been no really effective effort to oppose it. Stripping has increased since 1966, when the state legislature passed a law, of much-publicized toughness, to regulate the industry and improve reclamation. The law had the effect of driving out of business some of the smaller and least profitable companies and consolidating strip-mine production in the hands of a relatively few companies which were better financed. These companies continue to grow by virtue of landing long-term contracts with the principal consumers of strip-mine coal—including the Tennessee Valley Authority and a number of power companies in the South.

Strip mining's opponents admittedly won a major skirmish in 1967, when Pike county farmer Jink Ray blocked a bulldozer with his body and temporarily stopped the Puritan Coal Company from stripping his land. In the noisy publicity that followed, the then governor, Edward Breathitt, intervened and revoked Puritan's permit. It was an isolated victory. The strip-mine operators retaliated expertly with their sedition campaign against the Appalachian Volunteers staff members who had been working with Jink Ray, and the technique of civil disobedience has not been used since in eastern Kentucky.

But the general public received a much worse setback a few months later, in 1968, when the Kentucky Court of Appeals upheld the legality of the so-called broad-form deed, which divides land ownership between a surface owner and a mineral-rights owner. The traditional wording of such deeds predates the invention of strip mining by a half a century; most such deeds were signed before 1900. Since they were drafted by coal-company lawyers, they convey nothing of any value to the surface owner but give the mineral-rights owner free rein to remove coal any way he chooses.

Batteries of lawyers representing landowners, conservation groups and the Kentucky Civil Liberties Union tried to persuade the Court of Appeals that the broad-form deed had long since lost whatever validity it might once have had, but the Court turned a deaf ear. The test case had been pending for years; opponents of strip mining had pinned all their hopes on it. The Court's decision was a tremendous blow for them, especially since the case cannot be appealed to the U. S. Supreme Court because it was not argued on a constitutional issue.

The ineffectiveness of the 1966 law, combined with the negative ruling of the Court of Appeals, seems to have left strip mining's foes no gentlemanly way to fight the industry. In Kentucky, that means trouble. The technique that Jink Ray used to save his land requires great patience, tremendous publicity and a sympathetic governor. Most Kentuckians don't have the temperament for that kind of fight. Basically, they are inclined to think that long court battles are too risky and the science of publicity too obscure. Black powder is louder and simpler to handle, and the end results are more satisfying.

In Knott county, landowners have been sniping at bulldozers—sometimes with armor-piercing rifle bullets—and dynamiting heavy equipment for three years. As a result, coal operators have found it difficult to hire competent bulldozer operators, and some companies reportedly have been looking for quieter places to operate. Much of the stripping in Knott county is the work of Bill Sturgill, eastern Kentucky's biggest strip-mine operator, who has a 15-year contract to deliver two million tons of coal per year to TVA's Bull Run plant in Tennessee. For Sturgill, the stakes are high; nevertheless, when unknown saboteurs blew up his biggest single piece of equipment—a $90,000 diesel shovel, the largest of its kind in the Hazard coal field—no arrests were made. "And just suppose we did make an arrest," a state police detective said recently, off the record. "Try getting a Knott county jury to convict the guy. They never would."

In December, saboteurs struck Blue Diamond Coal Company's strip mines in Campbell county, Tennessee (just over the line from Kentucky), and destroyed a diesel shovel, six bulldozers, a truck, two core drills and a railroad car. The damages came to nearly a million dollars, according to the local sheriff's office. It's possible, of course, that attacks such as this one and the demolition job in Leslie county were not the work of peeved landowners (there have been no arrests in either of these attacks). But sounds of mutiny have become more audible among the citizenry since the Court of Appeals closed the door to legal protest. Landowners who used to meet openly two or three years ago to talk about court cases now meet clandestinely and talk about other things— the merits of black powder vs. nitroglycerin, for example. Conceivably, of course, their talk is no more than talk, and the actual demolition jobs are really being done by rebellious teenagers out looking for thrills. Conceivably.

STRIP MINING IN EAST KENTUCKY
David B. Brooks

Surface mining for coal is probably the youngest of the many problems in Appalachia. But it is no easier to accept for that. In fact there are times when strip mining so dominates description and discussion as to loom as *the* problem. Whether by use of shovels or draglines or augers or one of the new pushbutton miners, surface mining does seem to be the culminating burden on a region already too heavily laden.

But surface mining is nothing new. In fact, excavating from the surface rather than tunneling underground is the oldest form of mining. Nor is surface mining restricted to coal. More than 80 percent of the

From *Mountain Life and Work*, Spring 1967. Used by permission of the author.

minerals produced in the United States are mined by surface methods. Coal is not even one of the leaders; only 34 percent of our coal is mined from the surface compared with 80 percent of the copper ore, 90 percent of the iron ore, and essentially all the sand, gravel, clay and rock.

Yet it has been surface mining for coal far more than for any other commodity that has distinguished itself as a problem. One can go further. It is only a slight exaggeration to say that it has been surface mining for coal in East Kentucky that has drawn heaviest fire. Other states and other parts of Appalachia come in for some share of attention, but time and again the spotlight returns to East Kentucky. Is surface mining for coal different from surface mining for other commodities? Is East Kentucky different from other regions of surface coal mining? I believe the answer to both questions is a qualified "yes." That is, whatever problems may be common to all surface mining, they are accentuated for coal mining and further accentuated in the special case of East Kentucky. But by the same token we must be wary of dramatic overgeneralizations based on one commodity or one area. Perhaps if we can identify the distinctive features first of surface mining, then of surface coal mining, and finally of surface coal mining in East Kentucky, we shall be in a better position to deal with the resulting problems more successfully than we have in the past.

To start with, then, what are the differences between underground and surface mining? Or, what is more to the point, how do the advantages and disadvantages compare? The main advantage of surface mining lies simply in the fact that when mineral deposits occur near the surface, it is generally far cheaper to recover them in some form of an open pit than it is to go underground. To select just one reason, surface mining permits the use of larger equipment, equipment that can move about unhampered by walls and track. But it is not just cheaper in dollars; it is cheaper in human lives as well. Underground mining requires that meticulous attention be devoted to supporting the roof, to supplying miners with fresh air, and to ensuring that explosive gases are quickly exhausted. Surface mining avoids such problems; there is no roof to support and ventilation takes care of itself. Finally, surface mining permits the recovery of material that is too low in grade or too close to the surface to be mined by underground techniques. This means that surface mining results in a significant addition to coal reserves.

Evidence on each of these points is overwhelming. Productivity in strip coal mines averages nearly 30 tons per man per day, more than double the average productivity in underground mines. (Even this figure is well below the average of nearly 43 tons per man per day attained by auger mines.) Similarly, both the fatal and non-fatal accident rates in surface coal mines are well under half those in underground mines. And whereas underground mining typically recovers 50 to 85 percent of the coal in place, with strip mining 90 to 100 percent recovery is achieved. (Coal recovery by augers is equal to or a little less than that underground.) As a result of all these factors, strip coal has been able to undersell coal mined underground by more than a dollar per ton (about 25 percent of the f.o.b. price), a differential of considerable importance to the continuance of mining in some districts.

So much for the case for surface mining. There are also a number of disadvantages, only one of which needs be mentioned here. This is the all but overriding fact that surface mining of mineral resources causes, or at least can cause, incredible damage to land and water resources. Moreover, this damage is not necessarily restricted to the mine site itself but may proceed far downslope and downstream from the mine. The devastation left in the wake of poorly run strip mines has been too well publicized to require much additional comment. Suffice it to add that except for the ugly gash created at the mine site during mining, all of the common forms of air, land and water pollution can be prevented or greatly attenuated through careful mining and appropriate reclamation practice. Yet all too often high rates of sedimentation, devegetation, increased flooding, fire, erosion, and acid drainage combine to leave a legacy of tangible economic and physical damages. In addition, there may be intangible (that is, less measurable) effects on natural beauty and on the people and communities in surface-mined areas.

However one evaluates the merits of the case, he must recognize that powerful forces are leading to a resurgence of surface mining. Since 1945 the proportion of iron ore produced by surface methods has grown from 75 to 90 percent; for copper it has grown from 66 to 80 percent; and for coal from less than 20 to 34 percent. These trends are neither unique to the three commodities nor are they likely to diminish in the near future, for they represent the resultant of man's voracious demands for minerals and of his ability to cope with these demands by technological advances. Thus, as we exhaust the higher quality mineral resources in this country, technological advances more than make up the ground lost by permitting us to recover lower-grade materials, commonly occurring near the surface, more cheaply. There is no sign that we are anywhere near the end of strippable reserves of coal or of most other mineral commodities.

Our second question is why surface mining for coal seems to create more of a problem than surface mining for other commodities. One reason derives from a pair of pollution problems that are all but unique to coal mining: fire and acid drainage. Because coal is combustible, it can take fire after an explosion or through spontaneous combustion. Anyone familiar with coal regions knows of dozens of sites where either the mines themselves or waste piles have been smoldering for years. Not only is the coal lost, but a constant and evil smelling haze pervades the communities. Acid drainage—"the toughest resource problem in America today"—occurs when iron sulphide minerals like pyrite occur in coal or in overlying strata. Upon attack by air, these minerals decompose to form sulphuric acid, which is then carried by water along hillsides and into streams where, if the concentration is high enough, it is toxic to almost all forms of life. While both fire and acid drainage are most serious and most difficult to control with underground coal mining, they are far from unknown at surface mines.

Probably even more important than these special pollution problems is the coal operator's time horizon. Coal occurs in nearly two-dimensional sheets, six feet thick at most but generally less. Metallic ore deposits, in contrast, are more nearly spherical in shape, and the miner can gradually move to new (even if somewhat less rich) zones outward from the center. The typical iron or copper open pit may remain in existence for a generation or more, and after one pit is exhausted, others may be found nearby to support the community that has grown up around it. The situation for coal is wholly different. Once his seam is excavated, the operator has no reason to remain. Thus, the productive life of a strip mine is limited to a few years. And for exactly the same reason, more surface area is affected per ton extracted than for other forms of mining; a coal pit expands not by digging deeper but by spreading laterally.

There are a few exceptions to the general rule of short time horizon. The large mine-mouth power plants in Western Kentucky and elsewhere are served by strip coal mines that will operate in one area for many years. But there are few surface mines of this type in Appalachia. Mountain towns do not grow and sustain themselves on the basis of surface coal mining. In fact, as implied by the productivity figures above, surface mining requires fewer men than does underground mining. Surface mining yields over one-third of our coal production but accounts for only 18 percent of coal mine employment. On the other hand, it is worth noting that the skills learned in surface mines, such as operating bulldozers, are more useful in other industries than are those learned underground. Strangely, in a subtle way this training may work against the operator (and the union organizer), for strip mine employees do not identify themselves as "coal miners" but rather as "heavy equipment operators," and they exhibit no particular loyalty to the mining industry. Surface coal operators have often remarked on, and smarted under, the fact that criticism from local people is muted so long as the mine is supplying wages and jobs. But once he has moved on, the operator becomes fair game and the damages become the focus of attention.

Beyond these identifiable factors, a set of less definable influences exist that may originate in the historic animosity between coal operator and labor force or, more broadly, the general community. In short, surface mining adds a wholesale and rapid change in land use to what have seldom been amicable relations in the first place. Moreover, because of his short time horizon and his extensive use of land, the strip mine operator is peculiarly subject to the mountaineer's traditional distrust of outsiders.

Now this is getting into one of the special problems of East Kentucky, and before turning to that question, we might look once again at other forms of surface mining, for their problems are not going unnoticed today. The zoning restrictions confronting operators of sand and gravel pits near urban areas are well known. But less well known is the awakening of the iron mining towns around Lake Superior to the fact that unregulated mining has left them surrounded by enormous, barren holes in the ground. A national magazine devoted to land use recently described proposals for redeveloping the old pits, and new regulations may face those who open new pits. In California technological developments are permitting oil wells to be grouped so that once derelict and ugly land can be reclaimed. Closer to home, North Carolina, drawing upon the experience of other states, required detailed conservation plans from prospective mining companies before they were granted leases to mine newly discovered phosphate deposits occurring on the bottom of bays and rivers. Clearly, the United States is at a point where we no longer have any excess acres to waste, and recognition of this fact is spreading widely. It is as if a second frontier were passing, one related not to the quantity of land but to the quality of land use.

Despite this generalization, we must still face the final question: what factors set East Kentucky apart from other surface coal mining regions? In focusing on East Kentucky, I do not mean to imply that similar problems are absent from other areas or other portions of Appalachia any more than the focus on coal means that similar problems are absent from other forms of surface mining. In fact, East Kentucky is well behind several other portions of Appalachia in both the absolute tonnage and the proportion of coal produced by stripping. But nowhere else, it seems, do so many problems converge to magnify the difficulties to the extent that they do in East Kentucky.

Certainly first among the problems is topography. Anyone who has climbed the slopes of the Cumberland Plateau knows that this is steep country. With the possible exception of southern West Virginia and parts of Tennessee, it is the steepest country in Appalachia. Moreover, the coal seams tend to be thin, though of fine quality. As a result, mining methods, pollution problems and reclamation techniques all differ from those in flatter country.

The contrasts between East Kentucky and West Kentucky, while greater than those within Appalachia, are particularly striking. (The East Kentucky coal field includes only the mountain counties; it is separated by the Blue Grass region from the West Kentucky field which centers around Muhlenberg County.) The thick seams and gently rolling topography of West Kentucky permit the use of the mammoth shovels, some taller than Niagara Falls, that are so often pictured in magazines. No such shovels work in the mountains. Where would one find a flat area big enough to erect them? Nor can the shovels proceed back and forth in a series of rows, much like a giant plow, as they do in West Kentucky. The small shovels of the Cumberland Plateau must "contour" around the mountains in a thin shoe-string-like belt. This sets the stage for the next and most significant difference: disposal of over-burden, the unwanted soil and rock on top of the coal. In West Kentucky it can be used to fill up the row last excavated, which leaves a furrow but one that can be shaped and revegetated relatively easily. Each acre mined results in one acre of disturbed, but readily reclaimable, land.

The situation in East Kentucky is quite different. The obvious and cheapest thing to do with overburden is push it over the side of the mountain. Then the serious problems emerge full blown, for rapidity of runoff, susceptibility to flash floods, landslide damage, and many other phases of strip mine pollution are directly related to the steepness of the land. On the average, each acre mined in East Kentucky results in three acres of disturbed land. And, though strides are being made, we are still novices at reclamation in mountainous areas. A recent study based on a sample of 56 strip mining sites in Appalachia reported no successful reclamation where slopes were greater than 28 degrees.

Topography is not the only physical characteristic to hinder reclamation efforts in East Kentucky. Few coal regions are so fortunate as to have two minable seams close to one another, but in East Kentucky and a few surrounding counties one can find as many as four seams on a single hillside. The result is that the waste from one contour strip merges with the waste from the strip below it, creating an almost entirely denuded mountainside. Another difficulty is the seasonal character of rainfall, and still another is the acid-producing sandstone that overlies the seams in certain areas.

The difficulties besetting East Kentucky can be brought into sharp focus by juxtaposing two statistics. First, except for Alabama and Tennessee, which are relatively small producers, production of coal per acre mined is lower in East Kentucky than in any other area of Appalachia—lower by almost a thousand tons. Second, according to the best available information, the cost of reclamation per acre is higher in East Kentucky than in any other state except for Pennsylvania where (at the time data were collected) reclamation requirements were much higher. In sum, costs are higher and returns lower than in most other areas.

Partly as a result of the above factors, and partly because of the coincidence of thin but rich seams, East Kentucky is practically the home of the small, locally-owned "truck" mine. These mines, whether surface or underground, use small-scale equipment, require very little capital investment, and operate on a narrow margin (obtained partly by paying wages below the union scale). Hundreds of truck mines dot the East Kentucky counties, and any study of the regional coal picture must reckon with their presence. Despite the many charges against absentee ownership, it is likely that the small mines are responsible for more than their share of surface damage. There are two reasons to suspect that this is true. First, recent measurements indicate that the amount of disturbed land does not increase in proportion to production. That is, one surface mine producing ten times as much coal per year as another mine disturbs considerably less than ten times as much surface land. Second, large producers generally have funds enough to engage in reclamation associations, and to seek out the best techniques through research; small producers seldom do. It is significant that the first case brought by the Kentucky State Division of Strip Mine Reclamation for mining contrary to provisions of the new 1966 strip mine law was brought against a firm based in Prestonsburg, Kentucky. It is also significant that when Pennsylvania tightened its reclamation requirements several years ago, there was a sharp drop in the number of strip mine operators, but only a small drop in total strip coal production.

If physical and economic conditions underlie East Kentucky's strip mine problems, man has until recently done little to help the situation. First and foremost in this dubious record must come the Broad Form Deed. This remarkable legal instrument, which on its face only grants mineral rights to the holder, in actuality gives the miner the right to do anything necessary to recover the coal without compensation and regardless of surface damage. These deeds, as is well known, were obtained before surface mining was a common method for recovering coal, and on this basis the courts in most states have declared that they cannot be enforced. But Kentucky courts have consistently upheld the Broad Form, and the legislature has just as consistently (even in 1966) ignored or tabled measures that would force a reinterpretation. (Western Kentucky was spared from the Broad Form Deed because in 1900 no one was so foolish as to think that coal would ever be mined out there.) As for legislation, Kentucky was the last of the major coal producing states to pass a strip mine control law. And it took until 1964 to get a really satisfactory law. Not only were the early laws inadequate— grading, for example was required only "where practical"—but they could not be satisfactorily enforced because of inadequate staffing of control agencies.

There are other human factors that center in East Kentucky, factors that must be put into the nebulous category of sociological and psychological influences. Even the strongest supporters of the mountains admit that destructive exploitation of natural resources has been a way of life. Life has been hard, and the mountaineer has perhaps acted toward natural resources as he felt life was acting toward him. Whether it was the soil he was farming, or the hillside he was overgrazing, conservation has been a little-heeded virtue. Even local extension agents report great difficulties in gaining cooperation on reclamation projects. In some of the worst instances, land on the way to being reclaimed was so quickly grazed that it actually returned to its immediate post-mining conditions.

These human problems associated with surface mining and surface mine reclamation can no doubt be traced to several sources. They may be related to the mountaineer's "independence," as described by Jack Weller; they may be related to the exceptionally low per capita incomes in East Kentucky (the lowest by far for any portion of the Appalachian region) so that the mountaineer can literally not afford to look at the long-term benefits promised by conservation; or they may be related to some highly personalized tie to the land, perhaps even to existing land forms. One cannot help contrasting the attitude of the mountaineer-miner in the Appalachians with that of the miner in western United States who felt no association with the land and moved on to a new mining district as fancy took him or higher wages attracted him. If this analysis has substance, it implies that indigenous objections to strip mining derive less from the pollution problems so often identified than from the far less tangible effects of a changing landscape and loss of subsistence farm land or homesite. In short, the mountaineer may object more to intrusion into an accustomed way of life than to the erosion and sedimentation per se. Even those who would contemplate a change, deeply feel that the Broad Form Deed has cheated them of the right to make their own bargain with the coal company.

Whatever the reasons, and we have found many, no other region of the Appalachians has known the ravages that East Kentucky has suffered. Parts of southern West Virginia, Virginia and Tennessee show similar effects but on a smaller scale. Even today, there is a larger percentage of land in East Kentucky that is "totally unreclaimed" than in any other Appalachian state except Tennessee. West Virginia in contrast is gradually catching up with its problem through money paid into a special fund by strip mine operators.

To summarize, then, surface mining while more efficient, safer, and more conservative of mineral resources than underground mining, carries with it a whole set of problems related to other natural resources and to the people who live in surface mined areas. To some extent these problems are inherent in the method of mining and occur at the mine site itself, but to a very significant degree, they result from poor mining or reclamation practices and are most offensive downslope and downstream from the mine site. For several reasons coal accentuates these problems found to a greater or lesser extent with all surface mining: Its combustible nature, acid drainage, the short time span of mining, and the large surface area affected. Again, all of these problems common to surface coal mining everywhere can be found in East Kentucky, but they are further accentuated as a result of certain geological, legal, and cultural factors. Pollution of all types is much more difficult to control in the steep country of the Cumberland Plateau, and multiple seam mining compounds the difficulties. The thin but high quality seams of East Kentucky have led to the formation of a multitude of small companies that have not done all that they could to improve mining and reclamation practices. The upholding of the Broad Form Deed by the courts removed the normal judicial means for compensation, and (until 1964) weak laws and limited enforcement budgets removed the legislative and executive means of redress. Finally, the very character of the mountaineer and his attitude toward natural resources has led to a disregard of pollution problems.

Clearly, the era just described is over. We are learning to cope with the tangible damages associated with surface mining in such a way that land can be reclaimed after mining. The 1964 Kentucky law is a strong one, and the state gives every indication that it intends to enforce it. (It is only fair, however, to recognize that the state laws are not designed to, and cannot, cope fully with the intangible but nevertheless real sociological and psychological effects discussed at several points above; these lie fundamentally within the domain of a broader program for Appalachia.) There is no reason to think that this law, strict though it may be, or any of the other state laws foredoom the industry. In fact, there is reason to think that the reverse is true, that the surface coal industry will grow despite, or more likely because of, these laws.

Most of my past writings represent attempts to seek a rational intermediate position with regard to stripping in the mountains, a position that would balance added employment and taxes plus potential reclamation against the immediate and longer run damages to communities and to the environment. Briefly stated, my position has been that Eastern Kentucky could have most of its strip mines (assuming reclamation were strictly enforced) without irreparable losses. I have now come to the conclusion that something approaching the proposal to prohibit strip mining on slopes greater than 18 degrees is necessary. (I don't think, however, that the regulation would need to be so strict for auger mining.)

My position has shifted because it now appears unrealistic to attain the balance I was seeking. First, the benefit-cost calculations used to evaluate strip mining increasingly appears to be incomplete. In some cases tangible damages, notably those stemming from erosion and sedimentation, are partially or completely ignored; in other cases, insufficient weight is given to intangible impacts on people and aesthetics. Second, the local employment benefits of strip mining appear to be partially illusory as the firms bring in much of the skilled labor they need. Third, there are grounds for thinking that strip mining also works against longer term development prospects as well. (I refer here both to tourism and to industrial and urban development.) This is not because the coal itself is taken from the region, which is probably necessary in any case, or because of absentee ownership, which is a false issue, but because the conditions created by strip mining are not conducive to the development of satellite industries or of permanent communities. In sum, I have come to the conclusion that some strip mine damages in the steep mountains of central Appalachia *are* irreparable.*

* From a letter to *The Mountain Eagle*, March 12, 1970. Used by permission of the author.

Migration:
Take It or Leave It

A LOOK AT THE 1970 CENSUS
James S. Brown

By "Southern Appalachians" here we mean "Appalachia" as deline-
ated by the Appalachian Regional Commission with, however, the Appalachian counties of New York, Ohio, and Pennsylvania (the "Northern Appalachians") omitted. The ARC's definition of "Appalachia" is
primarily a political delineation, a collection of counties declared "Appalachian" by the governors of the various states. This is, therefore,
not a uniformly determined, carefully worked-out area occupied by
persons with homogeneous social, cultural, and economic characteristics nor a group of areas which function as a social or economic system. Instead, it is a loose collection of counties with very diverse characteristics which function in a variety of systems and subsystems. This
should be borne in mind in interpreting data both for the Southern Ap-

This is a revised version of an article from *Mountain Life & Work*, July–
August 1970. Used by permission of the author.

palachians as a whole and for the counties in each state taken as a whole.

The population of the Southern Appalachians on April 1, 1970, according to final census counts, was 10,096,119, a gain of 419,955 since 1960 (4.3 percent). The increase, in both numbers and percentage, is greater than from 1950 to 1960 when the increase was 35,154 (0.4 percent). The Appalachian rate of increase in the 1960s, however, was less than a third that of the United States as a whole (13.3 percent).

Appalachia's greater increase in population from 1960 to 1970 than from 1950 to 1960 is due to a tremendous decline in net loss through migration from 1,569,000 in the 1950s to only 592,000 in the 1960s, a decrease of 977,000 (62 percent). The rate of loss through migration in the 1950s was 16.3 percent, in the 1960s only 6.1 percent.

The region's population would, then, have been much greater except for a 37 percent decrease in natural increase (excess of births over deaths) in the 1960s (from 1,600,000 to 1,012,000) which occurred because births declined 19 percent (from about 2,410,000 in the 1950s to about 1,950,000 in the 1960s) while deaths increased 17 percent (from 804,000 to 940,000).

Both the decline of loss through migration and the decline of natural increase in such a short period are great, even dramatic, changes and call for much more investigation than could be done for this article. For these abrupt changes cannot be simply explained and their significance for the future is even more difficult to fathom. But we can at least suggest, more or less knowledgeably, some of the reasons for them.

CHANGES BY STATES

From 1960 to 1970, the Appalachian section of seven of the ten states had population increases. Numerically, Alabama's Appalachian counties gained most—155,000—closely followed by Georgia's with 139,000. West Virginia's counties lost most heavily (116,184) with Kentucky's and Virginia's also losing (46,000 and 30,000, respectively).

As for percentage changes, Appalachian Georgia increased most by far (21 percent), followed by South Carolina (12 percent) and North Carolina (10 percent). West Virginia lost most (6.2 percent), closely followed by Virginia (6.0) and Kentucky (5 percent). Six of the seven states with increases from 1950 to 1960 had even larger percentage increases in the 1960s, the most striking change being the increase in Georgia (from 9 to 21 percent). South Carolina's percentage increase stayed about the same.

Of the four states with population declines from 1950 to 1960, one, Mississippi, shifted from a loss of 5 percent in the 1950s to a gain of 3 percent in the 1960s. But the other three states continued to lose, Virginia's rate of loss staying about the same (6 compared to 5.9 percent), West Virginia's decreasing slightly (from 7 to 6 percent), and Kentucky's declining sharply (from 14 to 5 percent).

In the 1950s all the states had had net losses through migration, their rates ranging from 8 percent in South Carolina and Maryland to 32 percent in Kentucky. In the 1960s nine states still continued to lose through migration, though numbers lost as well as rates of loss of all dropped significantly. One state, Georgia, had a net gain through migration (8 percent compared to a 9 percent loss in the 1950s).

In all ten states birth declined (ranging from 5.4 percent in Georgia to 31 percent in Kentucky) and the number of deaths increased (from 8 percent in Kentucky to 29 percent in Georgia) so that natural increase fell at least 20 percent in every state (21 percent in Georgia, the lowest; 53 percent in West Virginia, the highest).

As a result of these varying declines in losses through migration and also decreases in natural increase, perhaps the most remarkable changes by states, then, in the 1960s were: (1) the rapid growth of Appalachian Georgia, both in numbers and percentage; (2) the great decrease, both in numbers and percentage, in the loss from Kentucky's counties; and (3) the continuing decline in Virginia's and West Virginia's counties, somewhat less in numbers but at almost the same rates as in the 1950s.

CHANGES IN METROPOLITAN POPULATION

More and more of the United States' population in recent decades has been concentrating in metropolitan areas, which today contain more than two-thirds of the nation's total population. Much of the growth of these metropolitan areas has been due to an influx of migrants from rural areas. Hundreds of thousands of migrants from the predominantly rural Southern Appalachians have moved to metropolitan areas; most of them, however, have gone to cities outside of Appalachia.

Table One

Population of the Southern Appalachians by States with Percentage Change

	1950	1960	1970	Percentage Change	
				1950–1960	1960–1970
Southern Appalachians Total	9,640,910	9,676,164	10,096,119	0.4	4.3
Appalachian Counties of:					
Alabama	1,860,829	1,982,286	2,137,278	6.5	7.8
Georgia	619,766	675,024	813,596	8.9	20.5
Kentucky	1,072,750	922,152	875,922	–14.0	–5.0
Maryland	189,701	195,808	209,349	3.2	6.9
Mississippi	426,076	406,187	418,644	–4.7	3.1
North Carolina	881,560	939,740	1,037,212	6.6	10.4
South Carolina	523,265	586,523	656,126	12.1	11.9
Tennessee	1,529,762	1,607,689	1,733,661	5.1	7.8
Virginia	531,649	500,334	470,094	–5.9	–6.0
West Virginia	2,005,552	1,860,421	1,744,237	–7.2	–6.2

Table Two

Population of Metropolitan Counties by States with Percentage Change

	1950	1960	1970	Percentage Change 1950–1960	Percentage Change 1960–1970
Southern Appalachians Total (27 counties)	2,704,286	3,031,821	3,269,958	12.1	7.9
Appalachian Counties of:					
Alabama (8)	981,361	1,111,619	1,211,221	13.3	9.0
Georgia (2)	70,518	88,805	123,040	25.9	38.6
Kentucky (1)	49,949	52,163	52,376	4.4	0.4
Maryland	—	—	—	—	—
Mississippi	—	—	—	—	—
North Carolina (3)	292,671	342,306	384,003	17.0	12.2
South Carolina (2)	208,210	255,806	299,502	22.9	17.1
Tennessee (4)	545,360	605,985	654,573	11.1	8.0
Virginia	—	—	—	—	—
West Virginia (7)	556,217	575,137	545,243	3.4	−5.2

The Appalachian metropolitan areas—mostly small and with economies not demanding large numbers of unskilled workers—have not attracted most of the vast migratory stream from the rest of Appalachia. In 1970, only one-third of Southern Appalachia's population (3,269,958) lived in its metropolitan counties, counties in Standard Metropolitan Statistical Areas (SMSA's). This is an increase since 1960 of only 238,137 (8 percent, less than two-thirds the rate of increase of the nation's metropolitan areas as a whole). Indeed, in the 1960s, growth of the twenty-seven Appalachian metropolitan counties slowed down, for from 1950 to 1960 they had increased 328,000 (12 percent). Though net loss through migration was 61,000 less in the 1960s than in the 1950s, metropolitan population grew more slowly because natural increase dropped about 150,000.

The metropolitan population of each of the seven states with metropolitan counties (Maryland, Mississippi, and Virginia had none) grew from 1950 to 1960 in spite of the heavier migration during that decade, increasing 10 percent or more in four states, declining in two—Kentucky and West Virginia with gains of only 4.4 and 3.4 percent, respectively. Georgia's and South Carolina's metropolitan counties gained most (26 and 23 percent, respectively). From 1960 to 1970, Georgia's metropolitan counties grew even more rapidly (39 percent) than in the 1950s; in each of the other states metropolitan growth was less rapid, ranking from greatest to least gains in exactly the same order as in the previous decade, from a gain of 17 percent in South Carolina to a loss of 5 percent in West Virginia. Clearly the metropolitan counties of the Piedmont Crescent running from North Carolina through South Carolina to Georgia grew most rapidly. These counties had net gains through migration large enough to offset losses in natural increase. Metropolitan counties in all the other states had combinations of declines in losses through migration and decreases in natural increase so that rates of population growth decreased.

Of the twenty-seven metropolitan counties, sixteen were in nine SMSA's wholly in Southern Appalachia. Seven of these SMSA's had population increases, led by Huntsville, Alabama, with an increase of 74,000 (48 percent) followed by Greenville, South Carolina, and Asheville, North Carolina, with increases of 16 and 12 percent, respectively. Two SMSA's, Gadsden, Alabama, and Charleston, West Virginia, had population declines of 3 and 9 percent, respectively.

The nine SMSA's continued to have a total net loss through migration in the 1960s (84,000), but it was 34 percent less than in the 1950s (127,000). There was much variation among them. Four had greater net losses through migration in the 1960s than in the 1950s (Birmingham, Charleston, Chattanooga, and Tuscaloosa). Two, Gadsden and Knoxville, had smaller net losses in the 1960s. Asheville, with a net gain in the 1960s, had had a net loss in the 1950s. Two, Greenville and Huntsville, had even larger net gains in the 1960s than in the 1950s.

Births in the nine SMSA's decreased 14.9 percent, from 578,000 in 1950–1960 to 492,000 in 1960–1970. Deaths increased 19.4 percent, from 186,000 in 1950–1960 to 222,000 in 1960–1970. Consequently, natural increase fell 31.1 percent, from 392,000 to 270,000. Only one of the SMSA's had a gain in natural increase (Huntsville, 46 percent). All the other eight had decreases (ranging from Gadsden's 25 percent to Charleston's 49 percent).

CHANGES IN NONMETROPOLITAN POPULATION

Since metropolitan counties in Southern Appalachia during the 1960s gained very slowly, Appalachian population continued to be overwhelmingly nonmetropolitan—68 percent in 1970 (compared to 69 percent in 1960 and 72 in 1950). The nonmetropolitan areas (276 counties and five independent cities in Virginia) had a total population in 1970 of 6,826,161, an increase since 1960 of 181,818 (2.7 percent). Though small, this was a significant change from the decrease of 292,381 (4.2 percent) in the previous decade. After a sizeable loss in the 1950s, then, the nonmetropolitan population seemed to be stabilizing and even growing slightly (3 percent) in the 1960s, persistently continuing to constitute more than two-thirds of the Appalachian population. There were, however, some important variations among the states.

The nonmetropolitan counties in the five states which had population increases from 1950 to 1960 also increased from 1960 to 1970, all at higher rates (Georgia's counties from 7 to 18 percent, Maryland's from 3 to 7, North Carolina's from 2 to 9, South Carolina's from 5 to 8, and Tennessee's from 2 to 8). Two of the five states with losses in nonmetropolitan population from 1950 to 1960 had gains during the 1960s (Alabama, changing from −1 percent to 6 and Mississippi from −5 to 3). In three states, nonmetropolitan population continued to decrease, Kentucky's and West Virginia's at notably smaller rates (the former dropping from 15 percent in the 1950s to 5 percent in the

Table Three

Population of Nonmetropolitan Counties by States with Percentage Change

	1950	1960	1970	Percentage Change	
				1950–1960	1960–1970
Southern Appalachians Total	6,936,624	6,644,343	6,826,161	-4.2	2.7
Appalachian Counties of:					
Alabama	879,468	870,667	926,057	-1.0	6.4
Georgia	549,248	586,219	690,556	6.7	17.8
Kentucky	1,022,801	869,989	823,546	-14.9	-5.3
Maryland	189,701	195,808	209,349	3.2	6.9
Mississippi	426,076	406,187	418,644	-4.7	3.1
North Carolina	588,889	597,434	653,209	1.5	9.3
South Carolina	315,055	330,717	356,624	5.0	7.8
Tennessee	984,402	1,001,704	1,079,088	1.8	7.7
Virginia	531,649	500,334	470,094	-5.9	-6.0
West Virginia	1,449,335	1,285,284	1,198,994	-11.3	-6.7

1960s, the latter from 11 to 7) but Virginia's percentage of loss remained almost the same (5.9 percent from 1950 to 1960, 6.0 percent from 1960 to 1970).

In spite of these variations there were only slight decreases in percentages of total population constituted by the nonmetropolitan counties in any of the states. Appalachian Maryland, Mississippi, and Virginia continued to be totally nonmetropolitan; Kentucky's Appalachian population was 94 percent nonmetropolitan, Georgia's 85, West Virginia's 69, North Carolina's 63, Tennessee's 62, and South Carolina's 54 percent. Only in Alabama was the nonmetropolitan population less than half the total (43 percent).

Again, as in Southern Appalachia as a whole and in the metropolitan counties, births in the nonmetropolitan counties fell from the 1950s to the 1960s (21 percent) and deaths increased somewhat (16 percent) so that natural increase dropped from 1,117,000 to 675,124 (40 percent). Similar decreases in births, increases in deaths, and consequent decreases in natural increase also occurred in the nonmetropolitan counties of each of the ten states.

During the same period, losses through net migration continued but declined remarkably from 1,409,000 in the 1950s to 493,000 in the 1960s. The rate of loss through migration dropped from 20 percent in the 1950s to 5 percent in the 1960s. Georgia's nonmetropolitan counties actually had a net gain through migration in the 1960s; in each of the other states nonmetropolitan counties as a whole had net losses, but the percentage losses strikingly declined.

CHANGES IN THE POPULATIONS OF COUNTIES

Variations in population change among the 303 counties and five independent cities (in Virginia) included in the Southern Appalachians are myriad. Consequently only a few of the most important differences will be discussed here.

By states the number of counties and independent cities which gained and lost are:

	Total Appalachian Counties	Number of Counties	
		Gained	Lost
Alabama	35	25	10
Georgia	35	33	2
Kentucky	49	15	34

	Total Appalachian Counties	Number of Counties Gained	Lost
Maryland	3	2	1
Mississippi	20	12	8
North Carolina	29	22	7
South Carolina	6	6	0
Tennessee	50	36	14
Virginia	26	9	17
West Virginia	55	15	40
TOTAL	308	175	133

COUNTIES WITH POPULATION INCREASES

The 173 counties and two independent cities with population increases gained a total of 714,006. About 78 percent (21) of the 27 metropolitan counties had increases compared to only 55 percent (154) of the 281 nonmetropolitan counties. Many of the nonmetropolitan counties with increases, furthermore, had large urban populations. For example, Douglas County, Georgia, with the greatest percentage increase of all (71 percent), adjoins the Atlanta SMSA and obviously is becoming an integral part of it.

More counties in the states along the southern and southeastern border of Southern Appalachia were growing than in other parts of the region. More than four-fifths of the counties in Georgia, South Carolina, and North Carolina and 60 percent of Mississippi's Appalachian counties had population increases. But of the 130 counties in Kentucky, Virginia, and West Virginia only 30 percent gained. Counties with the highest rates of increase were also concentrated along the southern and southeastern border—Georgia alone had 15 of the 39 counties gaining 15 percent or more; Alabama, South Carolina, and North Carolina had ten more. Kentucky, Virginia, and West Virginia together had only five such counties.

All the above suggest that Appalachian population increase was relatively concentrated in a few counties. One county alone (Madison, Alabama, part of the Huntsville SMSA) accounted for nearly 10 percent of the total gained by the 175 counties with population increases. The emergence of Atlanta as the rapidly growing, regional capital of the Southeast is obviously a major reason for the concentration of population increase of Southern Appalachian counties. The one Appalachian county in the Atlanta SMSA (Gwinnett), the nine counties adjacent, and twelve counties within commuting distance (twenty-two counties in all) alone accounted for about 117,000 (16 percent) of the total gained by the 175 counties. Much of the Appalachian population gain was concentrated in the growing belt of counties (including nine SMSA's) called the Piedmont Crescent which extends through North Carolina, South Carolina, and Georgia from Raleigh, North Carolina, to Atlanta. The Appalachian counties included in the Piedmont Crescent (four metropolitan, twenty-seven nonmetropolitan) had a total increase of 195,041 (27 percent of the region's total increase).

COUNTIES WITH POPULATION DECREASES

The 130 counties and three independent cities with population decreases lost a total of 294,051. Forty-five percent (127) of the 281 nonmetropolitan counties had decreases compared to only 22 percent (6) of the 27 metropolitan counties (5 of the 6 metropolitan counties losing were in West Virginia). The counties losing population from 1960 to 1970 were concentrated in the northwestern part of Southern Appalachia, Kentucky (34), Virginia (17), and West Virginia (40) including nearly 70 percent of the 133 with losses. The western part of Appalachian Tennessee, adjoining Kentucky, had fourteen counties with losses. Counties with the highest rate of loss were also concentrated in the northwestern part of Southern Appalachia. Kentucky (14), Virginia (9), and West Virginia (16) had 39 of the 44 counties losing 10 percent or more, and adjoining Tennessee had three.

The 91 counties in Kentucky, Virginia, and West Virginia losing population from 1960 to 1970 lost a total of 262,313, nearly 90 percent of the 294,051 lost by all the 133 counties with decreases. For that reason special attention will be paid to these 91 counties, particularly to the coal mining counties, where losses were heaviest. Twenty-six counties (10 in Kentucky, 4 in Virginia, and 12 in West Virginia) have been classified as *mining counties*. Twenty-four of these counties lost population from 1960 to 1970, a total of 143,322; two gained (Leslie, Kentucky, and Grant, West Virginia) a total of 985. Altogether then the counties lost 142,000 (16 percent), nearly half of the total lost by all Appalachian counties. From 1960 to 1970, Kentucky's mining counties lost 49,000 (17 percent), Virginia's lost 18,000 (14 percent), and West Virginia's 75,000 (16 percent). In 1950–1960 these twenty-six counties had lost 206,000 (19 percent)—Kentucky's counties 79,000 (21 percent), Virginia's 15,000 (11 percent), and West Virginia's 112,000 (19 percent). From 1960 to 1970 seven counties had percentage losses of 20 percent or more: Harlan, Perry, and Letcher in Kentucky; Dickenson in Virginia; and McDowell, Logan, and Fayette in West Virginia. From 1950 to 1960, eleven counties had had decreases of 20 percent or more (including all of those above except Dickenson, Virginia, which had replaced Wise, Virginia; plus Floyd and Leslie in Kentucky; Barbour and Calhoun in West Virginia).

As in Southern Appalachia as a whole, from the 1950s to the 1960s births declined in the mining counties (from 283,000 to 168,000—41 percent), deaths increased (from 74,000 to 79,000—7 percent) so that natural increase dropped (from 201,000 to 98,000—51 percent). Meanwhile, net loss through migration dropped from 409,000 in the 1950s to 231,000 in the 1960s, a decline of 44 percent, though the rate of loss dropped only from 37.3 percent to 25.8 percent. Kentucky's rate of loss through migration decreased from 42.5 to 29.9 percent, West Virginia's from 36.1 to 23.3, and Virginia's from 27.2 to 25.7 percent.

SUMMARY

In summary, the population of the Southern Appalachians (as defined here) has increased slightly from 1960 to 1970, gaining at a rate less than a third that of the United States as a whole. The greater increase in the 1960s is primarily due to the tremendous drop in loss through migration (a 62 percent decline). Migration loss dropped so much that it offset another astonishing change, a drop in births and an increase in deaths which together resulted in a 37 percent decline in natural increase.

Clearly the various parts of the Southern Appalachians are developing quite differently. The three great physiographic divisions of the Southern Appalachians—(1) the Cumberland and Allegheny Plateaus of the west separated by (2) the Great Valley from the (3) Blue Ridge on the east—give us one useful pattern of organization. These divisions enable us to see changes in greater sections and thus simplify the complex picture, for it is uncanny how relevant these physiographic divisions and subdivisions are. For many decades researchers on Southern Appalachia have said that the greatest development of the region would be in the Great Valley and along the outer fringes of the area—not in the Allegheny and Cumberland Plateaus on the west nor in the Blue Ridge on the east. This is what has happened.

Consequently, the Appalachian counties with population increases are concentrated in (1) the Great Valley running, roughly, from Birmingham and Huntsville in the south northeastward through Tennessee (including Chattanooga, Knoxville, and the rapidly developing counties of east Tennessee) and going on to the Valleys of southwestern Virginia; (2) the Southern Piedmont Plateau including counties along the Alabama border, a number of counties in Georgia (including the counties around Atlanta, Greenville, and several surrounding counties), and a number of North Carolina counties in both the Southern and Central Piedmont Plateau; (3) the Highland Rim counties of Appalachian Tennessee and of Kentucky, which also tend to have population increases, though in general not such great increases as along the Piedmont fringe in the east—no doubt because no such great metropolis as Atlanta is nearby nor even smaller metropolitan areas like Winston-Salem, High Point, and Greensboro. Counties in the Bluegrass of Kentucky also showed gains.

On the other hand, the counties with losses in population are concentrated in the Cumberland and Allegheny Plateau sections of West Virginia, Kentucky, Virginia, and Tennessee, including the sixty counties which the ARC calls "Central Appalachia" but including many other counties too, especially in West Virginia. All but two of the counties among the 303 in Southern Appalachia having population losses of 10 percent or more from 1960 to 1970 are in these parts of Kentucky, Virginia, and West Virginia. (The exceptions are in Mississippi.)

Along with the physiographic pattern, another significant pattern in county gains and losses during the 1960s was related to the presence of SMSA's nearby. Almost all the counties gaining 14 percent or more from 1960 to 1970 were parts of SMSA's or adjoining or were within commuting distance of SMSA's. Even though the SMSA itself might not be growing very fast, in a number of cases nearby counties were.

In eastern Kentucky, southern West Virginia, and southwestern Virginia the drastic decline of employment in coal mining during the 1950s continued into the 1960s as a result of mechanization and the growth of strip mining. Together with availability of employment in metropolitan industrial centers outside Appalachia itself, notably in the Midwest, this resulted in a virtual stampede of migrants out of the region in the 1950s. Although the number of migrants leaving declined in the 1960s, the rate of migration loss from most of this area was still very high. It takes no great foresight to see that heavy migration from the coal mining area will continue during the 1970s, though the number and rates will fall as the number of young people in the prime migratory ages decreases in both numbers and proportions of the total population. Obviously, too, the economic depression now affecting employment in the cities to which these migrants ordinarily go may further slow down migration and lead to a "piling up" of people in these counties rather like that of the 1930s. Because of these areas' heavy population decreases it will certainly not be as great as earlier.

The increase in deaths throughout the region is due principally to the increasing numbers and proportions of old people in the population. The decline in births is harder to explain. Undoubtedly part of this decrease is due to the migration of such large numbers of young people in the child-producing ages (and it is notable that areas with the heaviest migration tend to have the greatest declines in number of births). Some have suggested that migration is less responsible for the decline in birth and fertility rates than many suppose. In the counties of eastern Kentucky, southern West Virginia, and southwestern Virginia, I think migration has been the prime factor. We are now studying this phenomenon more carefully.

Finally we must say that these data tend to support Ben A. Franklin's assertion that for hundreds of thousands, perhaps a million of the poor in the ridgelands of Kentucky and West Virginia, opportunity is still like the rider of the six white horses in the old mountain song: perpetually coming "when she comes." As he also points out the Appalachian program was largely conceived for these people in the hollows. "And yet 10 years later they remain largely untouched by it, while to the north and south less impoverished fringe areas are making significant economic progress." Part of the reason that these really needy people in Kentucky, West Virginia, and Tennessee have been helped very little is that, to quote Franklin again, "the boundaries of the region were drawn so generously that its $7 billion in aid has come to only $390 per man, woman and child over the last 10 years." The reason for inclusion of so many less impoverished areas, including, for example, part of the Atlanta SMSA, is, Franklin quotes officials as saying, "that the need for sweeping, regional 'scale' in planning together with the need for congressional support has frankly required some 'logrolling.' " The addition of Mississippi, for example, "was dictated largely by the fact that Sen. John Stennis of Mississippi is a key member of the appropriations committee."

The saddest part of this story of population change is that the fringes and the "better off" areas are the ones progressing, partly because they are getting Appalachian funds, while the neediest areas are being neglected. With the declining attention being paid to Appalachia this situation will probably continue and even worsen. The economic and social conditions in the "hard core" counties of Southern Appalachia continue to be a national disgrace.

THE UPTOWN STORY
Bill Montgomery

If President Johnson's Commission on Rural Poverty had elected to dramatize its findings on film rather than issue them in a written report, the camera could have lingered long on a Chicago ghetto called Uptown. Urban and rural poverty, the Commission theorized, are closely linked by migration. Uptown is the urban end of that theory tested and proven.

The Commission in its film might also have cast Anna Bland in a featured role. She knows a lot about migration. Staring through the window of her small, third-floor Uptown apartment, Anna said what could have been her opening lines: "We nearly starved to death down there last winter. Things aren't much better here, but I wouldn't go back. I sure do miss the hills, though."

"Down there" is Clarksburg, West Virginia. Twice before, Anna Bland has missed the West Virginia hills and, twice before, she has returned to them. The Bland family—Anna, her husband, Jim, and their three small children—is caught on the treadmill of never-ending transiency that often is the fate of the rural Southern white who migrates to the industrial North. Of the many ethnic groups that make up America's cities, few experience the difficulty in becoming "urbanized" that besets the migrant Southerner. In the city, virtually every

From *Mountain Life & Work*, September 1968. Used by permission of the author.

principle of his life becomes a rural value struggling to retain its identity against an urban value that demands precedence. It is a cultural struggle: the personal against the impersonal, independence against regimentation. It is the casual laborer learning that in the city jobs do not wait for those who do not report to them every day. It is the fear and distrust of the formal, signed-paper society of the city; a man must sign a lease to rent a good apartment, a mortgage to own a home.

Unable to make a quick adjustment to the urban way of life, many Southerners become bogged down in a much worse kind of poverty than that they sought to escape. They fall into a pattern of moving from one slum dwelling to another but always remaining in the ghetto, of holding a job a day at a time and receiving their wages the same way, never accumulating any money; it is a "stumble-around" kind of living that prevents them from ever achieving any degree of social or economic stability, the things they came North to find. In the end, the Southerner has only exchanged the open-space poverty of the rural South for the ghetto poverty of the northern city. Whether or not he ever adjusts to urban life depends largely on his own endurance and how much help he can find along the way.

Those who experience the most difficulty in adjusting are the Appalachians. For more so than any other present-day ethnic group in America, the Appalachian seems to consider home to be where the heart is, and no matter where he might go the Appalachian nearly always leaves his heart behind in the hills. That point is illustrated graphically every Friday night by the long stream of automobiles heading south from Cincinnati on Interstate 75. License plates identify the vehicles as being from Ohio, but the people inside them are Appalachians heading home, if only for the weekend.

Southerners began migrating to the cities in large numbers during the World War II industrial boom. Today, jobs are still the magnet that pulls Southerners to the cities. Many come from the farmlands of Alabama, Mississippi and Arkansas; others, like the Blands, from the rural nonfarm areas that comprise much of Appalachia.

A Southerner's decision to migrate is usually preceded by a lot of thought but by less actual preparation than the average suburban family would devote to a weekend outing. In the end, he simply scrapes together what money he can get his hands on, loads his family and a few possessions into a bus or an old car and heads north for Cincinnati, Cleveland, Chicago, Dayton or Detroit. Anna Bland, for instance, had tried for months to persuade her husband to return to Chicago. Jim didn't relent until after he and Anna had separated, Anna and the children having moved in with her mother. Then Jim just appeared one day and announced, "I'm going to Chicago. You wanna come along?" The Blands packed what few possessions they hadn't lost during the hard winter into two suitcases, loaded them and the children onto a bus and were off. Fifty of the $120 they had managed to scrape together went for the bus fare.

Arriving in Chicago, the Blands headed straight for Uptown and straight to the same rundown apartment building they had abandoned the previous fall to return to the hills. It is not by chance that the Blands always go to Chicago when they leave the hills. One of the phenomena of the migration movement is the "Southern grapevine," a remarkably reliable word-of-mouth form of communication that enables Southerners to keep track of the friends and relatives who have migrated before them. Thus the Blands go to Chicago because that's where most migrants from the Clarksburg, West Virginia, area go.

Uptown is a 120-block ghetto into which are jammed just under 100,000 people. Southerners comprise almost half of Uptown's population, the rest being divided among Spanish-speaking people, the largest community of American Indians outside the reservations and a growing Negro population.

Uptown is the real face behind the mask of affluence that Chicago turns to the east. High-rise—and high-rent—apartments stretch block after block along Lake Michigan to greet visitors who arrive by way of Lake Shore Drive. It's a welcome that's roughly withdrawn once the visitor turns west into Uptown. There the new arrival runs headlong into a mass of rundown apartment buildings, vacant storefronts, flophouse hotels for men only, "greasy spoon" restaurants, skid-row-type bars and "daily pay" employment offices where a man can get a job if he promises not to keep it.

Uptown is not Chicago's only ghetto, but it has recorded some dubious "firsts." It is first among Chicago neighborhoods in the number of senior citizens, and it provides the most patients for Illinois mental institutions. Uptown is also the city's largest dumping ground for abandoned automobiles, most of them having barely made it in from the South before the transmission gave out or the last tire went flat. With today's automobile travel geared to the high-speed, limited-access highway, one of the wonders of the migration movement is that so many Southerners actually reach their destinations.

Uptown probably could also lay claim to having more alcoholics than any other section of the city were it not for West Madison Street, a longtime haven for the derelict. As it is, Uptown has its own skid row, a two-block section of Wilson Avenue where a dozen or so bars open early to compete for a beer-and-cheap-wine trade that is generally brisk enough to keep the bartenders active. There are also a lot of jukeboxes on Wilson Avenue and they're seldom ever silent. For a dime the Southerner can have his miseries put to music by a whining steel guitar and a nasal voice that sounds even more miserable than he is. Country-and-western is the "soul" music of the rural Southern white, and its popularity will never be more in evidence than it is currently on Wilson Avenue. There the Southerner can virtually relive his life in song if he doesn't run out of dimes. There's a song for every mood. For the new arrival lost in the aloof city, there's:

> Don't get no attention from the people that we meet.
> They don't even see us, they just step right on our feet.

For the homesick:

> I wanna go home, I wanna go home.
> Ooooh Lord, I wanna go home.

And over at The Old Homestead, a bar aptly named since many of its customers have little place else to go, a bewhiskered Southerner who long ago surrendered his life to Uptown stares into the bottom of an empty wine glass while the jukebox admits for him that "What made Milwaukee famous has made a loser out of me."

This is Uptown, only a port of entry for some, a final resting place for others. A composite picture of a newly arrived family's first day in Uptown would begin at five A.M. A family of five stirs from a sleep that never really came, inside a late-50's model automobile parked alongside a row of three-story apartment buildings, each looking exactly like the other, give or take a few broken windows. The family has arrived in Uptown during the night and decided to "sleep" on this particular street because the mother and father think a friend or relative lives here who might find them a place to live, in the same building if possible. The parents are between 35 and 40 years old. Their education is at the eighth-grade level by Southern standards, fifth-grade by Chicago standards. The father instructs the mother to take the children and begin looking for the friends or relative. Hopefully, she will have found an apartment they can rent by the time he returns in the evening. The father then goes off in search of either a blood bank to sell a pint of his own or a daily-pay employment office, maybe both. He must satisfy what he feels is the family's most pressing need, immediate cash. And he is doing it the way he has heard about through the grapevine. When he returns in the evening, he and his family will rent a cubicle-sized apartment in one of the three-story buildings, because rent can be paid by the week there and children are welcome, he has also learned from the grapevine. Both the tiny apartment and the daily wages are temporary measures, he tells himself—breathing room. But it may be months, if even then, before he and his family escape either of them.

James R. Grisham, an executive director of the Chicago Southern Center, a private, nonprofit organization that attempts to provide "instant stability" for migrants, has seen the above scene repeated time after time. Often, he says, it could have been avoided had the families come straight to the center. There, free food and clothing are available to the migrant. The center can also direct him to the "right kind" of job and housing.

One of the reasons more migrants don't contact agencies such as the Southern Center is simply that they don't know about them; the agencies have yet to be included in the grapevine. So the center, as has other Uptown agencies, has begun advertising its services through "flyers," one-page handouts that are circulated throughout the neighborhood. In addition to services, the flyers note, the center has regularly scheduled programs of sewing, quilting and guitar instruction, recreational activities for children, a weekly community open house, a young marrieds' club and country-and-western music sessions—anything that will bring a touch of home to the migrant during his adjustment period.

One of Grisham's full-time employees is Father Joseph Dunne, a native Chicagoan who became concerned with the plight of the southern migrant while serving as a Catholic priest in Eastern Kentucky. Wondering what became of the migrants from his area, Father Dunne used a vacation earlier this year to come to Uptown and find out. He never returned to Eastern Kentucky. Instead, he became field director of the Southern Center's new Outreach program. "It became quite obvious to me that urban and rural problems are directly linked by migration," Father Dunne explained. "I predict the trend will reverse if the Appalachian economy is ever uplifted. We may face a new problem then: what effect has the city had on the migrant, what is he coming back to? The church can play an important role. It is, after all, in both places."

Father Dunne accepted his position with the Southern Center because the possibilities it offered "struck me as being the best vehicle to accomplish what I wanted to do—to help the migrant retain his dignity and self-respect, not try to make a Chicagoan out of him. If Outreach is successful, he'll return without the scars of city life."

Simply stated, Outreach is designed to turn a 30-block area in Uptown into 30 one-block communities, the citizens of each block working to solve the problems of the block as a whole rather than being concerned only with their own. In short, Outreach encourages the migrant to retain his help-thy-neighbor spirit rather than throw it off for the every-man-for-himself attitude of the city.

It's not as easy, though, as it may sound. Father Dunne's immediate task is to find a leader for each block, that one person willing to lay aside his own frustrations long enough to become at least a little concerned with those of his neighbors. It requires a lot of door knocking and a lot of street walking. Once Father Dunne finds such a leader he instructs her—it's usually a housewife—on what programs are available to assist the migrant during his period of adjustment, where they are located and how to bypass the complex system of referrals surrounding such programs. The block leader then becomes a kind of community information center. But with the transiency of the migrant not stopping with his arrival in Uptown, today's block leader may be tomorrow's new arrival on another block. So Father Dunne has cultivated relationships with a number of people who, while they aren't willing to serve as block leaders, do keep him informed on new arrivals in the area who need help.

A health problem about which there is growing concern in Uptown is a form of lead poisoning contracted by young children who have eaten plaster from window-sills or paint from walls. During a two-week period in July, three children died from it. One of the agencies concerned is the Montrose Urban Progress Center, one of seven neighborhood arms of the Chicago Committee on Urban Opportunity, the Chicago war-on-poverty program. Montrose poverty workers have spent a good deal of time in the field publicizing the symptoms of lead poisoning—heavy vomiting and severe headaches. Montrose workers also give regularly scheduled examinations to discover the presence of lead poisoning. At a recent examination 54 of 60 children tested had some degree of it.

The Chicago Committee on Urban Opportunity places great stress on the neighborhood Urban Progress Center concept. Jesse Escalante, director of the Montrose Center, describes the concept as "a multitude of agencies under one roof." Indeed, a representative of virtually every city service being dispensed is housed at Montrose. The hoped-for effect is that with so many representatives of city government headquartered at Montrose, Uptown residents will come to regard Montrose as being city government, hence their own government.

One of those headquartered at Montrose is Miss Sylvia Swidler, long-time manager of the local office of the Illinois State Employment Service. She has studied the work habits of Southerners over the years and feels she has an understanding of migrants and their problems that prevents her from "becoming impersonal." She is especially sympathetic toward the Appalachian. She explains him thus: "The Appalachian simply is not familiar with the urban way of life. To him time is not important. In his home town everybody took time to sit or visit with his neighbor. It is not unusual for an Appalachian to work for a few days just to pay the rent and eat and then not show up for a few days after payday. He will return to his job when his money is gone and expect it to still be there." Such matters, Miss Swidler said, must be dealt with through "education and patience." She has brought some Chicago industries slowly around to accepting that theory. "It's an education program for them too," she said. "It's cheaper for them to go along with the individual than it is to fire him." Accordingly, some Chicago employers have initiated work-orientation programs for Southerners in cooperation with the Chicago chapter of the National Alliance of Businessmen.

Miss Swidler has also opened a "day labor" office in an effort to keep Southerners from becoming entrapped by the privately operated daily-pay employment offices, labeled in some circles as "slave-labor markets." Miss Swidler calls her program a "try-before-you-buy concept." Under it, an employee is hired for a job on a one-day basis at salaries ranging up to $3 per hour. He receives his wages direct from the employer at the end of the day. If both he and the employer are satisfied he can be hired on a permanent basis.

The 20 daily-pay agencies in Uptown operate somewhat differently, the main difference, of course, being the profit motive. Outside estimates place the portion of an employee's daily pay retained by the employment agency as between one-third and one-half. Agency managers, though, offer much more conservative figures. "If we net a buck and a half a day per head, we're lucky," said Saul Wallace, president of Alhelp Labor Service. "It's a volume business with us." According to Wallace, Alhelp charges employers $15 per day for unskilled labor sent to them. Of the $15, he said, the employee receives $12.80 less social security. Alhelp, it should be noted, is doing well enough to be able to transport its people to their jobs in a fleet of five buses. "We get the biggest pay of all of them," Wallace boasts.

The daily-pay offices have also come under fire for an agreement they require each employee to sign. Under it, the employee agrees to a 90-day ban on accepting permanent employment in any job to which the agency sends him. Wallace claims the daily-pay offices need the agreement as a device to build up labor "pools."

"If an employer wants six employees I have to develop a pool of 12 just to meet the demand," he said. "It's because of the drinking problem. Some of these people couldn't hold a steady job because they drink 75 percent of the time." Critics insist that the 90-day agreement often keeps the migrants in a low-pay situation just long enough to destroy their spirit and initiative. "Look, I know some people think of us as slave dealers," Wallace counters, "but they don't understand the kind of people we're dealing with. A person coming from a foreign land adjusts better than some of these people."

In the final analysis, Wallace figures, "we're doing a little bit for the community. Basically, we're selling it bodies. We're not an AA [Alcoholics Anonymous] and don't try to be. Every major triple-A .company in this city uses this type of service sometime." Wallace declined to name any of them. Alhelp is located on Wilson Avenue. Its immediate neighbors include several bars, a couple of restaurants, a

men-only hotel and a Goodwill Industries store. "You can get drunk for 24 hours for 50 cents on this street," Wallace observed. A man not only can get drunk there, he can draw his pay and grab a greasy hamburger beforehand, go sleep it off afterward, and never have to leave the block.

It is significant that with so many restaurants in Uptown, everything from bagels and lox with sour cream to Spanish and Oriental delicacies is available—but nowhere can the Southerner sit down to a meal of black-eyed peas and cornbread. "He probably couldn't afford it anyway," was the guess of one hash-slinger in the neighborhood. His restaurant was only a couple of blocks away from an equally nonaffluent section where the Puerto Rico theater was offering movies with Spanish subtitles to area residents, some of whom were named Garcia and lived in a rundown building that struggled for dignity under the name Carlos Hotel. One gets the feeling that what Uptown really needs is a theater named the Hatfield or McCoy that doesn't show anything but filmed versions of the "Grand Ole Opry" and serves only moonshine and hominy grits at the concession stand.

It is this disregard for the southern culture that a small group of former nuns is combatting at the grassroots level. Located on the top floor of one of Uptown's six-flatters is the one-year-old Federation of Communities in Service (FOCIS). Its members are expanding to the ghetto a mission of service to the Appalachian people that has been conducted in Appalachia by the Glenmary order, from which FOCIS sprang. FOCIS members live in the neighborhood with the Appalachians and try to bridge the gap between the person-oriented culture of Appalachia and the cold indifference of the city. FOCIS spends a lot of time trying to "get people in touch with each other," explained Miss Elizabeth Roth, who is still called "Sister" by the Appalachians. "The Appalachian culture is so kin-oriented. We know that if we can organize a recreation session for the kids the parents will soon join us. It's a way to get them acquainted."

Miss Roth talks a lot about "misunderstood Appalachian values." She'll probably never forget one lesson in Appalachian values. It concerned a music-loving Tennessee family of six who had decided to return to the hills and asked her to accompany them to help with the driving. The family had packed all its belongings into an uncovered trailer. Included among their possessions were two guitars, a banjo, an accordion and a stack of phonograph records. "The trip took nine-teen hours," she recalled, "fourteen of them in a driving rain. Naturally everything the family owned got soaked. But when we arrived the only thing they were concerned about was their phonograph records." Laughing, she added, "I spent an hour drying off records."

Knowing the Southern migrants' history of continuing transiency, Miss Roth had asked when the family might return to Chicago. "When the notes are right," the father replied.

THE FAMILY BEHIND THE MIGRANT
James S. Brown

One of the most important things about the Appalachian family, as far as both the country at large and Appalachian people themselves are concerned, is its role in the process of migration. This isn't really recognized as it ought to be, though every single one of us has probably observed this process. Let me tell you what I mean. When people go out, when people migrate, they don't go through the United States Employment Service or some recruiting agency; they go because some relative "out there" has written and told them, or come back and told them, that there are jobs available. Or if there aren't jobs, they have told the young brothers or sisters, neighbors or friends in the mountains that they are welcome to come out and, "We'll look for you a job." And they do go out and stay until they are located, and then in time another brother or sister reaches the age of migration and goes out and so on. Thus the family forms a real bridge from Beech Creek, in the case I'm describing, to Hamilton and Dayton and Cincinnati. As a result, you can find clusters of people in Ohio or Indiana or Michigan or many other places in the Midwest who are from certain com-munities or counties in Eastern Kentucky or West Virginia. Clay County, Kentucky, migrants go, for instance, to Cincinnati, Hamilton,

From *Mountain Life & Work*, September 1968. Used by permission of the author. This paper is based on the Beech Creek Study, which was sponsored by the National Institute of Mental Health in cooperation with the Kentucky Agri-cultural Experiment Station. The findings and conclusions reported here are de-rived from the work of all three researchers involved in this study: James S. Brown, Harry K. Schwarzweller, and Joseph J. Mangalam.

Middletown and Dayton. Migrants from southern West Virginia counties go to Columbus, Akron and Cleveland. They go to these specific places because of kinship ties.

Now, the family not only performs the function of telling potential migrants at home about jobs and getting them out there but educates and socializes them after they arrive so that they learn how to behave in this greater society. We have studied this process intensively for a number of years, and it is truly a very effective contribution the kinship structure of Appalachia makes to the nation as a whole. This is one reason we don't hear so terribly much about this great migration which, in scope, dwarfs a lot of the movements of people we do hear a whole lot about. It is amazing how fast the migration can be turned off if there aren't jobs out in the Midwestern cities. Family members pass the word back home, and migration is delayed until times get better.

We were intrigued by this kinship and migration relationship. We were also aware that Frederick Le Play, a French sociologist who lived from 1806 to 1882, had been much concerned about maintaining the strength of the nation. He thought that the way the family operated, the way the family was functioning, had a great deal to do with the strength of the society; so he began to look around to see what kind of family best maintained this strength. Eventually he developed the idea of what he called the *"famille souche"* or "stem family." This was a kind of family in which the stem "stayed put" back in the home community and sent out branches to the industrial cities. This stem family not only encouraged and got the people ready to go out but also maintained itself as a haven of refuge if there were difficulty in the cities, so that family members could come home and stay for a while, lick their wounds and then perhaps return to the urban fray. This was a good kind of family, he thought, to have in a modern, industrial society, and he noticed that there were many families of this kind in areas that were particularly strong and healthy, areas that didn't seem to have the weakness and instability connected with other types of families.

Well, now, we have followed this general idea through in our Appalachian studies. It is true that in many ways the Appalachian family operates as a "stem-family system." This doesn't mean that the people in Appalachia go to a completely new and different area, but rather they move, for example, from one sub-system, the Beech Creek sub-system or the Kentucky sub-system, to the Ohio sub-system. They're part of a single area of interaction, a single system if you please. The migrants and the home folks interact back and forth between Ohio and Kentucky.

Many of you who have seen the traffic crossing the Ohio River at Cincinnati going to Kentucky on Friday nights and then on Sunday nights returning from Kentucky to Ohio know the extent of this interaction. But there is much more to it than just that: all sorts of visiting back and forth that you don't see, letter writing, and money (and this is terribly important, not just from the standpoint of the migrant but also from the standpoint of the people back at home). Many, perhaps most, of the significant social changes that have come about in the mountains have been brought about through this very channel of the migrants bringing back new ideas, new patterns, new values, or having their kinsfolk come over to their new homes where they learn about "outside" folkways and norms, in fact all sorts of things that they take back with them.

There are many cultural patterns that I'd "just as soon" had not been imported to Appalachia, but the whole process means that for better or worse Appalachia has joined modern American society.

Now, under these circumstances we thought a good general hypothesis to test would be this: The more these migrants were involved in kinship groups out in what we call "areas of destination" (or the Ohio sub-systems), then the more adjusted, or the more rapidly adjusted, Beech Creek migrants would be in this greater society.

That is a very difficult research problem. In the first place, you've got to figure how you're going to measure "adjustment," how you are going to measure kinship involvement, and so on. We worked out indices of each of these and related them. Though about half of the Beech Creek population has moved out of the original neighborhoods in the 20 years since I first studied the area, we still have 161 informants, and they are all kinds, young and old; upper-class and lower-class; men and women; members of churches, nonmembers of churches, and so on. It is difficult, therefore, to determine whether their adjustment is due to the kinship system or something else. We have done a good bit of "methodological hocus-pocus" to try to take care of this, and I can say, in general, that my colleagues and I are convinced that the Appalachian kinship system has in many ways contributed significantly to the adjustment of Beech Creek migrants and to their personal stability. This is a tremendous contribution, one that should be repeatedly underlined (as I have done) because I think it is an overlooked and unappreciated function of the Appalachian family.

Though it isn't good puritanism (which tends to see things in mutually exclusive ways with no transitions between polar types—black and white, good and bad, moral and immoral)—I mention this because Appalachia has a strong strain, or dose, of puritanism in its culture—there is "bad" even in this "good" of familistic solidarity. The tendency to form tight clusters of relatives and close friends from Eastern Kentucky in Southern Ohio does ease the transition from one subculture to another, but it also delays integration and assimilation into the greater society and clearly often puts brakes on movement toward goals most of us consider highly desirable. You are aware, of course, that preservation of Appalachian traits may be considered to be a good thing, even if it does slow down mountain people's coming to be "like everybody else" in their new urban homes. No one who has studied and lived among Eastern Kentuckians can fail to have regrets about their loss of many distinctive social and cultural traits. But I must also say that my Ohio friends have a much shorter list of such characteristics than I.

I want, however, to finish with a quotation that "accentuates the positive" aspect of the Appalachian kinship structure. Dr. Robert Coles, the Harvard psychiatrist, is impressed with many things, and I consider him a keen observer of the poor. With a colleague, Dr. Joseph Brenner of M.I.T., Dr. Coles went with a team to help "unfortunate, deprived" children in poverty-stricken areas of Appalachia. From a newspaper account come these comments about their trip.

They did find people in need of help. But they found other things.

They said: "We have seen few 'neurotic' problems in mountain schools. Teachers do not describe and we have not seen that mixture of ability and nonperformance that characterizes the child with a 'learning block.'"

"We have to comment," they noted in describing the poverty of Appalachia, "on the difference between a [poor mountain] youth who may have 'little' in the economic sense ahead of him, but a firm idea of exactly who he is, where he comes from . . . and what he would like . . . and a [city middle class] youth who has a 'lot' [but who is uncertain] . . . about where he will go or what he will do."

They found a "greater sense of family, of shared allegiance to parents and grandparents that somehow makes for relatively more cooperative activity, frolic and eventually work than one sees among many other American children."

They found brothers and sisters living and playing together "without evidence of the charged defiant 'individuality' one finds so often in middle-class city homes."

They believe "a nation that knows wide-spread delinquency" and which has "almost made a virtue of youth's rebellion and fast departure from home" will be interested in what makes these Appalachian youth stick to the family and strongly want to return home if they do move away.

The secret, the two men found, was that these young men and women have strong ties to cousins, to neighbors, to a host of relatives as well as parents. These ties come, said the psychiatrists, because "even before adolescence, mountain children learn that a family is no laughing matter, no temporary arrangement characterized by divorce, constant movement and a strictly limited membership, lucky to include anyone outside a set of parents and . . . a matching set of children. Kin—relatives of one sort or other—have a real and well-known meaning."

Since families mean a lot, in old age they continue to mean a lot. The elderly are usually spared that final sense of abandonment and uselessness so commonly the fate of the middle-class suburban aged.

That, I believe, neatly summarizes many of the things I have been saying. In other words, the Appalachian family has a lot of strength, it has contributed a great deal and is continuing to contribute a great deal to this nation. It is largely unappreciated, but it deserves to be evaluated realistically, and seen in its rightful place in the scheme of things.

Part Three

Lessons in Fighting Poverty

Organizing at the Grassroots

A ROPE TO JUMP, A WELL TO DIG
Thomas Parrish

In the situation, one wants to remind oneself that politics is the art
of the possible. One wants to quote this worn dictum not to suggest
the limits of political action but to draw on its underlying implication
that in political situations some action is possible. It's the sort of reassurance this particular situation needs.

The situation: Ten persons sit in a basement room, down a flight
of stairs from a general store—Plummer's Store, which is also the
United States post office for Battle Fork, Kentucky. Battle Fork is
down a road off a road up a road, back in the hills—a long way back.
There's a TV set in the room, and chairs around the walls, and a lino-
leum "carpet." It's a comfortable room for Battle Fork, though the
ceiling is low, in mountain style. It's closed in, like Battle Fork, like the
whole county.

The ten persons speak slowly, a slow give and a slow take, not
always with a return. A visitor is telling them that he's arranged some
shipments of books for the schools. The teacher thinks the news is
wonderful. The visitor, who has just come from a stop at the teacher's

From *The Reporter*, November 19, 1964. Used by permission of the author.

one-room school, feels that he's perpetrating a fraud, as though he had promised a potato chip to a man dying of malnutrition. There's nothing wonderful about a single potato chip or even a bag of potato chips.

"The books will be wonderful," the teacher says again.

"What about the well?" says a middle-aged man, after the books have been nodded to.

The well—that's the real crisis.

"Where do you get water now?" asks the visitor.

"They have to go 'bout a quarter of a mile," says the teacher. "I bring my own in a jar. Helps out that much, anyway. I send the children out with a bucket. But we can't get enough that way."

The visitor says, "Did you talk to the superintendent about the well?"

Another man, who prefers to stand, says, "We talked to him. Promises—he's a great one for promises."

The man's wife agrees: "He promises you, but it don't mean nothin'. We went down and told him the school didn't have no water, but that's all that happened."

"How about the county judge?" asks the visitor. "Does he have anything to do with this kind of thing?"

"Well," says the standing man, "he's got the dollar-an-hour fathers—the stickweed gang. They could dig a well, I reckon. But he don't have nothing to do with the schools. That's the Board of Education."

"That means the superintendent, I guess," the visitor says.

The man nods. Nobody speaks. They need a well dug, so that the thirty kids in the one-room school can have water to drink, so that it won't have to be fetched from a spring about a quarter of a mile away. Winter is coming, and springs freeze in the winter.

"We can't have the hot-lunch program, either," the teacher says. "I don't know if I could take care of it myself anyway, but I sure can't do any cooking without water."

So without the well there's no lunch as well as no water for drinking. And pans have to be washed.

"You've got to put pressure on the superintendent," says the visitor, feeling that a generality will clear the air. "That's the way things get done anywhere—Washington, Frankfort, anywhere. Most things that happen are in response to pressure. Look at the Negroes: they've found kinds of pressure they can exert, and many of them couldn't even vote. Yet they've achieved a great deal."

A very tanned woman next to the visitor nods agreement. "They sure have," she says, as if glad of it—glad that some chronically voiceless somebodies have found a way to shout.

"We ain't got no pressure," says a man who hasn't spoken before.

Assent in various shades comes from everyone present. The visitor listens for a moment. He wants to express disagreement. He begins to say, "But you are ten separate persons—ten units of pressure." Here is where the dictum about politics comes to mind, as he looks at the faces of persons who are getting precisely what they seem to expect—which is nothing.

"You can bug the superintendent," the visitor says. "You can stay on his back—worry him to death. He might give you the well just to get rid of you." That, surely, is a mild suggestion, the visitor thinks. It's a simple form of group action.

The listeners find the suggestion amusing.

"Bug him," repeats the tanned woman, seeming to like the word.

"We did that once," says a woman across the room. "I went down there to his office and told him 'bout the well and us needing it."

A man says, "Bet he told you he'd take care of it, didn't he?"

The woman nods yes, and everyone laughs, the kind of laugh that is a wry smile made audible.

"You could go see him again," the visitor insists. "You could see him day after day, if you had to."

"I s'pose we could," says the woman who had once gone to the superintendent's office. "Maybe it would get us something." There are other maybes. But there isn't much conviction—the words are spoken flat, with no inflection—and by some non sequitur the gift of books comes back into the discussion. It is generally agreed that the books are wonderful.

"We need anything," the teacher says. "Anything would help—a rope to jump, even. And the softball came apart. The dew got to it."

The visitor scans the ten patient faces. Is it possible, he wonders, for a pressure group to be established for the purpose of obtaining a seventy-nine-cent softball, if a well is such an impossibility? Maybe not. Maybe a pressure group can't function unless it believes there is such a thing as pressure. Maybe it needs help and advice, an experienced counselor, so that it will come to believe that some of the desirable things in the world are for it, and that some of the time the school superintendent has to listen to his constituents (which is what superintendents have in the mountains).

Or, the visitor thinks, maybe the group could decide to dig the well itself. That wouldn't put the superintendent in his place, it wouldn't release any accumulated resentments against "the county"—but it would provide the school children with water to drink, and water for lunches, and water for washing pans. It might also yield psychological by-products for the group, though its members wouldn't be aware that they were participating in dynamics.

Maybe . . . maybe a whole lot of things. It's a maybe place, the mountains, back up the creeks and hollows.

FAIR ELECTIONS IN WEST VIRGINIA
K. W. Lee

The faces were sallow and white—pale under an early spring sun, but the gazes were defiant. In chant-like unison, they shouted "No, No, No!" They held signs high saying, "Down with the Machine," "People Want Honest Elections," "County Court is a Pawn in the Machine."

On a crisp morning in late March 1968, 700 mountain folk packed the street in front of the same courthouse steps where the late John F. Kennedy, on his 1960 vote-getting trail to the White House, had vowed to "do something" for Appalachia's forgotten people. The crowd—a motley army of disabled miners, pensioners, housewives, and children too young to vote—was protesting the entrenched Democratic county court's plan to take over a poor-people-run poverty program which, among other things, had generated a clean election drive.

Down along the lower banks of creeks, the azaleas and dogwoods were budding. The long winter of discontent was over and the spring of rebellion had broken out in Mingo County, West Virginia, a land where the ghosts of the McCoy-Hatfield feud and bloody union strife

From *Appalachian Lookout*, April 1969. Used by permission of the author.

still haunt the surrounding hills, and where what is undoubtedly the most persuasive political machine east of Mayor Richard Daley's Chicago has reigned comfortably for decades through well-oiled machine politics and crooked election practices.

Inside the courthouse, the politicians and their hangers-on looked uneasily out of windows. Armed constables and deputies swarmed the halls but didn't venture out. A delegation of the organized poor walked into the room where the county court was in session and demanded that the three commissioners come out and address their unhappy constituents. The officials refused. Returning to the street, protest leader Herbert Meade, a grizzled, ex-coal miner, shouted to the roaring crowd: "We know what we've got to do, so let's get back into the hollows and do it."

Thus, on March 30, 1968, deep in the mountains of the Appalachian South, was launched the open challenge of a county machine—and of a sordid tradition which has enslaved the once-proud mountaineers in the vote-rich southern coal fields of West Virginia for nearly a half-century.

In electoral fraud, Mingo County is a microcosm of its mother state, whose bizarre voting behavior is a cruel joke on its state motto, "*Montani Semper Liberi*." Some observers even trace the flagrant corruption to West Virginia's own constitution which allows voting by "open, sealed, or secret ballot." Open balloting—shunned even in the one-party dictatorship of Russia—has been the standard procedure in most of the county fiefdoms.

As early as the 1940's, elder statesmen of both parties conceded expansively that votes had been bought in their state for as long as they could remember. They offered this redeeming argument: since both parties compete to buy an equal number of votes in the contested precincts, the non-bought votes really decide the election outcome.

In his 1946 visit to the state, *Nation* magazine editor Carey McWilliams wondered incredulously: "What a visitor to West Virginia finds mystifying about the politics of the state is how the citizenry really know who won the election. . . . It would be accurate to say," he reasoned, "that there are rotten boroughs in West Virginia, but it would be closer to the truth to say that the state itself is a rotten borough." McWilliams confessed he was "impressed with the nonchalant manner in which voting frauds are taken for granted."

In the intervening years, corrupt election practices have been fused with the state's political system as hallowed custom and technique. A few editorial statistics in this never-never land of wild politics:

The state's population fell 7.2 percent from 1950 to 1960 (West Virginia was one of three states losing population in the United States), but registered voters increased 2.4 percent during the same period. The 1960 census counted 1,083,347 voting-age persons, but 1,090,042 were registered to vote.

In Mingo County, the 1960 gap was even more pronounced: there were 19,879 eligible voters, but 30,331 were registered.

In 1964, registered voters outnumbered eligible voters in 29 of the state's 55 counties, and four years later the strange disproportion spread to 33 counties.

In neighboring Lincoln County, the voting-age population numbered 10,516, but 14,279 were registered. Although its population dropped from 20,267 in 1960 to 19,900 in 1966, registration increased from 14,279 to 16,233 in the six-year span.

Present West Virginia political practices are an out-growth of the early politics of coal which developed as the vast untapped underground was first opened by enterprising businessmen from out of state. These mine operators built their own little Balkans in which they owned everything—including politicians, law enforcement officers and judges. In time, as automation put thousands out of work, courthouse jobs became the main source of employment in some counties, enabling the state machines to keep these little kingdoms loyal through patronage in the state liquor commission, state road commission and other agencies. The political harvest is reaped in every primary race.

West Virginia's 1960 presidential primary—the one that made Kennedy a President—exposed to the nation such well-weathered habits as the half-pint-vote, "slating," "lever brothers" in voting booths, and prolific absentee balloting. In his classic book *The Making of the President, 1960*, Theodore H. White was moved to observe: "If one were to choose those states whose politics . . . are the most squalid, corrupt and despicable, then one would add West Virginia to that Jukes family of American politics that includes Indiana, Massachusetts and Texas."

What was well on its way to being a movement that early spring of 1968 had actually begun the summer of 1967 when 400 anti-poverty grassroots representatives from ten southern counties convened at Concord College in a "Poor People's Congress."

The delegation tackled four issues of immediate concern: dirty elections, an unfair tax structure, backward school systems and a politics-mired state road commission. The Mingo delegation's interest was captured by a fair elections workshop in which the former candidates John Callebs and the Democratic Party's angry young man, State Senator Paul Kaufman, briefed them on the state election laws.

James Washington, the black, 52-year-old former coal miner who was to become chairman of Mingo County's Fair Election Committee (FEC), compared the laws with his county's election practices: "Until that time I didn't realize how bad the things were in Mingo." His right-hand man, Okey Spence, also upset, commented, "Somebody has messed up with my rights and I'm going to get them back!" Upon their return, these men and others began calling meetings in hollows where both Republicans and Democrats discussed just what was wrong with their elections and decided that the fault was as much with the people as the politicians. In the final analysis, they realized, it was up to the mountaineers themselves to restore, or, more accurately, initiate honest elections.

Long winter nights were spent studying the loophole punctured election laws, sometimes with election experts. Small in the beginning, gatherings began to swell in size. At one study session, 400 showed up. Warm bodies were recruited and a dozen "core" leaders emerged. As the snow started melting, they were on their own.

Their first job was to purge the hopelessly padded registration rolls. Their initial difficulty: many were afraid to enter the courthouse to check the registration books for challenging purposes. They had good reason; armed officials were everywhere. Some actually attempted to intimidate Callebs and state Republican lawmaker Cleo Jones—the only lawyer in the state to volunteer help for the FEC—within the courthouse itself.

The FEC resolved to overcome this fear of "confronting the system face to face." A small group of spunky housewives who knew districts like their own backyards entered the courthouse and began challenging hundreds of names on the rolls. It was not long before they were arrested, but there were others to take their place. Mrs. Alma Jean

Justice, long active in Democratic politics, alone challenged 400 names. Mrs. Lerly Murphy, a petite Republican worker, scored 700 challenges.

To the machine, the bold challenge presented a clear and present danger to its rule. Hundreds of political jobs were on the line. The apparatus, with its allies in the Statehouse and Congress, lashed back with numerous arrests. This raw display of power, however, only gave credibility in the eyes of resigned residents to what the FEC was trying to do, and helped the embattled volunteers pull themselves together.

Sympathetic outsiders came to their aid. "Mingo County isn't part of the United States," Callebs declared. He offered to go to jail with the arrestees. Former Republican Governor Cecil Underwood and Democrat Kaufman, both opposing organization candidates, made trips to Mingo to give their moral support. After attending a rally of the Political Action League (a spin-off organization of the county's anti-poverty group), Underwood told a statewide TV audience, "It's one of the most inspiring things that I have seen." Kaufman called them "freedom fighters."

Unobtrusively, millionaire John D. Rockefeller, who was seeking the Democratic nomination for secretary of state showed up at meetings of the county's underdogs. The former antipoverty worker quickly developed working relations with the Fair Election people. At FEC gatherings, he listened with an ear for legislative reforms. On his own, he probed into the intricate workings of machine politics and vote frauds. On the eve of the May primary, he condemned the practices as "a national disgrace and a local tragedy" and called for vigorous enforcement of the election laws.

The arrests continued, escalating into what FEC lawyer Jones charged was "political repression." "These people are people of little financial means but are tired of being held in political bondage," he said.

The Fair Electioneers hurriedly organized a trip to Washington to appeal for an FBI investigation into what they believed were flagrant violations of civil rights and the 1965 federal Voting Rights Act. A group of 38 members, including 74-year-old Mrs. Ethel Wren, spent two days in the capital visiting the Justice Department and the state's congressional delegation. A 26-member contingent met with Senator Robert Byrd, a strong "law and order" advocate, but six of them walked out in disgust, grumbling that the Senator was unresponsive.

Those who'd been arrested were hauled into Justice of the Peace courts for acts state officials say they didn't commit. They were accused of maliciously challenging a voter's right to vote on election day, even though the election was more than a month away. Most of them were tried, despite the fact that a JP has no authority to hold trials in election-related cases.

In one instance Mrs. Judy Trend was given the maximum penalty of a $100 fine and 60 days in jail, after a trial in which, according to her lawyer, she was ordered to prove her innocence. She appealed the conviction. Three other workers—Mrs. Alma Jean Justice, Mrs. Lerly Murphy and Hiram Marcum—were determined to go to jail. They refused to sign bond when they were bound over to the grand jury, and the JP let them go. Their open demonstration of contempt for the county's JP system—long regarded as a tool of the machine among Mingo's trampled people—was something that had never happened before.

Despite intimidation and threats, the challenges continued. "There's not enough space in the county jail to halt the people willing to fight for clean elections," a brief statement from FEC headquarters said. Shortly, the group announced it had removed nearly 3,000 names from the list of 25,566 names.

The stepped-up antifraud drive—and the accompanying glare of publicity—didn't seem to slow the pace of absentee voting, a favorite means for chalking up a decisive margin of the votes before an election takes place—and popular because votes can be bought easily that way. As the May 14 primary approached, hundreds of mountain folk, most of them on welfare rolls, were being herded like cattle in truckloads to cast their absentee ballots. Circuit Court Clerk John Keesee—the only cooperative county official, according to the FEC—glumly noted he was powerless to stop "open balloting." "Most of them voted right before the eyes of the election officials," he said. "I've never seen so many blind people in my life—they say they couldn't see well and would have to have assistance."

On heavy days, dozens of cowed voters stood outside in the halls waiting their turn. At one point a party boss, irked by the slow-moving line, walked into the circuit court clerk's office where the balloting was going on and demanded that Keesee let the two ballot commissioners mark the ballots to speed things up. Later Keesee wryly commented that Harvey District, one of the three lower end districts, didn't need an election. Most of the voters there had cast their absentee ballots. And most such voters, he added, had no intention of leaving the county on election day. FEC observers estimated that about two-thirds of the votes had been bought, at $3 to $10 per vote. They noted that some enterprising voters would wait all day outside the courthouse for the highest bid.

In the Mingo primary, at least one out of every 10 voters—well over 1,000—cast absentee ballots. This figure, though, was an improvement, thanks to FEC activity. In the primary four years earlier roughly 4,500 absentee votes were cast in Mingo, about 25 percent of the total.

During the 29-day absentee voting period, the FEC collected 13 affidavits of vote buying and voting by dead people and non-residents, which they submitted to the FBI. According to the FEC, many individuals were afraid to sign affidavits for fear of being taken off the welfare rolls.

At the height of the influx of votes, clusters of protestors gathered in front of the courthouse in pouring rain and demonstrated. Some of their signs read, "Let's Stop Voting Dead People," "Blood Has Paid for Your Right to Vote—Does It Sell for As Cheap As $5?" Their young spokesman said, "A lot of good people are aroused by this stuff going on for so long." "But they won't fight," a housewife added, "—just talk."

On the eve of the primary, rumors of killings at polling places ran rampant. The FEC grew alarmed at the possible risk of the lives of nearly 100 volunteer poll-watchers. Turning to Governor Hulett Smith, an organization Democrat, for help, the FEC drafted a six page letter listing incidents of threats, vote-buying and voter-hauling by state employees and pleaded with Smith to dispatch outstanding citizens as poll observers. "The citizens of Mingo County need your protection," the appeal said.

Smith declined the request, claiming it would be illegal for him to post such observers inside the polls. Although the FEC didn't expect much from Smith, they were flabbergasted at the reason for his refusal. "We are well aware of the West Virginia election laws," FEC chief James Washington told the governor. "We realize that poll observers couldn't be inside the polling places. We wouldn't be foolish enough to ask you to violate the law. We are asking you to uphold the law." He continued, "Our federal government found it possible to send observers to a foreign nation (South Vietnam) to insure fair elections. Are you telling us that a state government here in the United States can't do the same for its own citizens?"

Appeals to Attorney General Ramsey Clark and the White House, for federal observers to "protect the lives of our citizen poll watchers" were no more successful. Finally the FEC mailed out requests for volunteer poll watchers to the state's chamber of commerce, junior chamber of commerce, labor unions, civic groups and colleges. There were no responses.

Mingo's disenfranchised voters were obviously going to be largely on their own. A few outside sympathizers came to join their watch, including a dozen AVs and VISTAs from throughout the state who appeared at dawn on election day. Two campaign volunteers for Kaufman and one Rockefeller aide teamed up with the local people. Later, a contingent of Underwood, Callebs and FEC legal counsel Jones arrived and proceeded to visit "problem" precincts.

May 14 was a day filled with an incredible display of machine power in an unreal world of sheep-like people. At one precinct, the ex-governor and his fellow poll-watcher suddenly found themselves confronted by a glowering, pistol-packing constable. Inside the courthouse, a young poll observer was taking pictures of candidates electioneering within the 60-foot limit among lined-up voters, when he was attacked by a deputy. A similar incident occurred at a remote precinct.

At still another poll, Mrs. Murphy's intrepid husband, Sid, was photographing a group of people gathered at the door to the building. A deputy sheriff tackled him in an attempt to confiscate his camera, then threatened to shoot. Murphy didn't retreat. (It wasn't a new experience for Murphy. In 1966, he was serving as a Republican poll worker when he was forcibly taken out of the polling place and put in jail. His crime was refusing to offer illegal assistance to voters who could vote on their own.)

Mrs. Justice, the mother of seven children, was threatened with rape by a constable and his cronies who taunted her for two hours after her fellow watcher had gone. She later told state officials that he had approached with several "roughneck" boys and said, "Boys, which one of you wants to be first?"

Political candidates, deputies and constables freely entered polling places. Election officials forced voters to accept their "assistance" in voting booths. Polling officials left polling places to carry messages to outside workers. A police car was seen hauling voters to the polls. In one precinct independent voters, who had been waiting in line since 5:30 P.M., were turned away at the 7:30 P.M. closing, but continued standing in protest until midnight. Poll observers were commonly the target of constant verbal abuse and threats.

In a good many precincts, there were discrepancies between the number of signed poll slips and the number of votes cast. At the "problem" Wharncliffe precinct all of the Republican poll slips were missing and didn't turn up for two days. Elsewhere, an open voting machine in a van was seen being "worked on" by three men with tools while on the way to the canvass at the courthouse. In a lighter vein, when a VISTA dressed in a three-piece business suit and carrying a briefcase appeared at one rural precinct, the constable, who had made the threat to a local poll watcher to "lock him up until sunrise" suddenly became exceedingly courteous, taking the VISTA for an FBI agent.

These incidents and numerous others were reported to state authorities. Washington told Secretary of State Robert Baily that his group estimated about 80 percent of the votes were bought one way or another on May 14. What he witnessed on that day shocked Underwood: "Armed constables trying to push people like cattle—this kind of thing has to be eliminated from American politics. It just isn't part of America." "I felt very depressed about the whole day," said Callebs.

Out of the primary landslide, Rockefeller emerged as a rising star of incorruptibility in a state recently shattered by a scandal in which six men, including five Democratic officials, had been indicted by a federal grand jury on bribery conspiracy charges involving state contracts. One of them, a former Democratic governor, was later acquitted, and another official was granted a mistrial. The remaining four were convicted.

The Rockefeller mystique—he doesn't have to steal taxpayers' money—and his evident concern for the state's problems brought him victory in all but one of the 55 counties. In Mingo, Rockefeller lost to a nameless candidate—and learned a lesson. "I am proud because I lost in Mingo County," he told a summer picnic of Fair Election people. The only way to beat the machine, he went on, is for the people to organize and fight. "The easiest thing is to get discouraged and do nothing—that's what the machine is hoping for you to do."

During the summer months, Washington's group concentrated its efforts on a comprehensive proposal for removing numerous loopholes in the existing law and preventing election violations. "Our ideas didn't come from some big shot lawyer or even college-educated people, but from ordinary citizens of Mingo County," Washington explained in announcing the proposals. Among its key measures were selection of election officials by lottery, a requirement that absentee voters submit sworn affidavits, prohibition of assistance by poll workers in voting and open balloting and a recommended change in the role of secretary of state to make him the chief election officer, not simply a registration officer. At the same time they were formulating the proposed changes, the Mingo Fair Electioneers busily exported their own missionaries to six other counties for a coordinated drive.

As the fall election season began, absentee voting again moved into full swing, despite the public uproar over the May primary. Captive voters by the hundreds were herded into the courthouse. The circuit court clerk said about 90 percent of the absentee voters sought assistance from election officials. In 11 warrants, several Democrats, including T. I. Varney, a constable, state road employees, and a committeeman were charged with vote-buying—largely absentee ballots at $5 apiece. All the charges were later dismissed in JP courts.

On the eve of the November election, the FEC again sent appeals to Washington for federal observers, saying, "Already efforts to steal this upcoming election are well underway," and adding that the state and county governments had been totally unresponsive. The FEC had not heard from either the governor or the state attorney general since requesting a special grand jury on the Mingo situation.

The November 5 election was less violent, but, according to Washington's estimates, about half of the total votes were either bought or influenced under the machine pressure. Fair Electioneers said their campaign had produced little or no effect on vote frauds. One Republican poll worker challenged countless voters seeking assistance on voting machines only to have the challenged voters, despite a law requiring them to cast challenged paper ballots, escorted to the machines by the Democratic poll workers who "helped" them vote. Many with high school educations claimed they couldn't see well and needed election officials' assistance, among them high school teachers. Said Mrs. Murphy, a former poll worker, "They aren't scared of voting machines but they are scared of election officials." After the hectic election, Washington concluded glumly, "The machine people here know how they can get away with anything, and nobody at county, state and national level wants to help us—nobody gives a damn for what we have been doing."

If the results were discouraging, the FEC could claim some small credit for its past labors: for the first time in the county's history, its registered voters dropped below the number of eligible voters. In 1960, the county had 19,879 voting-age people, but 30,331 were registered. The registration number had fallen to 19,248 for the November election. County Clerk Thomas Chafin now publicly challenged anyone to find the names of dead people on the county rolls.

Armed with his Mingo experiences, the newly elected Secretary of State Rockefeller returned to the county in mid-January to hold fair elections hearings in the first leg of his search for legislative cures. On hand were 150 citizens, including a number of business men. Rockefeller heard emotion-choked witnesses relate how elections were stolen from the people. Most of their testimony was familiar, but one witness —a shriveled old man—spoke movingly for the county's disenfranchised. He was a life-long Democrat, he said, who had voted in the county for 20 years, and "I have never seen a fair election in our county." His voice trembling in helpless anger, the old man asked the young secretary of state how any Mingo County citizen could expect to do something about elections when the Democrats named the county Democratic chairman as chairman of the Senate Election Committee, which had happened several weeks earlier. Then almost in a whisper, he said, "I hope you live up to your word. That's all I ask you . . . I may not live too long. I am 74 years old."

After a second hearing in Charleston, attended mostly by those who administer elections, Rockfeller hammered out four priority bills for legislative action, measures (1) tightening the rules governing absentee voting, (2) restricting assistance in voting to only the disabled and illiterate, (3) prohibiting government employees and their wives from serving as election officials, and (4) giving authority to the secretary of state to subpoena records, investigate irregularities and hold hearings on election matters.

Rockefeller, in fact, introduced nine election reform bills, most of which, including the priority bills, were bottled up in committees in both houses. The state's lawmakers returned to their homes, leaving the "priority" bills to die the traditional lingering death of their countless predecessors.

To the outside world, which is how the West Virginian conceives all that is not Appalachia, the Mingo revolt demonstrates the lack of even the most basic elements of democracy. Impoverished, apathetic and isolated, most people in the mountains live in cruel political bondage. Ironically, the greatest poverty and the most durable political machines are found where some of the richest natural wealth lies underground.

In Appalachian colonies—and Mingo is a salient case—many of the problems of the poor are easily traced to the doorsteps of the courthouse and statehouse. Any community action program which ignores this factor would have as much effect as giving aspirins to a cancer patient. Mingo's poverty group, under Huey Perry, has emphasized the development of viable groups among poor people who can themselves exert pressure for effective institution and political changes. The Fair Election test proved poor-run community action can take place in an Appalachian setting. It was also a historic breakthrough in the barren field of election law enforcement. For decades, the feeling had prevailed among the populace and, more importantly, among politicians that elections may be violated without any fear of prosecution. There are no known cases of election violators going to jail. But persistent prodding and determined field work by the Mingo people have produced a full-scale FBI investigation of election troubles, hopefully for grand jury action.

The emergence of a Political Action League in the May primary as an independent arm of the poor, separate from the poverty group, was the first test of Poor Power in West Virginia elections. PAL supported reform candidates in both parties for county and state office. Few won, but its influence is certain to mount in future tests.

The clean election campaign has drawn on resources ignored by or unavailable to some other reform movements. From the beginning it has been run by local organizers—housewives, ex-coal miners and other trampled people who had come to realize that only through an honest election could they hope to correct unfair treatment in welfare, social security, social service, schools, law enforcement, road services and public financing. Moreover, Fair Election leaders drew their main strength from the most active community action organizations in the state. The FEC could count on 300 to 400 volunteers in a countywide project from a pool of 30 groups.

Perhaps the most significant was the "clean"aspect of the issue in the eyes of the general public. Few politicians dared attack the FEC directly because of the "clean" cause it was championing. Instead they were forced to go after VISTA, a favorite scapegoat in Robert Byrd's Bible Belt, and to harass the poverty agency through interminable federal investigations. A coalition with the middle class was possible because the clean election issue was without the stigma of giveawayism so often attached to the poverty programs. The FEC successfully sought tacit support from business, professional and middle-class people who were anxious to see honest elections but reluctant to work openly for fear of reprisal from the machine. At the same time, the reform group learned exactly how much to expect from these elements. Basing his experience on the clean vote drive, Huey Perry now declares he has little faith in the middle class. "They are always obsessed with economic security and social standing. They are afraid of community action. They don't want to get involved. If there is any controversy, they draw back from it. It's always, 'Let George do it.' "

In the final analysis, the Mingo lesson suggests mountain people must learn to "do it" for themselves.

ON THE OUTSIDE LOOKIN' IN
Jeanne M. Rasmussen

"I sat right there by him for three weeks and watched him slowly die. If I'd had the money to put him in the hospital . . . if the union had still let him keep his card . . . he might be alive today."

Francie Hager's face is as lined as a washboard and as brown as the muddy waters of the Kentucky River. Her gray hair is pulled tautly into a no-nonsense knot on the back of her head, and when she talks about her coal-miner husband—who died in 1962—her voice becomes as bleak as the scarred Kentucky hills around her.

From *Mountain Life & Work*, September 1969. Used by permission of the author.

The story is a familiar one, repeated frequently in varied form by different faces, different names; but to 52-year-old Mrs. Hager, it's a personal tragedy that left her husbandless, homeless, penniless and on the edge of hopelessness. Her three-room frame house perched on the bank of a small creek at Lothair Station, just outside Hazard, Kentucky. It was flooded twice and was burglarized, and finally it burned to the ground. At present, it's being rebuilt by volunteer workers and a few financial contributions. It isn't the lack of personal comfort that brings raw anger to Francie Hager's voice, nor is it self-pity that clouds her eyes with sudden tears: "See, when the International took their cards, I didn't know they'd took his'n. I did know they knocked him out of his miner's retirement. One day, my husband got a real bad spell. My brother drove him over to the Appalachian Hospital at Harlan, but as soon as I walked in, they told me he didn't have no hospital card. That was in May, and I had his union dues paid till October. They said there was nothing they could do for him with no hospital card and me not able to pay a fifty-dollar deposit. All we had to live on was a forty-eight dollar Social Security check. We took him home. Doc Green said my husband had got so much of that rock dust and that old black coal dust in his lungs that it turned 'em like concrete. He said if we could take a hammer to 'em, it would be like breaking a saucer or a piece of dish."

When Hager applied for his retirement pension in the early 1960's, he discovered he wasn't eligible because he had not been working in a union mine in 1946—the year the UMWA Welfare and Retirement Fund was established. He was told that in order to qualify, he would have to go back and work an extra year in the mines. Hager worked for seven months—"till he got smashed up in an accident."

Francie Hager's hands are calloused from hard work, yet they cup around a memory with unbelievable gentleness. "I remember how bad it was—he couldn't hardly walk across the house without having to stop a spell and rest. Two or three days before it changed weather, he'd have these smothering spells—couldn't sleep. I'd wash his face with those wet cloths but it didn't really help much. Those bad weather days, when it rained or snowed, that's when they really do suffer. Makes me freeze just to think about it."

When Hager died in 1962, Francie Hager was destitute. "I told Billy Engles—Engles Funeral Home—I said, 'Billy, the county's going to have to bury him.' But Billy—he were so nice about it, and he let me pay him ten dollars a month. I told Billy I'd kinda like to put him away nice—after he'd raised his family and worked hard in the mines all those years. He was a good man and there was always something to eat and a home and clothes to wear. It cost $690 and I still owe $252. It was a just debt." Social Security paid $186 death benefits, but Francie Hager's income is limited to what she can earn (usually fifty cents an hour) taking in washing.

"I'll tell you another thing!" she said, her voice shaking with anger. "Back then, the International paid a thousand dollars on a man's death; but when they'd see a person that was really sick, they'd cut him off—take his miner's card away from him. When they did that, they didn't have to pay no burial fee. See, the International is supposed to write you a check immediately for this one thousand dollars. It's to be used for the deceased. But what they done, they cut him off, because they knowed it wasn't going to be too long. After they take your hospital card, that settles it. You don't pay no more union dues." The anger drained from Francie Hager's voice as quickly as it had come, and in its place . . . resignation. "You're just out, that's how I figure it," she said softly; "you're just on the outside lookin' in."

Although no one seems to have an accurate estimate of just how many disabled miners and widows make up this select population of the Appalachian coal-mining regions, West Virginia—the leading coal producer in the nation—unofficially claims 51,000, as compared with the state's 43,000 who are still working miners.

They, too, feel that they're on the outside looking in. For over two decades since the United Mine Workers Welfare and Retirement Fund was established, miners have pried black coal out of the hills to pay a royalty fee (now forty cents a ton) into the fund, only to learn that the "security" their labor bought was a gamble—a game of chance, where the rules were based on the whims of the fund's three elderly trustees: the late John L. Lewis, whose position is filled by W. A. (Tony) Boyle, UMW president; Henry Schmidt, who resigned in 1969 and was replaced by George L. Judy, who served for only one month and was then replaced by Guy Farmer; and Josephine Roche, listed as a "neutral" trustee, but known to have played a strongly influential role in the Lewis administration.

"I belonged to the UMW for the last forty years," a miner from Fayette County, West Virginia, stated recently, "and their conventions was always controlled like a political machine. One they had in Cincinnati a few years back, some man got up and tried to make a speech to help the widows and orphans and the disabled, and John L. Lewis said, 'Brother, sit down! You're outta order! That's not charity, it's royalty that's been paid by the operators!'"

Many older and now disabled miners remember when they fought to organize the union, and later the Welfare and Retirement Fund. "We was ignorant of the facts back when we first started and Franklin Delano Roosevelt give us the right to go out and organize," one old miner recalls. "I wasn't quite old enough to go to work, but I was hiding in the paw-paw bushes with the older men, trying to help organize while my father was working. If the yellow-dogs had knowed it, my pa would have been throwed out. I'm only fifty-two years of age, but I remember it very well. The men today is just as ignorant of the facts as we was back when it first started."

Other miners learned the "facts" the hard way. Charles Ingles of Oak Hill, West Virginia, was one of many who were assessed twenty dollar payments back in 1946 and 1947 to help get the Fund started. "And I have the receipts to prove it!" he declares. Yet when Ingles mentioned this "fact" to a UMWA Fund official, he was curtly told that "nobody contributes anything to this welfare fund."

Another disabled miner who was "cut off work in 1958" and went back again in 1960 was not reissued a welfare card. After repeated attempts to be reinstated (while working and paying union dues), he became so exasperated that he admits to writing "a very nasty letter" to Fund trustees. "I got just as nasty a one back," he said. "It stated: 'You contribute nothing to this fund; therefore we can take your welfare card on any grounds that we see fit.' "

When Iva Pearson Fine, a disabled coal miner, died in a West Virginia nursing home because he was too ill to be cared for at his own home, his wife was denied death benefits on the grounds that she was "not his dependent." In a letter signed by Eugene F. McAndrew, Supervisor, Review Unit, UMWA Welfare and Retirement Fund, Mrs. Fine was informed: "You do not meet trust fund requirements as an eligible dependent of the deceased. Accordingly, survivor's benefits may not be authorized on your behalf." The standard "explanation" which accompanies such pronouncements was printed at the bottom of the letter: "This benefit is subject to suspension or termination at any time by the trustees of the fund for any matter, cause or thing, of which they shall be the sole judges, and without assignment of reason therefor."

In 1966, the Association of Disabled Miners and Widows (ADMW) was organized in West Virginia. It now has 17 chapters and a membership of over 3,000. The association describes its primary purpose as securing "the right to be heard." A mimeographed paper, addressed to "all members and future members" explains: "We want to state the purpose of this organization, it being [the case that] under the present setup of the administration of the Miners Welfare Fund, the claimant has no right to be heard—in the case of the UMW Welfare Fund there is no hearing in which a claimant has a right to be heard and we are trying to get these rules changed so the claimant can be heard. Shouldn't there be some sort of hearing to allow testimony to be offered?"

For the most part, however, the UMWA Welfare and Retirement Fund hierarchy turned deaf ears to members' pleas to be heard. Testimony was limited to small gatherings held once a month, attended by a faithful few who came limping, leaning, wheezing—the disabled, the destitute—seeking a "miracle cure" for their private tragedies, finding only the shared solace of common circumstances.

The plight of the disabled miners, widows and pensioners might have remained forever ignored had it not been for the revolution staged early this year by miners of the southern coal fields, who came out of the pits demanding safety and health reform. While the ADMW lacked the "big stick" power employed so effectively by the UMW, they gained a number of champions. Two of the strongest allies were Congressman Ken Hechler, D-W. Va., and safety advocate Ralph Nader.

Members of the news media, as well as other investigative teams, probed into the UMWA and its sister, the Welfare and Retirement Fund. They found incompetence, mismanagement and negligence. Among other facts upturned, a 1968 audit showed some $67 million sitting idle in a checking account at the National Bank of Washington, not drawing interest. It was also learned that a "special retirement fund" had been set up to guarantee the three officers of the Welfare and Retirement Fund $40,000 to $50,000 annually for life. "Apparently," Congressman Hechler commented, "it takes very high-paid employees to figure out the arbitrary and unfair rules by which thousands of coal miners are deprived of their medical cards, as well as retirement pensions."

To the discarded victims of the coal industry, however, the support of men like Hechler and Nader was a shot in the arm. Disabled miners and widows journeyed to Washington to tell their stories before subcommittees. They appealed to Federal and state legislators. For the first time in a long time, they were granted the right to be heard—and somebody listened.

Behind the scenes, a young Washington attorney, Harry Huge, was retained as legal counsel by the ADMW. Huge, considered by Washington associates to be one of the most qualified and capable of the new breed of socially conscious lawyers, accepted the burden willingly. On August 4 a press conference was held at the Mediterranean Room of the International Club in Washington, to announce the filing of a class-action lawsuit in the U.S. District Court of the District of Columbia. The suit was filed by Huge and two attorneys who are well known for their previous efforts in representing Appalachian coal miners—Paul Kaufman of Charleston, West Virginia, and Harry Caudill of Whitesburg, Kentucky. The class action was filed on behalf of some 4,000 disabled miners, widows, union members and pensioners from the Appalachian coal fields—"on their own behalf and on behalf of all others similarly situated who are now receiving, or should be receiving, or will, upon retirement or becoming disabled through sickness or injury, be eligible to receive, pensions and other benefits from the Welfare Fund."

Named as defendants were the United Mine Workers of America, the United Mine Workers Welfare and Retirement Fund of 1950, the Bituminous Coal Operators' Association, the National Bank of Washington, and certain individuals, including W. A. (Tony) Boyle, George Titler, Josephine Roche, and presidents of nine UMWA districts. The suit charged that "the Welfare Fund has not been and is not presently being operated or administered . . . for the sole benefit of the beneficiaries of the Fund" and that "Trustees have violated their duties as Trustees for their own or others' profit and benefit, and they have exploited, made use of, and permitted the use of the assets of the Welfare Fund." Stating that "regulations of the Welfare Fund are arbitrary, capricious and unreasonable and have been deliberately designed by the Defendant Trustees wrongfully to exclude Plaintiffs," the document cited specific examples and accused the UMWA Welfare and Retirement Fund Trustees of "granting or withholding benefits—which has been used and is used as a weapon of intimidation." Compensatory damages in the amount of at least $75 million were demanded, not counting "punitive damages" for "willfully defrauding" the membership. The U.S. District Court was asked to place the Welfare and Retirement Fund in Federal receivership to prevent "further plunder" of the members' assets.

UMWA spokesman Rex Lauck, associate editor of the *Mine Workers' Journal*—a publication that up to now has been dedicated to admiration of W. A. Boyle—termed the lawsuit "politically motivated" and, at least publicly, dismissed the charges as "pure hogwash."

But Howard Linville, a 58-year-old disabled miner from Peytona, West Virginia, disagreed. Listed as one of the plaintiffs, Linville is the father of four children under 18 years of age. Permanently disabled because of a back injury suffered in 1958 as a result of his job, Linville was denied his pension despite 21 years in union mines, because he did not work 20 years in a union mine within the 30-year period immediately preceding his pension application to the Welfare Fund. "After giving our lives to the United Mine Workers and the mines," he stated at the Washington press conference, "we now have nothing. We feel that this is wrong and the union and Welfare and Retirement Fund which we helped found did not intend that its members and its disabled and its widows and its retired should be denied their pensions and hospital benefits."

In a fiery statement before the House Labor subcommittee, April 3, 1947, volatile John L. Lewis once thundered: "If we must grind up human flesh and bones in an industrial machine—in the industrial machine that we call modern America . . . then before God, I assert that those who consume coal, and you and I who benefit from that service—because we live in comfort, owe protection to those men first, and we owe security to their families after, if they die. I say it! I voice it! I proclaim it! And I care not who in Heaven or Hell oppose it!"

Twenty-two years later, John L.'s successor—William Anthony Boyle, reigning monarch of the UMWA, anointed himself as Trustee and Chairman and Chief Executive Officer of the Welfare Fund and promptly waved the magic wand to increase pensions from $115 to

$150 per month. Ironically, only three months earlier Boyle had stated that pensions could be raised to $150 when the union "brings 75 million more tons of scab coal" into royalty payments for miners' benefits.

"I think it was just a gag . . . for election, you know," one disabled miner commented stoically. "Now he can just come up with all this money all at once . . . and that still leaves something like 100,000 miners not able to work and widows going without anything. He could have put that $35 a month on some of these widows and disabled miners not getting any pension. . . ."

O'Dell Gwynn, a tall, dignified black man who is president of Chapter 5 of the ADMW, Beckley, summed up the situation at a recent meeting: "The UMWA Welfare and Retirement Fund promised to take care of miners, widows, children," he told members, "but we've been left by the wayside. We're not asking for anything that we don't believe we're entitled to; we're just asking for what belongs to us. We've got to fight for it. We're too close to the door to turn around."

Meanwhile, fund officials issued their fiscal report for the year ending June 30. It stated that the fund paid out $158.6 million in pensions, hospital and medical benefits, funeral expenses and widows' and survivors' benefits; spent $5.2 million on administration; took in $157.4 million from soft coal operators (at forty-cent-a-ton royalties); had an income of $5.7 million from interest and dividends; and ended the year with an unspent balance of $179.4 million. As the result of criticism previously leveled at the $67 million not drawing interest in the National Bank of Washington, the amount in the noninterest checking account was said to have been pared to $32.7 million.

Such statistics, however, mean relatively little to the widow who must scrub floors or take in washing to support herself and her orphaned children. To the miner who wheezes and gasps and "smothers slowly to death," $32 million is a lot of money that would buy a lot of needed medicines. To many of the working miners who face the prospect of being on the outside looking in at the age of 40, the money represents a deposit earned by the blood, sweat and tears of their own labor, and a balance to which they feel wholly and justifiably entitled. Beneficiaries have been locked out in the cold for too long. Now, they hope the key of legal justice will open doors formerly slammed against them.

Local Reactions:
Outside Agitators, Subversives,
& Other Helping Hands

KENTUCKY'S COAL BEDS OF SEDITION
Paul Good

Tourists driving mountain roads in Eastern Kentucky's Pike county see billboards picturing a proud mare and foal gamboling in blue grass with the slogan: "Kentucky—Great for Family Vacations." It's a lovely image. But in recent weeks some ugly Kentucky realities have come to the fore in that vacation paradise where 40 per cent of the nation's one-room schools are found and children have the highest TB rate in the nation. It was in Pike county on August 11 that three anti-poverty workers—one an Appalachian Volunteer—were arrested on sedition charges. Underlying the arrests is a story of the cruellest white poverty, of rapacious coal-mine operators, and of right-wing politicians whose shopworn smear tactics would be laughable if they weren't so effective.

So effective that on August 18 OEO Director Sargent Shriver cut off all funds to Appalachian Volunteers in Kentucky. AV has received

From *The Nation*, September 4, 1967. Used by permission of the publisher.

funds from such respectable sources as the Field Foundation, but depends heavily on OEO money for training hundreds of VISTA workers who assist Kentucky's legions of poor. Shriver, in a craven display of instant capitulation to the growing forces of reaction, canceled funds without any hearing and without even notifying AV head Milton Ogle in Bristol, Tennessee, that action was being taken.

Ogle, an unradical Kentuckian, protested unavailingly that volunteer Joe Mulloy wasn't guilty of sedition or anything else. But neither Shriver nor his office spoke to Ogle. When Shriver threw the Child Guidance Development of Mississippi Head Start program to the state's political wolves last year, he at least went through the motions of an investigation. It is a commentary on the current Washington climate that this was thought unnecessary in Appalachia.

The separate midnight arrests of Mulloy and Mr. and Mrs. Alan McSurely of the Southern Conference Educational Fund (SCEF) were made by a dozen men led by Pike county prosecuting attorney Thomas Ratliff. He has long been a coal-mine lease operator and presently is the Republican candidate for lieutenant governor. His running mate, Louie Nunn, has pledged that if elected governor he would run SCEF out of the state along with other "subversives." What constitutes a subversive today in Kentucky (and possibly in Washington, to judge from Shriver's action) may be gleaned from the evidence seized from Mulloy. Ratliff described materials taken from him and the McSurelys as a "Communistic library out of this world." Mulloy's total contribution was:

Great Russian Short Stories, the poems and sayings of Mao-Tse-tung, Pushkin's short stories, Lenin's works, *Catch-22* by Joseph Heller, and an account of the Berkeley Student Movement. Some of this material was on the reading list of Mulloy's political science class at the University of Louisville. Prosecutor Ratliff left behind in Mulloy's room and did not mention *The Conscience of a Conservative* by B. Goldwater, John Stormer's *None Dare Call It Treason*, something by William Buckley, The Complete Works of Thomas Merton, the works of Carl Sandburg and Robert Frost, and two Bibles.

The chain of events behind the arrests started millions of years ago when nature formed an estimated 35 billion tons of soft coal under the lushly green hills of the Appalachian chain in Eastern Kentucky. More than half a century of mining has removed only 2 billion tons, the extraction enriching giant absentee-owned corporations like U. S. Steel, Republic Steel and Ford, while leaving the area impoverished. John L. Lewis' United Mine Workers of America unionized many Eastern Kentucky fields in the thirties and forties after violent and bloody opposition from operators. During World War II and briefly afterward, miners were among America's highest paid industrial servants. Eastern Kentucky knew sufficiency if not prosperity, while wholly dependent on the mineral version of a one-crop economy.

All those years coal operators paid the state a pittance in taxes and the counties virtually nothing, while reaping fortunes through depression allowances and capital gains. Harry Caudill described one industry tactic in testimony before the U. S. Senate Committee on Government Operations last June:

> It is as easy to rob a little Appalachian county of its revenues as it is to rob a child of his candy. For example, an immense firm once bought a modern continuous coal mining machine . . . the machine cost $75,000 and was used by the parent firm for a few months. It was then sold to a Kentucky subsidiary for $5,000 and this amount was stated in the bill of sale. On the next assessment date the bill was produced to the Tax Commissioner. By that time the machine had depreciated for an additional six months and so its value was fixed at $3,000. Since the county's rate was 40% of the fair market value, it entered the assessor's books at $1,200. At that time I was driving a Ford automobile bought 37 days after the (coal) machine was sold as new. I wound up with my car assessed for more than a mining machine that had cost nearly as much as a railroad locomotive.

Meanwhile, Kentucky's educational system was stagnating with counties unable to scrape up enough taxes to run the schools more than a few months of the year. State and federal funds prevented a complete breakdown, but generations were born to live and die in ignorance (nearly a quarter of all East Kentuckians over 24 cannot read or write).

The final physical link to the August raid recalls the folk song *Sixteen Tons*. The miner who still owed his soul to the company store sang of Number Nine coal. This is a rich seam that runs at around 1,800 feet, mountaintop level in Eastern Kentucky. In the late fifties, strip-mining was introduced to the region. Techniques and machines were developed enabling operators to gouge coal from mountainsides without burrowing underground. The operators had bought mineral rights forty and fifty years ago from farmers who sold the rights to tens of thousands of acres for a paltry 25¢ or 50¢ an acre. They had envisioned the classic shaft-mining operations underground that did not disturb farm or woodland and signed so-called "broad forms" which only barred the operator from inflicting "malicious" damage on the property. But when strip-mining began in earnest, the result on the land was catastrophic.

Forty million tons of coal were stripped out of Kentucky last year. I saw part of the result in Eastern Kentucky on a recent visit to Young's Fork of Clear Creek, ten miles north of Hazard in Knott county. Picture a green hilltop raked by a giant claw uprooting every tree, bush and blade of grass and scraping the mountain down to the bone. The displaced earth and debris tumbles down a 30–degree slope in a massive landslide onto woods and streams below. Huge tree trunks protrude like match-sticks at crazy angles from a swath of earth and rock advancing relentlessly as heavy regional rainfall churns it into a mudslide. Far below is a small farm and a once clear stream. Its sedimentation rate has increased an incredible 30 thousand times, killing fish and polluting the farm's water supply. Above on the scalped mountain head, the exposed rock bears a resemblance to the glacial striations of the Grand Canyon. But there is no grandeur.

Instead, for as far as one can see in an area snaking through two counties, is a ribbon of moonscape desolation. Mile after mile of bulldozed road runs along the eerie lip of the Number Nine seam. Here and there machines have sculptured little buttes, raw earth and rock on the sides, and on top green caps where birds still sing in the desolation, a melancholy reminder of what all the mountaintop was like before.

It is a profitable operation requiring few men. One firm in Perry county alone holds orders from TVA for $100 million. To combat the devastation that immediately despoiled water supplies and woodlands, mountain people organized. They formed the 1,000-member Appalachian Group to Save the Land and People, a grass-roots organization that promoted the radical idea of taxing each ton of coal taken from Kentucky before the region's patrimony vanished without a trace of native profit. The group, composed of highly American, Daniel Boone types distributed pamphlets with the following questions and answers:

Q. Doesn't strip mining employ lots of Eastern Kentuckians?

A. No. A very large strip-mining operation bringing millions of dollars of profit to the operator can be run with a handful of men. They are paid whatever the operator feels he can get away with.

Q. Doesn't strip-mining help our economy in other ways?

A. No. In fact it costs the taxpayers of this state about a dollar every time a ton of coal is strip-mined. That figures out to millions of dollars a year—in expensive reclamation and reforestation, in road repairs [laden coal trucks chew up highways while their overloads are winked at by county judges "sympathetic" to the operators], flood-control projects, water-pollution control. We pay the strip miners to destroy us.

Q. What will happen to Eastern Kentucky if strip-mining isn't stopped?

A. In a few years, every coal-mining county will be a crisscross of shattered mountains and ruined valleys. Thousands of people will have to leave. [Letcher county population has gone from a peak of 44,000 to 24,000 while Leslie county lost half its population in ten years. General economic conditions along with strip-mining are factors in this exodus.]

The Appalachian Volunteers enthusiastically assisted the Appalachian Group, perhaps exceeding Washington's concept of the limitations that should be imposed on fighting poverty with tax dollars. But strip-mining in Eastern Kentucky is like laying a lash on the back of a dying man and the Volunteers felt that you had to stop new punishment while you treated old wounds. At any rate, the Appalachian Group with AV help fought against the "broad forms" which the prize-winning Louisville *Courier-Journal* called "a wretched document that has haunted Kentucky and brought ruin to its mountain people for long enough."

Democratic Kentucky Gov. Edward T. Breathitt agreed, although taking pains to point out that strip-mining in the flatlands of Western Kentucky could be carried out with reclamation safeguards. Last year the legislature passed a reclamation bill, remindful of those Con Edison signs in New York that say, "We'll clean up and move on." The bill outlawed stripping on slopes steeper than 33 degrees and prescribed mild penalties for operators who did not plant grass and trees to cover the ravaged hillsides.

But the insufficiency of this approach was evident at the Young's

Fork operation. Slides moved down the legally permissible slope. Locust saplings planted here and there, then uprooted by rain, dotted the landscape. Splotches of green furze sprouted on the hillside like a dime-size growth of hair on a bald man's head. But no grass could ever grow from the exposed rock or from the wasteland of coal, crushed rock and slag left behind by the bulldozers where a few brave saplings shivered in a wet wind.

So people at Young's Fork were moved to nonlegislative action. The shattered hulk of a $300,000 coal gouger lay 100 yards from the end of the scar. It had been dynamited a month before and totally wrecked. In its cab, the sprung controls (Swing Left, Boom Down, Engine Throttle) no longer moved the boom's pendulous might and the red steel snout that had been rooting in the mountainside capable of raising a 30,000-pound weight in one bite lay slack-jawed. Dynamite had carried a message that appeals could not get through, and the Mountain Top Stripping and Pine Bluff Augering Co. had suspended operations there.

Over the line in Pike county (where subversive-hunter and lieutenant governor candidate Ratliff was county prosecutor), opposition had taken a nonviolent form. Farmer Jink Ray and his neighbors had lain down in front of the bulldozers of the Puritan Coal Co., come with an ancient broad form in hand to strip-mine the land. The company obtained an injunction from the Pike county court, forbidding Ray to interfere. But Governor Breathitt bravely ordered a temporary suspension of the Puritan permit under provisions of Kentucky mining law. It was the first time in its history that the state government had so boldly challenged the divine right of mine operators.

On August 1, Breathitt made the suspension stick. The State Department of Natural Resources revoked the Puritan permit to strip mine in Pike county. It was a big political risk, calculated to rouse the wrath of the operators. And it came at a time when other elements were ruffling the *status quo* of the poverty-stricken scene in Eastern Kentucky. The Citizens Crusade Against Poverty, organized with strong backing from Walter Reuther, was looking into the scope of nation-wide poverty and planned to convene a "board of inquiry" in Hazard, Kentucky, on August 22 to sketch in that Appalachian phase of the overall poverty picture. Much of its Kentucky research had been organized by the Appalachian Volunteers, already anathema to the mining powers that be.

It did not take inspired investigation to recognize Kentucky poverty. Ten of the nation's twenty poorest counties are located there. In the four-county OEO area comprising Leslie, Knott, Letcher and Perry (LKLP) counties, an average of 60 per cent of the families make under the poverty minimum of $3,000 a year. Of Letcher county's 6,700 families, 1,470 make under $1,000. Shriver's office, with much ballyhoo, had allocated $6.5 billion to the eleven-state Appalachia area over two years with many millions going into Kentucky. But Edwin J. Stafford, director of the LKLP Community Action Program, declared: "About these programs I can say this flatly: they have not eradicated poverty in Eastern Kentucky."

Well, no one ever expected them to do this quickly, if at all, and it is not Shriver's fault that the Congress pinches poverty pennies when a massive and continuous flow of dollars is needed. But much of what is allotted never gets to the poor. All dole is divided into three parts by 1967 governmental ukase and the poor are supposed to have one-third representation on the OEO boards. This works out in practice only where strong mobilizing efforts are made by civil rights organizations or groups like AV to get poor people, often ignorant and universally intimidated, to press for a meaningful voice. OEO critics in Eastern Kentucky say with some justification that too many OEO dollars are going to fatten middle-class staffs as assistant directors and executive secretaries proliferate.

In Hazard, a straight-talking mountain man named Everett Tharpe, who directs the OEO program, sounds disillusioned. "There are long-range plans for highways to come in and dams to be built," he says. "Eventually that might help the economy. But it's a long way off. What I'd like to see—but I don't see it—is a broad, comprehensive manpower plan for these four counties. Like the Job Corps or WPA. Heavy-equipment training, mechanics, teach 'em a trade."

What he has been able to offer to any army of applicants are platoon-size programs that are barely stopgap. For example, only thirty-four chronically unemployed mountaineers, many in their 50s and 60s, were enrolled under OEO's pre-vocational training. This was hastily designed to absorb men from the Labor Department's work experience and training program (called Happy Pappies in Kentucky) which had been crimped by fund shortages. The men earned $64 a week for eight weeks. What did they learn? They were taught how to dress, and how to fill out job applications and income-tax forms. The irony, even the cruelty, of teaching men hungering for work how to fill out applications for nonexistent jobs and tax forms for income they do not make is too apparent.

Sitting on the swaybacked porch of his shack in a hollow outside Hazard, Grover Chandler, father of seven and a Happy Pappy graduate said:

About all I did in the vocation program was plant saplings. I don't want to lie about nothing. If I say it didn't he'p me, it didn't he'p me and that's the truth. They promised us a job when we came out. That's what got us all stirred up when there weren't none. I ain't had regular work in two years and with seven kids it's just hard, I tell you. What's aggravatin' me so much is school starts this months and we have four to be goin' and there isn't any money for shoes.

Chandler and his family are not starving only because of the Food Stamp program. During the brief time he was a Happy Pappy, his stamps were cut off because he was making too much money. Now the family gets $86 worth for $3 and these buy food for about two and a half weeks. Then they borrow from a friend who is working, the same friend who lends them money for the stamps. Since Chandler is employable the family can get no welfare under Kentucky law, despite the fact that his wife is chronically ill and needs help in caring for the children ranging from 2 to 10. Chandler, a fourth grade school dropout, recites his tale of woe in accents remarkably free of self-pity. This is common with these mountain people. Poverty has become a way of life as unremarkable as the morning sun.

But unrest has been increasing as SCEF workers and Appalachian Volunteers encourage the poor to press for whatever rights were left them and to demand significant national aid for a region whose mineral riches have helped to power America's wealth-producing industrial growth during this century. The successful unity of the Appalachian Group to Save the Land and the People encouraged the notion that the powers that be were not invincible. The group threatened to fill the jails to protest if strip-mining continued. So it was no accident that only eleven days elapsed between Governor Breathitt's revocation of the Puritan strip-mine permit in Pike county and the midnight raid by Pike county prosecutor Ratliff. The time had come to show who was boss.

Ratliff, past president of the Independent Coal Operators' Association, denied AV charges that his raid was politically or economically motivated to aid his coal-mining friends. "These are the smear tactics always used by their kind against anyone who exposes them," he said. "From what I have seen of the evidence in this case, it is possible that Communist sympathizers may have infiltrated the anti-poverty program not only in Pike Co. but in other sections of the country as well."

But Ratliff did not specify against whom sedition had been committed. Was it the county, the state or, perhaps, the Puritan Coal Co.? The question seemed academic since Supreme Court rulings in the past have found state sedition statutes unconstitutional. In 1954, for example, Carl Braden—present head of SCEF—was convicted of sedition after he had sold his home in a white section of Louisville to a Negro family. The conviction was later set aside by the Court of Appeals. Ratliff conceded that "the Supreme Court has made it very difficult to prosecute Communists." Nothing daunted, he pressed the central theme of his prosecution: "Every piece of evidence we have points to just one objective, to stir up dissention and create turmoil among our poor."

While it is Ratliff's prerogative to believe the poor should assent to orderly impoverishment, Shriver would seem in an awkward position if his precipitate cutoff of Volunteer funds signified agreement that his volunteer Mulloy was seditious. (Governor Breathitt had caved in and had officially requested Shriver to make the fund suspension. It is hard to be brave for long in a state that is the captive of America's largest corporations.) In the second annual OEO report, entitled *The Quiet Revolution*, posthumous praise was lavished on a Kentucky VISTA volunteer named Phil Johnson who died in an accident.

"When 22-year-old Phil Johnson arrived in Breathitt County," read Shriver's official report, "his first act was to knock the rotting wood steps off the local school and knock over the deteriorating outhouses behind the school. He went to the local school superintendent, a woman, and said that if she would send some lumber to the school, he would get some people to replace the wornout facilities. She was taken aback by this approach but agreed to his request.

"This act seemed to set Johnson's style as a VISTA in the county, a style which his field supervisor described as 'awkward but beautiful.'

"Phil Johnson showed more than style. Assigned to the Appalachian Volunteers, Bristol, Tenn., he talked to numerous people, listened to their ideas . . . he got people talking . . . when they began talking about forming a county-wide organization of their own, he became an effective organizer."

Phil Johnson was "beautiful" as he knocked down the steps of a public school without permission and organized poor people. But what a difference a year makes. Something ugly is loose when Appalachian Volunteer Joe Mulloy tries to organize poor people in 1967 without knocking down anything. Is it seditious to inquire where the ugliness lies?

A STRANGER WITH A CAMERA
Calvin Trillin

On a bright afternoon in September, in 1967, a five-man film crew working in the mountains of Eastern Kentucky stopped to take pictures of some people near a place called Jeremiah. In a narrow valley, a half-dozen dilapidated shacks—each one a tiny square box with one corner cut away to provide a cluttered front porch—stood alongside the county blacktop. Across the road from the shacks, a mountain rose abruptly. In the field that separated them from the mountain behind them, there were a couple of ramshackle privies and some clotheslines tied to trees, and a railroad track and a rusted automobile body and a dirty river called Rockhouse Creek. The leader of the film crew was a Canadian named Hugh O'Connor. Widely acclaimed as the co-producer of the Labyrinth show at Expo 67 in Montreal, O'Connor had been hired by Francis Thompson, an American filmmaker, to work on a film Thompson was producing for the American pavilion at Hemis-Fair in San Antonio. O'Connor went up to three of the shacks and asked the head of each household for permission to take pictures. When each one agreed, O'Connor had him sign the customary release forms and gave him a token payment of ten dollars—a token that, in this case, happened to represent a month's rent. The light was perfect in the valley, and the shooting went well. Theodore Holcomb, the associ-

From *The New Yorker*, April 29, 1969. Reprinted by permission; © 1969 by The New Yorker Magazine, Inc.

ate producer of the film, was particularly struck by the looks of a miner, still in his work clothes and still covered with coal dust, sitting in a rocking chair on one of the porches. "He was just sitting there scratching his arm in a listless way," Holcomb said later. "He had an expression of total despair. It was an extraordinary shot so evocative of the despair of that region." The shot of the coal miner was good enough to be included in the final version of the film, and so was a shot of a half-dozen children who, somehow, lived with their parents in one of the tiny shacks. After about an hour and a half, the crew was ready to leave, but someone had noticed a woman come out of one of the shacks and go to the common well to draw some water, and she was asked to repeat the action for filming. As that last shot was being completed, a woman drove up and told the filmmakers that the man who owned the property was coming to throw them off of it. Then she drove away. A couple of minutes later, another car arrived, and a man—a thin, bald man—leaped out. He was holding a pistol. "Get off my property!" he shouted again and again. Then he shot twice. No one was hit. The filmmakers kept moving their equipment toward their cars across the road while trying to tell the man that they were leaving. One of them said that the man must be shooting blanks. "Get off my property!" he kept screaming. Hugh O'Connor, who was lugging a heavy battery across the highway, turned to say that they were going. The man held the pistol in both hands and pulled the trigger again. "Mr. O'Connor briefly looked down in amazement, and I saw a hole in his chest," Holcomb later testified in court. "He saw it and he looked up in despair and said, 'Why did you have to do that?' and, with blood coming from his mouth, he fell to the ground."

Whitesburg, a town twelve miles from Jeremiah, is the county seat of Letcher County—headquarters for the county court, the sheriff, and assorted coal companies and antipoverty agencies. Word that someone had been killed reached Whitesburg quickly, but for a couple of hours there was some confusion about just who the victim was. According to various stories, the dead man had been a representative of the Army Corps of Engineers, a VISTA volunteer, or a C.B.S. cameraman—any of whom might qualify as a candidate for shooting in Letcher County. The Corps of Engineers had proposed building the Kingdom Come Dam across Rockhouse Creek, thereby flooding an area that included Jeremiah, and some opponents of the dam had been saying that the first government man who came near their property had better come armed. Throughout Eastern Kentucky, local political organizations and coal-mining interests had warned that community organizers who called themselves VISTAs or Appalachian Volunteers or anything else were nothing but another variety of Communists— three of them had been arrested on charges of attempting to overthrow the government of Pike County—and even some of the impoverished people whom the volunteers were supposedly in Kentucky to help, view them with fear and suspicion. A number of television crews had been to Letcher County to record the despair that Holcomb saw in the face of the miner sitting on the front porch. Whitesburg happens to be the home of Harry M. Caudill, a lawyer who drew attention to the plight of the mountain people in 1963 with an eloquent book called "Night Comes to the Cumberlands." Television crews and reporters on a tour of Appalachia are tempted to start with Letcher County in order to get the benefit of Caudill's counsel, which is ordinarily expressed in a tone of sustained rage—rage at the profit ratio of out-of-state companies that take the region's natural resources while paying virtually no taxes, rage at the strip mines that are gouged across the mountains and at the mud slides and floods and pollution and ugliness they cause, rage at the local merchants and politicians who make a good living from the trade of welfare recipients or the retainers of coal companies and insist that there is nothing wrong with the economy, and, most of all, rage at the country that could permit it all to happen. "Look what man hath wrought on that purple mountain's majesty," he will say as he points out the coal waste on the side of a mountain that had once been beautiful. "A country that treats its land and people this way deserves to perish from the earth."

In the view of Caudill and of Tom Gish, the liberal editor of the *Mountain Eagle*, a Letcher County weekly, the reactions of people in Jeremiah to the presence of O'Connor's film crew—cooperation by the poor people being photographed in their squalid shacks, rage by the man who owned the shacks—were characteristic of Letcher County: a lot of people who are still in Eastern Kentucky after years of welfare or subsistence employment have lost the will to treat their situation as an embarrassment, but outside journalists are particularly resented by the people who have managed to make a living—running a country store or a filling station or a small truck mine, working for the county administration, managing some rental property. They resent the impression that everyone in Eastern Kentucky is like the people who are desperately poor—people whose condition they tend to blame on "just sorriness, mostly." In Letcher County, fear of outsiders by people who are guarding reputations or economic interests blends easily into a deeprooted suspicion of outsiders by all Eastern Kentucky mountain people, who have always had a fierce instinct to protect their property and a distrust of strangers that has often proved to have been justified. All of the people in Letcher County—people who live in the shacks up remote hollows or people who run stores on Main Street in Whitesburg —consider themselves mountain people, and, despite an accurate story in the county paper, many of them instinctively believed that the mountaineer who killed Hugh O'Connor was protecting his property from smart-aleck outsiders who wouldn't leave when they were told.

The mountaineer's name was Hobart Ison. There have always been Isons in Letcher County, and many of them have managed somewhat better than their neighbors. Hobart Ison had inherited a rather large piece of land in Jeremiah—he raised chickens and rented out shacks he himself had built and at one time ran a small sawmill—but he was known mainly as an eccentric, mean-tempered old man. Everyone in Letcher County knew that Hobart Ison had once built and furnished a house for his future bride and—having been rejected or having been afraid to ask or having had no particular future bride in mind—had let the house remain as it was for thirty years, the grass growing up around it and the furniture still in the packing crates. He had occasionally painted large signs attacking the people he thought had wronged him. He was easily enraged by people hunting on his property, and he despised all of the local Democrats, whom he blamed for injustices that included dismissing him from a post office job. A psychiatrist who examined him after the shooting said, "Any reference to 'game warden' or 'Democrat' will provoke him tremendously." Once, when some local youths were taunting him, he took a shot at them, hitting one in the shoulder. "A lot of people around here would have welcomed them," Caudill said of the filmmakers. "They just happened to pick the wrong place."

Streams of people came to visit Ison in the Letcher County jail before he was released on bail. Women from around Jeremiah baked him cakes. When his trial came up, it proved impossible to find a jury. The Letcher County commonwealth's attorney and Caudill, who had

.

been retained by Francis Thompson, Inc., secured a change of venue. They argued that Ison's family relationship in Letcher County was "so extensive as to comprise a large segment of the population," and, through an affidavit signed by three citizens in position to know public opinion, they stated that "the overwhelming expression of sentiment has been to the effect that the defendant did right in the slaying of Hugh O'Connor and that he ought to be acquitted of the offense of murder."

Harlan County is a mountain or two away from Letcher County. In the town of Harlan, benches advertising Bunny Enriched Bread stand outside the front door of the county courthouse, flanking the First World War monument and the Revolutionary War monument and the plaque recalling how many Kentucky courthouses were burned down by each side during the Civil War. On the ground floor of the courthouse, the men who habitually gather on the plain wooden benches to pass the time use old No. 5 cans for ashtrays or spittoons and a large container that once held Oscar Mayer's Pure Lard as a wastebasket. In the courtroom, a plain room with all of its furnishings painted black, the only decoration other than pictures of the men who have served as circuit judge is a framed poster in praise of the country lawyer—and also in praise, it turns out upon close reading, of the Dun & Bradstreet Corporation. The front door of the courthouse is almost always plastered with election stickers. In the vestibule just inside, an old man sits on the floor behind a display of old pocketknives and watchbands and billfolds and eyeglass cases offered for sale or trade.

The commonwealth's attorney of Harlan County is Daniel Boone Smith. Eight or nine years ago, Smith got curious about how many people he had prosecuted or defended for murder, and counted up seven hundred and fifty. He was able to amass that total partly because of longevity (except for a few years in the service during the Second World War, he has been commonwealth's attorney continuously since 1933), partly because he has worked in an area that gives anyone interested in trying murder cases plenty of opportunity (the wars between the unions and the coal operators in Harlan County during the thirties were almost as bloody as the mountain feuds earlier in the century), and partly because he happens to be a quick worker ("Some people will take three days to try a murder case," he has said. "I usually get my case on in a day"). During his first week as commonwealth's attorney of Harlan and an adjoining county, Smith tried five murder cases. These days, Harlan County may have about that many a year, but it remains a violent place. The murders that do occur in mountain counties like Harlan and Letcher often seem to occur while someone is in a drunken rage, and often among members of the same family—a father shooting a son over something trivial, one member of a family mowing down another who is breaking down the door trying to get at a third. "We got people in this county today who would kill you as quick as look at you," Smith has said. "But most of 'em are the type that don't bother you if you leave them alone." Smith is known throughout Eastern Kentucky for his ability to select jurors—to remember which prospective juror's uncle may have had a boundary dispute with which witness's grandfather twenty years ago—and for his ability to sum up the case for them in their own language once the evidence has been heard. He is an informal, colloquial, storytelling man who happens to be a graduate of the Harvard Law School.

A lack of fervor about convicting Hobart Ison was assumed in Harlan County when he came up for trial there in May, 1968. "Before the case, people were coming up and saying, 'he *should've* killed the son of a bitch,' " Smith said later. "People would say, 'They oughtn't to make fun of mountain people. They've made enough fun of mountain people. Let me on the jury, Boone, and I'll turn him loose.' " Smith saw his task as persuading the citizens and the jurors that the case was not what it appeared to be—that the filmmakers were not "a bunch of privateers and pirates" but respectable people who had been commissioned by the United States government, that the film was not another study of how poor and ignorant people were in Eastern Kentucky but a film about the whole United States in which the shots of Eastern Kentucky would take up only a few seconds, that the filmmakers had behaved properly and politely to those they were photographing. "Why, if they had been smart-alecks come to hold us up to ridicule, I'd be the last man to try him," Smith assured everyone. It took Smith only a day or so to present his case against Hobart Ison, although it took three days to pick the jury. On the witness stand, the surviving filmmakers managed to avoid admitting to Ison's lawyers that it was the appalling poverty of his tenants that had interested them; they talked about being attracted by expressive family groups and by the convenience of not having to move their equipment far from the road. The defense asked if they were planning to take pictures of the Bluegrass as well as Appalachia. Were they going to make a lot of money from the film? How many millions of viewers would see the pictures of poor Eastern Kentucky people? Had they refused to move? Had they taunted Ison by saying he was shooting blanks? Did the people who signed the release forms really know what they were signing? (At least one of the signers was, like one out of four of his neighbors, unable to read.)

Except for the underlying issue of Eastern Kentucky v. Outsiders, the only issue seriously in contention was Ison's sanity. The director of a nearby mental-health clinic, testifying for the defense, said that Ison was a paranoid schizophrenic. He told of Ison showing up for one interview with long socks worn on the outside of his trouser legs and of his altercations with his neighbors and of his lack of remorse. The prosecution's psychiatrist—an impressive woman from the University of Kentucky who had been retained by Francis Thompson, Inc. —said that Ison had grown up at a time when it was common practice to run people off of property with a gun, and because he had lived with aging parents or alone ever since childhood, he still followed that practice. Some of Ison's ideas did have "paranoid coloring," she said, but that could be traced to his being a mountaineer, since people in isolated mountain pockets normally had a suspicion of strangers and even of each other. "Socio-cultural circumstances," she concluded, "lead to the diagnosis of an individual who is normal for his culture, the shooting and the paranoid color both being present in other individuals in this culture who are considered normal." In the trial and in the insanity hearing that had earlier found Ison competent to stand trial, Smith insisted that Ison was merely peculiar, not crazy. "I said, 'Now, I happen to like Mayonnaise on my beans. Does that make me crazy?' " Smith later recalled. "I turned to one of the jurors, a man named Mahan Fields, and I said, 'Mahan, you remember Uncle Bob Woolford, who used to work up at Evarts? Did you ever see Uncle Bob in the winter when he didn't have his socks pulled up over his pants legs to keep out the cold? Now, was Uncle Bob crazy? Why, Mahan, I bet on many a winter morning you wore your socks over your pants legs.' "

In his summation, Smith saved his harshest words not for the defendant but for the person who was responsible for bringing Hobart Ison, a mountaineer who was not quite typical of mountaineers, and Hugh O'Connor, a stranger with a camera who was not quite typical of strangers with cameras, into violent conflict. Judy Breeding—the operator of a small furniture store near Ison's shacks, and the wife of Ison's cousin—had testified that she was not only the woman who told the film crew that Ison was coming but also the woman who had told Ison that the film crew was on his property. "Hobart," she recalled saying, "there is some men over there taking pictures of your houses, with out-of-state license." Smith looked out toward the courtroom spectators and suddenly pointed his finger at Judy Breeding. He told her that he would like to be prosecuting her, that if it hadn't been for her mouth Hugh O'Connor would not be in his grave and Hobart Ison would be back home where he belonged. Later, Smith caught a glimpse of Mrs. Breeding in the hall, and he thought he saw her shake her fist at him, smiling. "You know," he said, "I believe the idea that she had anything to do with bringing that about had never occured to her til I mentioned it."

The jury was eleven to one for conviction, but the one held out. Some people were surprised that Ison had come that close to being convicted, although it was generally agreed that the prosecution's psychiatrist had out-talked the psychiatrist who testified for the defense. Smith believed that his case had been greatly strengthened by the fact that the filmmakers had been respectful, soft-spoken witnesses—not at all smart-alecky. "If there was anything bigheaded about them," he said, "it didn't show."

The retrial was postponed once, and then was stopped suddenly during jury selection when Smith became ill. On March 24th, Hobart Ison came to trial again. The filmmakers, who had been dreading another trip to Kentucky, were at the county courthouse in Harlan at nine in the morning, ready to repeat their testimony. Although Smith had anticipated even more trouble finding a jury, he was prepared to go to trial. But Ison's lawyers indicated to Smith and Caudill that their client, now seventy, would be willing to plead guilty to voluntary manslaughter, and they finally met Smith's insistence on a ten-year sentence. Ison—wearing a baggy brown suit, his face pinched and red—appeared only briefly before the judge to plead guilty. A couple of hours after everyone arrived, Caudill was on his way back to Whitesburg, where he was working on the case of a Vietnam veteran accused of killing two men during an argument in the street, and the filmmakers were driving to Knoxville to catch the first plane to New York.

The following day, the clerk of the court, a strong-looking woman with a strong Kentucky accent, happened to get into a discussion about the filmmakers with another citizen who had come to know them in the year and a half since Hugh O'Connor's death—a woman with a softer accent and a less certain tone to her voice.

"You know, I asked those men yesterday morning if they were happy with the outcome," the clerk said. "And they said, 'Yes.' And I said, 'Well, you know, us hillbillies is a queer breed. We are. I'm not offering any apologies when I say that. Us hillbillies are a queer breed, and I'm just as proud as punch to be one.' "

"Not all of us are like that," the other woman said. "Mean like that."

"Well, I wouldn't say that man is mean," the clerk said. "I don't guess he ever harmed anybody in his life. They were very nice people. I think it was strictly a case of misunderstanding. I think that the old man thought they were laughing and making fun of him, and it was more than he could take. I know this: a person isolated in these hills, they often grow old and eccentric, which I think they have a right to do."

"But he didn't have a right to kill," the other woman said.

"Well, no," the clerk said. "But us hillbillies, we don't bother nobody. We go out of our way to help people. We don't want nobody pushin' us around. Now, that's the code of the hills. And he felt like— that old man felt like—he was being pushed around. You know, it's like I told those men: 'I wouldn't have gone on that old man's land to pick me a mess of wild greens without I'd asked him.' They said, 'We didn't know all this.' I said, 'I bet you know it now. I bet you know it now.' "

CATALYST OF THE BLACK LUNG MOVEMENT
K. W. Lee

You can take the coal camp out of Craig Robinson but you can't take Craig Robinson out of the coal camp. That's the way it was for a young man from Buffalo, N. Y. From one coal camp to another, his trails ran deep in the Southern West Virginia coal fields.

From the Charleston *Sunday Gazette-Mail State Magazine*, November 2, 1969. Used by permission of the author.

When I caught the first glimpse of him one blustery winter day, Craig Robinson, hatless, overcoatless and shivering, was following, blocks away, marching columns of miners towards the capitol where the state lawmakers were sitting on their black lung bills. "No laws, no work," chanted the striking miners on the wind-swept steps of the capitol. The Movement had crested: Hominy Falls, Farmington's Consol No. 9, then Dr. I. E. Buff's barnstorming Physicians for the Miners' Health and Safety and finally the wildcat strike which bounded over the West Virginia hills like wild fire. Together, on that coal gray March afternoon, the doctors and the miners were storming the state capitol for an answer.

The miners' march mirrored national and worldwide concern for a dying race of black-lunged miners who numbered well over 100,000. Yet few—outside the scarred mountains and the dreary coal hamlets where people linger on the bitter heaps of old age, poverty and black lung—seemed to know his name. Robinson's shadowy presence among them had eluded the mass media which descended on the heartland of Appalachia. Not even House Judiciary Chairman J. E. "Ned" Watson, who thundered in the legislative halls that VISTA workers had agitated the miners to the crippling strike, could place his name. This quiet VISTA volunteer, only a year out of Oberlin College in Ohio, blended into the mountain scenery.

In retrospect, this young man from Buffalo, N. Y., emerges out of mountain witness accounts as the catalyst who helped forge a movement which, almost overnight, aroused a nation's conscience and global attention. Historians and students of social movements in post-World War II America may well discover a latter-day Johnny Appleseed in 25-year-old Craig Robinson's role for the Black Lung Rebellion —and an irony that so young an American, fresh out of college, made a difference in righting the wrongs so long perpetrated by king coal and ignored by the very institutions—unions, federal and state mine and health agencies and medical centers—which had been created to protect the miners' health and welfare.

"This young man was our vital connection between the physicians committee and the miners," booms Dr. I. E. Buff, father of the movement. With almost fatherly nostalgia, the 60-year-old heart specialist reminisces: "I don't forget that day—that was one January afternoon— when this boy showed up in my office and offered his help. He came by himself. He said he felt sorry for the coal miners. He felt in his heart something ought to be done for them, but no West Virginians would do this." The gruff-voiced crusader pauses here and chuckles. "I was very suspicious of this boy; I viewed his interest with suspicion." The doctor, wary of suppressive tactics in the coal counties, had "my own people check on this young man. My final conclusion was, 'Here is a rare American specimen.' This boy had thoroughly educated himself on the black lung disease."

Dr. Buff asserts Robinson's educational and organizational activities proved crucial for the movement's initial thrust. The coal miners tragically lacked the necessary information and understanding of the coal dust diseases. It had been for many years a practice of the coal companies to suppress any knowledge of this killing disease. They were saying coal dust was good for miners. "This young man," he says, "lived among the miners and spread this knowledge among them—this was powerful stuff." He insists, "This young man should be given a medal by this state's common people."

Dr. Donald Rasmussen, in charge of the Appalachian Regional Hospital's pulmonary laboratory, who stumped the mining fields with Dr. Buff, is no less impressed with the health volunteer: "This guy has done more things behind the scene than anybody I can think of in the movement." The red bearded man who looks more like a lumberjack than a world famous lung specialist unabashedly calls himself "one of many admirers" of VISTA Robinson. In the early days of the drive, he says, "Craig was in every situation, never runs out of energy and goes on all the time—and I remind you this guy was in on no less than three black lung bills." The miners are basically suspicious of outsiders but, he adds, "they were touched by his absolute modesty and sincerity. This guy speaks only when spoken to and mostly listens. He sits back and lets somebody take credit. He never brags." Rasmussen, with feeling, remarks, "He's the most underrated hero of the movement and the guy who would be the last one to admit it is Craig Robinson."

"There's something about this young man," mused stocky Negro miner Charles Brooks not long ago. Brooks, a 27-year veteran in the mines, spearheaded efforts of grassroot miners who sidestepped their own unions to form an ad hoc group called the Black Lung Association. The association Brooks heads has now spread into other mining states including Kentucky and Ohio. "In our earlier start," Brooks recalls, "this young man gave the miners a lot of information they needed badly. This young man cared deeply for the welfare of the humble people, and the miners felt the same way about him."

Robinson's fellow VISTA room-mate, John Lenti from Memphis, Tenn., remembers that Robinson began "reading everything on black lung" sometime last October. "A whole stack of literature—he read them day and night, getting in touch with doctors and going to meetings and more meetings." The wavy-haired artist from Tennessee continues, "He really believed in this black lung thing, living, breathing and sleeping it." Their home—a shabby, gray four-room frame job along a reddog road at an old mining town called Stanaford outside Beckley—soon turned into a bulging library on black lung. Lenti himself got swept in by Robinson's unrelenting pursuit and soon found himself producing black lung posters which became a grim symbol of the movement.

Another little-noted role belonged to VISTA lawyer Richard Bank who closely worked with Robinson in Raleigh County in the movement's infancy. "He brought me a whole bunch of materials on black lung and said he wanted to do something about the fact that black lung wasn't compensable under the then existing laws." Banks, a University of Pennsylvania law graduate, subsequently drafted the original black lung legislation. "Craig is the unsung hero," declares Bank, who now is associated with the Charleston law firm of Sprouse, McIntyre and Louderback. "He was the guy who put the doctors into contact with what had developed to be their constituency. Of course, this guy, Dr. Buff, was the one around whom the miners rallied. They believed in him like their Messiah. Craig was a broker, a coordinator, who put things together and established means of communication with all miners groups."

Ellis Bailey of Raleigh County, a gaunt disabled miner of 65, remembers: "This boy comes in and helps me out in any way he can. He just drops in. He will feed chickens and do other chores and go away." A union organizer in the bloody days of coal strife, Bailey lives on a Social Security disability pittance and bitter memories at a dead-end work off Clear Creek in the stripmining-gutted hills near the Boone County line. He echoes a familiar lamentation repeated hundreds of times in the sad coal towns. Bailey says he gave 46 years of his life to union mines. At 53 he quit because "I couldn't get no breathing." He looks back, "My Dad and I stood up with John L. Lewis in Cabin Creek when things were rough and I helped organize Cabin Creek. My lungs are drying up and one lung is covered with coal dust. Now I can't get a dose of medicine for my black lung from the pension fund, and if I die, they won't give me a dime for my burial." Staring into nowhere, he asks, "Why is it that nobody—except a young boy like him—cares for us?"

Levi Daniel of Beckley is a sturdy black man, a 32-year union veteran, who speaks of Robinson as if he were a union brother. Daniel was one of the early black lungers in a region where the historic black lung strike originated. Mrs. Daniel recalls Robinson "traveling a lot with my husband into the homes of miners in this part of the country."

A miner in another coal town, reports Daniel, introduced him to Robinson. "We got in touch with this young man and got from him what we needed." Says Daniel: "He is a close friend of the coal miners. He always tries to learn something from miners and comes up with wonderful ideas that helped our movement. A lot of miners would miss him if he leaves," he adds, wistfully.

Cabin Creek miner Arnold Miller, a 30-year man, first ran into Robinson at a meeting in the Cabin Creek Junction community building one cold Sunday. "This boy was listening, intent on finding out what was going on. There were about 250 people there, but I just had a feeling that he wasn't a miner although he looked pretty much like a mountain boy." A couple of weeks later Miller met him again at a black lung rally at Man in Logan County. "He was there all right. I asked him what he was doing. He said he thought he ought to be there. I haven't missed him in all meetings I attended since. I saw him on more than 30 occasions. Seems like he goes all over southern coal fields, always inquiring and trying to learn something about our problems. He stays in the background and, if somebody asks him, gives straight answers, good answers. One time I walked up to him and said, 'Someday the miners are going to recognize you because you are the one who did it.' He just laughed, a shy sort a guy."

Clifford Martin, an 18-year miner who lives in Coal City about 10 miles south of Beckley, met Robinson in a retired coal miner's home last winter. "He was trying to find out what miners thought of black lung and explaining the existing laws and the new laws which could help us. He seemed well educated, but talked like somebody you knew all your life. He would listen to anything you got to say, awful patient."

Robinson came to West Virginia at a time when it was more fashionable to club a VISTA's head than to bestow a cap. It became a fashionable vote-getting past-time for politicians and their redneck allies to bait VISTA workers. Some were jailed on dubious charges, and others were beaten. The Appalachian Volunteers had already been driven out of Southern West Virginia counties. Only a few diehard AV and VISTA holdovers stayed in the coal fields.

Robinson paused for candid reflection the other day in response to prodding inquiries. He says he signed up for a year's work as a health VISTA for two vague reasons: He was slightly bored with teaching after college ("I wasn't really interested in teaching—it was a kind of a one-year thing"); he was slightly more interested in VISTA's mental health program, because of his father's background ("I heard about mental health and I wanted to look into this field when I got here").

He grew up in Buffalo in the upper-middle class family of a psychiatrist with no inclination or orientation for social involvement. After finishing Oberlin with a major in government, he taught history a year at a Quaker private school in Philadelphia. He was neither a harbinger of a social upheaval nor a student activist eager for social action.

When he and another VISTA arrived in the former mining town of Lester in Raleigh County, their first assignment had remote connections with Robinson's first interest, mental health. "Our job was to get drinkable and safe water at nearby Fireco because there was no running water. First, we organized the little village. They bought pipe with a loan from a credit union and we did the work digging a 900-foot ditch. In a couple months, the people began to help. NYC (Neighborhood Youth Corps) boys and a couple other VISTAs joined. Women in town cooked meals. We did research on how to build a water system, but the people were worried when I presented the plan. First, we had to dig and install a 900-foot mainline through under the railroad. They had a lot of worries, but we found out we can beat them all. We dug through two reddog roads and had to shoot a few sticks of dynamite under the railroad. We had to make it sure that there were no leaks. It worked." The work started in August and was over in early November. "They were pretty happy. It was a real self-help, not a penny from government. It was my first organizing work."

It was during his stay at Lester, he reports, that brought his contact with the ravages of black lung. "I ran into human debris every day." The sad, troubled eyes of his black-lung afflicted neighbors began to haunt him. "You pick up a little bit all the time—their bitterness and helplessness—and when you live with miners, working and retired, you can't help but listen. I'm not exactly sure what especially spurred my interest in black lung," he wonders aloud. "But I believe it was meeting so many disabled men and listening to their stories about how they were 'beat out of compensation' and left with nothing but a stack of medical reports. These coal miners are great human beings," he said, with believable passion. " But I saw greater forces at work which were bringing destructive influences on these human beings." At a Disabled Miners and Widows chapter meeting in Beckley, Robinson faced "a pitiful group of broken men and destitute widows who were seeking the aid of someone with more leverage than they had over the process which had impoverished them." He says, "I told the leaders I would do what I could and began talking to former miners and studying the disease and the law."

Robinson held lengthy discussions with Dr. Rasmussen on the diagnosis of miners' lung diseases. "The doctor was eager to share the results of his research and introduced me to the expert medical literature that might help my understanding. I also sought help from Dr. Hawey Wells, the pathologist." Ceaselessly, he drew "hard information" from Congressional sources, medical and law journals and medical institutions and libraries. "There was no doubt coal dust was killing and maiming thousands of men and they were being systematically denied compensation, because of the insidious mating of a loosely worded law and a compensation department which saw its role as that of protector of the coal companies."

He and VISTA lawyer Richard Bank called their first meeting of disabled miners and invited Dr. Rasmussen to discuss his findings. "Many of the 35 men who attended," recalls Robinson, "had to rest several times on their way up the stairs. The meeting was very good. I led a lively discussion on how men were 'beaten out.' The doctor gave a good talk and showed some lung sections. Rich Bank explained how the law in a number of ways was weighted in favor of the coal operators. We decided to meet again and draw up some proposed changes in the law that would help make it more equitable." The next meeting was smaller but proved significant. At least six southern coal counties sent representatives. "This was a great meeting of minds. Men told of their stories about having been denied compensation and we all dis-' cussed how we might close that loophole that beat them. Pretty meaty stuff came out of that meeting," he says. "In fact, we developed at that meeting the major issues which were to plague the legislature for the next two months."

At this juncture, Robinson's one-man mobile library began its elusive but effective runs in the black-lung country—in Raleigh, Logan, McDowell, Fayette, Wyoming, Mercer and Kanawha counties. Early black lung organizers, he notes, were a curious collection of union miners, disabled miners, VISTA workers and antipoverty community workers and miners' widows. "Those meetings were intensely exciting meetings," says Robinson. Working relations with Buff and Charles Brooks developed shortly. "I had nothing to do with organizing the Black Lung Association which was the independent work of very concerned, quite intelligent and active miners."

While the Legislature was in session in early 1969, Robinson became a traveling missionary speaking to local union meetings in Raleigh and other counties. "It was always my concern that miners wouldn't know what specific provisions they must fight for and then be sold out in their unguarded moments." Many miners he talked with, he recalls, were grievously ignorant about the specifics of their demands. "They became increasingly sophisticated as the session wore on and by the end of the session, they were informing me more than I was them."

The three-week mine strike, he says, came as a surprise to him and the miners themselves. Miners shed their age-old fatalism and drowsy isolation and walked out, but, Robinson points out, the original strike which broke out in Raleigh County was the product of a series of grievances and fatal accidents. "But the men decided they might as well stay out to help the doctors, who were fighting so hard. The strike then leapfrogged around the state, with miners picketing at other mines." In Robinson's assessment, the black lung rebellion was "truly and really democratic. If you are close to the scene, what you saw was that nobody was in control of the thing. All over the southern part of West Virginia, local unions took initiative. That is what is so remarkable about this movement. Many men sacrificed. Locals would send their people to Charleston to talk to delegates and organize meetings and dig out information. It wasn't, as coal operators tried to depict, a highly controlled thing—really it was spontaneous."

Mountain life, he insists, suits him well. Contrary to popular belief, he says, he has found his adopted home "one of the most enjoyable places to live—mostly because of many friends I've made here." Before he signed up for VISTA work, he says, he thought of becoming a doctor like his father. He isn't sure now, he says. "I've learned a whole lot, and things have changed since." Robinson loathes labeling: "I just learn as I proceed. Being a liberal doesn't mean a thing. It doesn't describe a person as anything. I want to see improvements," he says, "and I want to get involved. That's all. I've learned the importance of organizing. If I want to be aspiring to be anything, I want to be an organizer."

Currently, he has been deeply involved in the first-hand documentation of the other scourge afflicting the miners—disability from injuries. Counties dominated by the coal industry, he observes, have a significantly higher rate of Social Security disability and welfare disability payments. In Logan County, he points out, one out of every five underground miners suffers a loss time injury each year and this doesn't include the pneumoconiosis (black lung) victims who must quit work each year.

He argues: "The dollar cost of supporting disabled miners, in an area already heavy with unemployment, places a great strain on the economy, as does the potential loss when a man is disabled. As tax revenue decreases, public facilities reduce their standards. This causes more people to leave the state and reduces the tax bases even further. Finally, the situation becomes cyclical—poverty multiplies and the community eventually deteriorates."

His future plans are not settled yet. "If I can be of any help, I will stay. I hope to stay for another year." The West Virginia miners, he believes, have learned a great deal from their earlier mistakes in the movement. "They tell me they are waking up now and aren't going to be 'beat out' this time. If they do, it could bode well for their future." As for Robinson the organizer: "My part in this movement is really quite small. I find that I learned much more than I passed on."

ROMANTIC APPALACHIA
Don West

Almost every day we get letters from those wanting to come to Appalachia to "fight poverty." They've read about the Southern Mountaineers. They've seen movies, comic strips or TV (Li'l Abner, Beverly Hillbillies). It's not that there's no poverty in New York, Philadelphia, Baltimore, Chicago and other parts. There is. But Southern Appalachia has that "romantic" appeal.

Just a few years ago it was the southern Negro, and dedicated (or adventure seeking) young "yankees" came trouping to the South on freedom rides, marches and such. Not that racism, segregation and even riots didn't exist in the North. They did. But since the black militants kicked the whites out, suggesting they go organize their own kind, the next most romantic thing seems to be the Appalachian South.

So we are "discovered" again. It's happened every generation, sometimes more often, since the Civil War. After a few people in the North, following Lincoln's awareness, realized how the mountain South played a strategic role in defeating the Confederacy, there was a tinge of stricken conscience. First came the religious "missionaries" from New England and other parts North to lift us up and save our "hillbilly" souls. They brought along their "superior" religion to do it —and were closely followed by corporation emissaries buying up mineral rights for 25 cents to 50 cents an acre.

The Union General Howard, marching through Cumberland Gap, had been so deeply impressed by the friendly spirit, aid and support given his soldiers by the mountain people that he communicated it to the President. Lincoln himself vowed that after the war something should be done for "the loyal mountaineers of the South." One eventual result was Lincoln Memorial University at Cumberland Gap.

Subsequently a whole passel of mountain missionary schools sprang up. The loyalty of the southern mountaineer, his antislavery sentiment and action, and the plight of the poor little mountain boys and girls in isolated Appalachia were told in lurid details at the North.

From *The West Virginia Hillbilly* and the Appalachian South Press, 1970. Used by permission of the author.

Many missionaries were New England women who, some of the romantic fables held, were disappointed in love. They came to the mountains to lose themselves. Nonetheless, they had "uplift" in their eyes. A few even married hill men. We reckoned maybe that was part of the "uplift" too.

I attended one of these mountain missionary high schools. I remember so well how the New England "Pilgrims" used to come down each year. A special train brought them on a siding to the campus. All of us little "hillbillies" were lined up with candles lighted on each side of the dirt road for half a mile with carefully coached greeting smiles. It was a "great day." We were supposed to be cheered when the "Pilgrims" told us how we were "the last remnants of the pure old Anglo-Saxons" who, of course, were the most superior of all peoples. This maybe ought to have made us feel good and "superior" in spite of our poverty. And we did have poverty then. It's nothing new in the mountains.

Our biggest show was reserved for the Henry Ford visits. The old oxen were yoked to a wagon loaded with wood to amble all the campus roads, managing to meet the Ford procession on numerous occasions. (Henry might give us a flivver, you see.) Oh, but we really got to do our stuff then, including the old mountain dances with Mrs. Ford and Henry. That, we learned, was Henry's favorite dancing, and he gave the school more than a flivver, too. Ford put millions into that school. He also gave jobs to graduates in his non-union Detroit Plant which, he vowed, would never sign a union contract. Though we walked out of Appalachian poverty through the slums of Detroit, Henry would protect us from all union evils.

Ford, we learned, was a tight lipped guy. He never bored us with speeches as others did. He was the "silent but strong" type. He also doted on our supposedly "pure old Anglo-Saxon" heritage.

When later at a mountain college (Lincoln Memorial) Henry and Mrs. Ford showed up, we sort of felt just like old friends. Dancing the mountain folk dance with Mrs. Ford again we could talk about back when. Henry didn't confine his southern mountain interests to high school. He beckoned to "the best" in our colleges, too. We were inspired to "make a success," "get ahead," "be somebody," just like Henry had. The dollar mark was the standard, always.

Each time we are "discovered" a passel of new missionaries invade the mountains. Old clothes, surplus food and such are made available and some temporary reforms may result—crumbs thrown to the poor who need whole loaves and some meat, too. Some stirring is stimulated. Hope flutters painfully to escape the lint covered mill-hills or dust blackened shacks behind slate dumps only to fall broken-winged in polluted air or rivers outside. The missionary effect is to dull the razoredge thrust of the people toward human betterment. Appalachia's colonial status—the ownership, production and distribution structure —is left intact, hardly shaken or questioned.

As the nation's awareness of the new "discovery" wanes and, despairing of saving our "hillbilly souls" anyhow, the "missionaries" begin to pull out again. In such manner went many Presbyterians, Congregationalists and other religious cults years ago. More recently it was the Appalachian Volunteers, SCEF, VISTAs, some CAPs and other assorted conglomerates of poverty warriors. Shortly we may be forgotten again, until another generation "discovers" poverty in Appalachia.

Yes, the southern mountains have been missionarized, researched, studied, surveyed, romanticized, dramatized, hillbillyized, Dogpatched and povertyized again. Some of us who are natives and have known this hard living all our lives and our grandpaw's life before, marvel that our "missionary" friends discover us so often.

Southern Appalachia is a colonial possession of Eastern based industry. Like all exploited colonial areas, the "mother country" may make generous gestures now and then, send missionaries with up-lift programs, "superior" religion, build churches and sometimes schools. They'll do about everything—except get off the backs of the people, end the exploitive domination. That the people themselves must eventually see to. The latest "missionary" move is the "War on Poverty." It was never intended to end poverty. That would require a total reconstruction of the system of ownership, production and distribution of wealth.

This is not the first time in our lifetime that big city folk have come down to save and lift us up. I remember the 1929–1930's. Southern Appalachia was discovered then, too. Young "missionaries" were sowing their "radical wild oats" from the black belt of Alabama and Arkansas to Harlan County, Kentucky, and Paint and Cabin Creeks in West Virginia. They were mostly transients as "missionaries" frequently are. I don't know a single one who remained. I do know quite a few who returned North and are now rich men, some multimillionaires. It was a thrilling experience to be in romantic Appalachia or other parts South for a spell, but it was nice to have a rich papa up North to fall back on.

Not long ago visiting in an affluent apartment house on Riverside Drive in New York our hostess asked if I knew who owned that building. I didn't, of course. "Well," she said, "It is your old friend Alex ————, and this is just one of several he owns."

I remembered Alex very well. Once I drove his car from New York to Birmingham. He was a super activist and articulate as big city folk frequently are. He was sure he had the answers, too, about solving the problems of the poor. If you disagreed you were just no doggoned good, maybe an enemy of the poor. But I went to see him there in New York recently. He is not interested in the plight of the poor anymore. His time is given to looking after his multimillion dollar real estate business. He sowed his "radical wild oats" down South years ago.

There is a qualitatively different situation for those who come to fight poverty in Appalachia now and back in the 1930's. Then they came (Theodore Dreiser, the great American novelist, brought a passel to Pineville and Harlan, Kentucky) on their own. There was no OEO, no VISTA, no Appalachian Volunteers. Nobody was paid a good salary to fight poverty. They made their own way, shifted as best they could. It was depression times, too. Some did good work—helped to smooth the way for a future union and such. Some were murdered by thugs. Others were beaten, crippled. Issues were sharp and violence too common. There was more to it than writing songs, though songs were written. "Which Side Are You On?" came from Harlan, Kentucky, "Solidarity Forever" came from the Cabin Creek Struggles. There were underground papers, too, that didn't have an address or editor's name. They were really underground, no romantic play-like. They who worked at organizing the poor had to keep a wary eye. The murder of the Yablonski family is a throw-back, a reminder that the billionaire coal operator families always play rough, and for keeps, against effective opposition.

I remember a night on a mountain road above Harlan town in the 1930's. Six operator gun thugs with deputy badges and a young native organizer. Beaten to unconsciousness, thrown in the brush for dead, he came to hours later, crawling from the nightmare, stumbling down the mountainside to where a friendly old couple tended him in their humble cabin. A few nights later in a fourth rate Hazard hotel, beyond sitting up, unable to pay for food or lodging, dirty, hungry, listening to every footstep in the hall outside with fearful uncertainty. Organizing the poor in the 1930's was risky and extremely uncertain. I speak from experience here.

But things are considerably different now. The young "missionary" in Appalachia has it comparatively easy. First, he is paid. He has food to eat regularly, a place to sleep. He goes to bed with scant fear of being murdered in his sleep. He holds meetings without slipping around secretly in the bushes or basements. His meetings are not liable to be broken up or machine-gunned by operator thugs with deputy badges. And in an area where tens of thousands of families live on less than $2,000 a year, poverty fighters may get much more. Some salaries are large—$10 thousand, $15 thousand, $20 or $25 thousand or more.

We know one poverty "consultant" who received $500.00 a day for his consulting. He was later hired by a poverty fighting agency to work 4 days a month at $10 thousand a year salary. Others received similarly outrageous stipends. And some of the bright young "missionaries" who came down in one of the poverty fighting brigades, perhaps despairing of saving our "hillbilly souls," certainly failing to organize the poor, now find money in poverty by setting up post office box corporations that receive lucrative OEO grants or contracts to train others to "fight poverty." If they failed to organize the poor themselves, they nonetheless can train others to go out and do likewise. They became "experts" in the process, and now get well paid for their "expertise."

Recently a new agency a-borning to "change the image" poverty creates in our area, to be financed by OEO "seed money," proposed to pay its director $25 thousand a year with $16 per diem; the assistant to receive $20 thousand a year and so on. The claim is that such salaries are essential to get "qualified" personnel. Some of us who have seen the "missionaries" come and go over the years may think that such salary demands are indicative of precisely the kind of quality not needed.

From their affluent middle class background so many do-gooders who come into the mountains seldom grasp the fact that the poor are poor because of the nature of the system of ownership, production and distribution. When the poor fail to accept their middle class notions they may end up frustrated failures. Some put their frustrations into a book. Others set up post office box corporations to get in on the "benefits" of the system. Both have been done.

Their basic concern was not how they related to the mountains but how the mountains related to them and their notions. With their "superior" approach they failed to understand or appreciate the historic struggles of broad sections of the mountain people against the workings of the system dating back beyond the 1930's: Early Paint and Cabin Creek battles; the armed march with five to seven thousand miners camped at Marmet in the Kanawha Valley, marching toward Logan to help fellow miners against gun thug terrorism; the Battle of Blair Mountain where the enemy dropped bombs from the air; the battle of Evarts, Harlan and Bell in Kentucky; Gastonia, Marion, High Point in North Carolina; Elizabethton, Wilder, Coal Creek in Tennessee and later Blue Ridge in Georgia and the Black Lung West Virginia Strike in 1969. And before that the mountain man's struggle against a slave system that oppressed both the poor white and black slaves.

These modern "missionaries" (some already "ex-missionaries"), despairing of us, may return home. Ten years from now—if the world still stands—they may look back from their affluence with nostalgia for the time when they sowed their "radical wild oats" in Appalachia. The "missionaries"—religious or secular—had and have one thing in common: they didn't trust us hill folk to speak, plan and act for ourselves. Bright, articulate, ambitious, well-intentioned, they became our spokesmen, our planners, our actors. And so they'll go again, leaving us and our poverty behind.

But is there a lesson to be learned from all these outside efforts that have failed to save us? I think so. If we native mountaineers can now determine to organize and save ourselves, save our mountains from the spoilers who tear them down, pollute our streams and leave grotesque areas of ugliness, there is hope. The billionaire families behind the great corporations are also outsiders who sometimes claim they want to "save" us. It is time that we hill folk should understand and appreciate our heritage, stand up like those who were our ancestors, develop our own self-identity. It is time to realize that nobody from the outside is ever going to save us from bad conditions unless we make our own stand. We must learn to organize again, speak, plan and act for ourselves. There are many potential allies with common problems—the poor of the great cities, the Indians, the Blacks and the Chicanos who are also exploited. They need us. We need them. Solidarity is still crucial. If we learn this lesson from the outside "missionary" failures, then we are on our way.

Part Four

Can We Get There from Here?

Education & Youth

THE SCHOOL & POLITICS
Peter Schrag

Education in the mountain counties of Appalachia is the product of a nearly perfect system. Poverty, politics, and the catatonic consequences of deprivation and exploitation have left most of the mountain schools generations behind the rest of the nation. In their isolation, they educate children for the community and for the futility that surrounds them. In preparing children for the larger world they deal with the irrelevant.

The symptoms of the disease are easy to enumerate. In virtually every category by which we measure educational achievement the schools of Appalachia represent extremes. Many of them lack the personnel and facilities for modern instruction in foreign languages and science—indeed many of their high schools teach no foreign languages at all; they rank low in the percentage of graduates going on to higher education but they are high in the percentage of dropouts—sometimes as high as 85 percent between first and twelfth grades; their students,

From *Appalachian Review*, Fall 1966. Used by permission of the publisher.

even those who finish, stand low on standard reading comprehension tests—low enough so that in most instances graduates of mountain high schools are on a par with tenth graders in other parts of the country. Many Appalachian school systems have no libraries, no laboratories, sometimes not even adequate gymnasiums despite the area's passion for athletics. Their teachers are undertrained, underpaid and—if they are conscientious—overworked. But the system rarely rewards the conscientious. Often it protects the incompetent.

To a visitor in the mountain schools, the discourse in the classroom has a kind of somnambulistic unreality about it, almost as if the participants were playing school or performing a little play purporting to represent real education. No one knows his lines well because the dialogue is about something far away and not understood by the participants: the French revolution, or the mechanics of city government as described in a civics text, or the economics of market capitalism as imagined by the Chamber of Commerce in 1928. Textbook cliches abound and no one makes much effort to relate them even to the limited experiences of the students in the class. Concurrently, the conscientious teachers find that their students cannot read or even speak adequately; their language is so remote from literate English that it sometimes appears like a foreign tongue. The words appearing on the students' papers come out as "attinshun," "mintion," the "Application" mountains.

But listing problems—the one-room schools, the children who lack shoes, the difficulties of transportation, the many small districts—does not explain the fundamental pathology of Appalachian education. It does not explain how new programs tend to become mired in the sump of old political styles, how the wives and brothers and cousins of the county politicians are suddenly put in charge of local poverty or educational improvement programs, or how the circle of futility seems to renew itself year after year, despite all the national attention that has been focused upon it. There are, without question, major exceptions to the general pattern, as well as significant efforts to upgrade life and education in the mountains. There are competent, dedicated teachers and principals, conscientious superintendents, and effective school boards. The Eastern Kentucky Resource Development Project, the Council of the Southern Mountains, and other state and private agencies have made an impact on the region. Yet most of these individuals and organizations have left the prevailing educational-political structures untouched: essentially they have conducted rescue operations, teaching skills and organizing small community development or rehabilitation projects while leaving the system unchanged.

What is the system? Basically it is a self-contained social mechanism isolated physically and culturally from the outside world, although partially sustained by the public funds for education and welfare that the outside world provides. Its elements include chronic unemployment of an industrial population, a historic neglect of formal education, a lack of cultural capital, a political structure founded on family associations and nepotism, an exploitative coal industry controlled by irresponsible absentee ownership, and, increasingly, a tradition of dependency and helplessness. Harry M. Caudill has called the region the "vast paleface reservation"—an area exhibiting all the signs of institutional dependency associated with people who have adjusted to a life where all decisions, and even identity itself, are determined by the keepers of the institution. Some of the outside poverty workers who have come to the mountains in recent years have been continually frustrated by their inability to convince mountain people that they have (at least in theory) rightful access to school superintendents, county judges, and other local officials. The eminences of the county seats—small-time politicians, all of them—have attained Olympian stature in the eyes of many of their oppressed mountain constituents. For years they have been taught to depend on the small blessings that trickle from these lesser village gods: jobs as bus drivers and lunchroom employees, leniency in misdemeanor cases, perhaps a little extra welfare assistance for a needy cousin. People who question or criticize lose favor with the powers, and even tenured school teachers, presumably protected by law, can be exiled to one-room schools in distant hollows. Thus much of the new money—and therefore the power—is not associated with the federal government. It does not come from Washington, or even from the state capital, but from the county courthouse and from the office of the county school superintendent.

From such a base the remainder of the system can operate without disturbance. The better graduates of the mountain schools either leave for the cities in the North and West or they continue their education at the mountain teachers' colleges, from which, after four years of poor training, they return to their home counties to take charge of the classrooms they had left as students not many years before. "Outsiders wouldn't be happy here," said a county superintendent, explaining why he was not interested in recruiting beyond his own area. Outsiders, of course, are reluctant to come in anyway, given the pay and the conditions. But the few who might are generally suspect: they have strange ideas, they are not beholden to the local machines and they may be interested in change. And there is always somebody's cousin who needs a job.

Because of physical and cultural isolation, the view of these communities is limited. Nothing comes in, while the best of the local resources—the coal, the human energy, the talent—flows out of the region with little or no return. The middle-class burghers of the county seats—small businessmen, coal operators, lawyers—who often congratulate themselves on their generosity, behave with the wisdom of a lumpen proletariat when it comes to the genuine problems of the community. Dependent themselves on the existing structure, they often tend to deny the existence of chronic unemployment, of regional decay and of home-grown corruption. Like those of the federal government, their charitable acts leave the essential structure untouched; rather, they serve simply to keep the waste and misery from becoming too unconscionable. The effect, if not the intent, is to keep the natives sufficiently dependent in order to prevent any fundamental change from taking place.

As so often happens in every isolated depressed society, the most fearful are often those who have risen a notch above the rest, and who are now in a position to act. Their ability to effect changes is also the ability to repress and to maintain the status quo, and this is the course they often take. No foreign industry—whether it is a coal company or a crowd of banana imperialists—can operate successfully without native allies, without a local army of lawyers, foremen, and judges who can enforce the laws and customs perpetuating the system. In Appalachia, those laws permit the extraction of coal almost untaxed and they permit strip mining to be carried on with only the barest regard for the land and streams and homes that it ravages each year. (Recently Kentucky adopted legislation to control some of these activities. The question is whether succeeding administrations will enforce it.)

The local leaders permit—even encourage—irrelevant education based on books and classes that kill questioning and curiosity, that discourage change and that reinforce existing fears and superstitions. As

a consequence, no cultural capital has been accumulated. Each generation begins with the ideas and attitudes of those that preceded it, lacking the resources, the books, the ideas and the experience to go beyond
the highest point reached by the one before it. Thus the cycle is repeated. Appalachia is now raising its third welfare generation.

Within this system, education is only a sideline, while schools, as
sources of power and income, are major institutions. Political dynasties
are founded on the job of the school superintendent who often controls
not only his own school board and the jobs the schools provide, but
other county offices as well. The addition of federal funds, as presently
allocated, merely reinforces the existing structure.

It is impossible to break this system by attacking it on one place
only. The construction of a few schoolhouses, the assignment of
VISTA workers, or even the development of a huge new highway program are likely to be encapsulated in old political structures and practices. It is only at the point when a significant number of local individuals begin to develop a sense of control—and enough anger to act—
that changes are likely to begin. The Kentucky strip mining laws
passed within the last year were the product of local organizations and
local power, people who discovered almost accidentally a common
sense of anger over the destruction of their land. Their subsequent
march on Frankfort and the pressure they exercised on the legislature
appear to be a model for similar political acts in other areas and on
other problems.

The average mountaineer is fully committed to the idea of education for his children, but often he does not know, and cannot know,
what effective education is, or how it can be achieved. One of the prime
tasks of any social action program is to describe to him how his children are being systematically cheated, and how his own commitment
to existing political practices has undermined education in the classroom. He has to learn that a high school diploma from a mountain
school is not enough, that it symbolizes little unless it is backed by the
hard currency of good teaching. He has to learn that education in the
mountains can no longer be merely education for the mountains, that
it must also be education for the economy and the society and the problems of the world beyond. He must, in a sense, be made the agent of
change, must discover, as the Southern Negro has discovered, that he
can develop political muscle, and that if he chooses to act the world will

respond. In this respect any social action must be subversive. As long as new support and new programs are simply tied to old machines, the machines will use them as they always have in the past, and the system will continue forever.

THE CRISIS OF APPALACHIAN YOUTH
James Branscome

The child was diseased at birth, stricken with a hereditary ill that only the most vital men are able to shake off . . . I mean poverty—the most deadly and prevalent of all diseases.

Eugene O'Neill

In Appalachia today more than three-quarters of a million young people sit in the hollows and hills unmotivated, uneducated and unemployed. Poverty, that "most deadly and prevalent of all diseases," still leaves its crippling marks on the youth of the Region—leaves them, essentially, in young people's inability to profit from the educational opportunities which are open to them. To see this vital young talent atrophying at home is a loss the Region cannot afford. The threat of creating a future welfare generation is a real one unless the vicious cycle can be broken. A unique and imaginative solution to the problem must be found.

In an age when a high school diploma is a requirement for almost any but the least skilled job, 65 percent of the Region's students still do not graduate from high school. The bulk of students drop out between seventh and ninth grade. Of the rural dropouts (and Appalachia's population is still over 50 percent rural), less than 30 percent of farm students and only about 40 percent of non-farm students complete ten grades of school. In some counties in the Region the dropout rate has reached an alarming 71 percent, double the already high national rate. While college graduates are demanded as leaders for the Region, only one out of ten Appalachian students goes on to college.

No single factor causes the Appalachian young man or woman to leave school so early. Difficulty in reaching the schools, the attractions

From *Appalachia*, May 1969. Used by permission of the publisher.

of out-migration, local politics, low parental educational attainment—all of these have an effect. Almost certainly one other factor is the failure of education to respond to the particular need. In the words of the Education Advisory Committee to the Appalachian Regional Commission, "the differences between the family, culture, social setting and mores of the urban and the Appalachian youth are demonstrable and significant. The educational effects of these differences, however, have not been studied. We can only say that the character of the 'deprived' Appalachian probably demands a different system and different approach to education."

The teacher and the school system are at times at the root of the problem. In some areas inadequate educational attention has had grave adverse effects; standardized tests have shown that the I.Q. of school children has actually been declining from ¼ to ½ point annually for some thirteen years. A comment from educator Robert R. Bell in his book *The Sociology of Education* provides an insight into the damage that the attitude of educational personnel may be:

> Because the middle class teacher from lower class origins has in her own mind been socially successful through the means of formal education as an occupation, it may seem that this is the correct behavior pattern to be followed by all "worthwhile" young people of lower class background.

The resentment such an attitude may arouse is all too easy to imagine.

The Region is not always the gainer when one of its young people does complete his education. Demographic studies indicate that those trained in the Region's colleges migrate in significant numbers to other areas. For example, 85 percent of the teachers in the Hamilton County and Cincinnati, Ohio, school systems are Appalachian immigrants. Nearly 70 percent of the young teachers returning to or remaining in the Region leave after their first four years. The results are the steady aging of Appalachia teachers and a tremendous loss of talent which can scarcely be spared.

The young Appalachian who is neither a migrant nor a dropout is nonetheless likely to be less well equipped to face the competitive business world than his contemporary outside the Region. Vocational education, viewed by many as a panacea for the Region's educational problems, has not done the job it should have. The first problem is that all too often secondary schools are out of touch with the realities of the labor market. Students are frequently trained for jobs which do not exist, and are not trained to fill those that are available. A much higher proportion of students are enrolled in agriculture or home economics than in trades and industry courses, but most job openings occur in the latter field. The Educational Advisory Committee commented fittingly, "No greater harm could be done to a youngster than to train him for a job soon to become obsolete." The recent report of a manpower research agency showing that a young person entering the work force can expect to be retrained eleven times before he retires indicates that perhaps this harm has been more widespread than many have realized. Unfortunately there is evidence to indicate that merely making vocational courses available in schools does not significantly lower the dropout rate. One may guess that a more judicious offering of vocational courses would lead to a different result.

Another difficulty in the current vocational education setup lies in the Region's failure to receive a fair proportion of Federal funds in this field. Although Appalachia has 13 percent of the national enrollment in secondary school vocational education, it receives only 7.3 percent of the Federal funds available. Finally, the Region is not keeping pace with the Nation in advancing to higher levels of vocational education. Secondary school enrollment still accounts for nearly three-quarters of the Region's total vocational enrollment, while the Nation is moving on to post-secondary and adult vocational training.

It has often been pointed out that the character and motivation of the individual may have a far greater effect on his future than the opportunities he has enjoyed. In the case of Appalachian youth, this is borne out by two studies. The President's Advisory Commission on Rural Poverty commented in its report *The People Left Behind*:

A very significant finding of the Coleman study (Equality of Educational Opportunities, prepared for the Office of Education by James S. Coleman, Ernest Q. Campbell, et al., 1966) is that factors associated with the individual student were more important in explaining differences in educational achievement than factors associated with the schools. For example, all the "school factors" combined, such as the training of teachers and quality of facilities, were not as important in explaining differences in achievement scores as the student's attitude regarding the amount of control one has over his or her destiny. Students, regardless of race, who had a strong conviction that they could control their future achieved at a higher rate than those who did not. The importance of this finding is illustrated by the fact that the variability among individual pupils within the same school was about four times greater than the variability among pupils between schools.

The Educational Advisory Committee makes the same point in a more specific connection: "Appalachian youth in Job Corps camps most frequently drop out, apparently because of homesickness and inability to cope with the active aggressiveness of the urban youth. However, once convinced that they are trained to perform a task, they persevere and demonstrate considerable energy and integrity."

It seems clear that the Region has untapped potential in its youth, but it is failing to meet the challenge they present. It is failing to develop and hold the corps of leaders it will soon need to replace its present aging leaders. New major programs have begun to promise relief to the youngest of the Region's citizens: Head Start, day-care centers, early-childhood education centers. But for the young people of high school and college age new and creative assistance is imperative.

One program which has proved surprisingly effective elsewhere might solve part of Appalachia's problem. The admission of significant numbers of "high-risk" students (of whom there are many thousands in the region) to the Region's colleges and universities through special consideration programs might open a brighter future to many young Appalachians. Too many Appalachian students are denied entrance to college under present rigid rules and are presented with only two alternatives: vocational training or unemployment. By furnishing special assistance, the Regional institutions of higher learning can exercise their responsibility in this area.

High-risk students are those who lack the usual credentials of acceptable grades and test scores, not the ability to succeed in college. They are, as John Egerton of the Southern Education Reporting Service has stated,

... the long shot prospects of success, but who demonstrate some indefinable and unmeasurable quality—motivation, creativity, resilience, leadership, personality, or whatever—which an admissions office might interpret as a sign of strength offsetting the customary indicators of probable success.

Simply stated, a high-risk Appalachian student is one who can expect to gain admission—if he bothers to seek it—only at a junior college or a small black college in the South. To the college admissions department or a high school guidance counselor, his records usually show that he:

... is from a home where low economic standing is only one of many socially complicating problems;
... has an erratic grade school and high school record, showing alternatively high and low achievement;
... has had at least one major discipline problem during his school career;
... has low standardized test scores but a high I.Q. if tested nonverbally.

He is, in short, the product of a deprived environment, and unless some special action is taken, his talent will be untapped and his future blocked.

Because the weaknesses in development and education displayed by the high-risk student in Appalachia reflect in large measure the weaknesses native to the community and Region which produced him, the regional colleges and universities have a special responsibility to provide for the development of his potential. Until now, no significant effort has been made by either public or private educational institutions in the Region to seek and educate these students.

Institutions of higher learning have a natural reluctance to use limited faculty and facilities for training students whose success potential seems limited. Experience in other areas of the U. S. indicates, however, that high-risk programs may well represent one of the most promising and exciting ways to invest our educational capital. John Egerton, in his study for the Southern Education Foundation, reviewed 86 different programs in both public and private predominantly white four-year colleges and universities. These programs represented a wide range of effort in this experiment—high-risk and low, large numbers and small, substantial and modest institutional commitment. Although the study did not attempt to make a formal evaluation of the effectiveness of the program, reactions of responsible officials were obtained and frequently cited in the report. In many institutions program officials reported solid results.

An important high-risk program is OEO's Upward Bound, which began on a national basis in 1966. Like the individual institutional programs described by Egerton, this federally financed program operates on the premise that a very high percentage of rural and urban youngsters from poverty backgrounds have the ability to succeed in college if they are provided with the necessary stimulation and academic and cultural preparation.

In a typical program the students, most of whom have completed their sophomore or junior year in high school, live for six to eight weeks in the summer on college, university and secondary school campuses. During the academic year the students continue in their regular high school classes, but meet with the Upward Bound faculty in Saturday classes, tutorial sessions after school hours during the week and periodic cultural enrichment programs. Upward Bound, like other high-risk programs, uses a wide variety of teaching techniques and places great emphasis on developing basic skills, individual counseling, and nurturing the students' self-confidence.

OEO's 1968 year-end report cites statistics which indicate the success of the program. Almost two-thirds of all Upward Bound graduates have gone on to college. At the end of the year more than 11,000 students were enrolled in more than 800 two- and four-year accredited colleges and universities across the U. S., including several in Appalachia. The 1965 Upward Bound graduates entered their senior year of college in the fall of 1968, and their retention rate was 54%, just two points below the average for all seniors nationally. For the class of 1966, now juniors, the retention rate thus far is 57%; and for the 1967 group, now sophomores, the retention rate is 77%.

Experience has already given us some guidelines in the successful design of high-risk education. It is important that the faculty of the participating college or university should be properly prepared to accept the new program; special orientation and training of participating faculty members should be completed before the program begins. Students should be carefully recruited, with emphasis on potential rather than past performance.

For the high-risk student it is important to create an environment which the student does not view as hostile and which in itself contributes to removing his social, emotional and intellectual blocks against development. It should be an environment in which change is the norm and personal growth is encouraged at an accelerated rate. The program —academic as well as extracurricular—should be structured to meet individual needs rather than to insure conformity and administrative efficiency.

A staff should be recruited which is sensitive to the problems of high-risk students and which is varied in age, experience, training, cultural and racial background, and political, educational and social viewpoint. The program director should be experienced, dedicated and resourceful. He should be sensitive to both staff and students to the degree that he can channel and motivate them all to their fullest capacity without creating conflict.

The staff must be totally involved with the students. Staff should participate with students in all academic and extracurricular activities wherever possible. Individual instruction and counseling should always be available for a student when needed. The program should be so directed that the student is made to feel a necessary part of the program, not solely an object of the experiment. Program responsibility should be shared with the students, allowing them to govern themselves to the highest degree possible. Members of the staff should avoid forcing cultural identity or value judgments on the students.

The curricular and extracurricular program should be geared toward development of the whole person—emotionally, socially and intellectually—rather than merely developing his academic expertise. This means careful selection of subjects to be taught, emphasis on problem-solving rather than discipline mastery, dialogue rather than lecture as the teaching method and revision of academic testing, grade assignments and other activities which create competition and break group feeling and solidarity.

Special remedial programs should be incorporated into the program from the beginning. These programs should cover reading comprehension and speed, English usage and expression, auditory and visual perception, verbal and physical expression, mathematical and abstract thinking, and cultural and social understanding and appreciation.

Another answer to the crisis of Appalachian youth would be to establish a program to develop civic and governmental leaders in the Region from among the young. There are bright and talented young people in the Region who need to see their own potential and importance to Appalachia as leaders. At present they either leave the Region for "some brighter clime" or resign themselves to self-effacement, convinced that their salvation will have to come from outside.

What is needed is a pragmatic, positive program with a basic double objective: First, to help the young participant to see himself as a leader worthy of respect, to recognize his talents and to help him channel these talents into programs of action; second, to develop in the participant sufficient pride in and appreciation of the Region so that he feels a commitment to its future.

Such a program must be flexible, as the leaders developed by it will not be intended to fit one particular slot but to fill needs wherever they arise. It must teach relevant technical knowledge about leadership, preferably through such techniques as apprenticing young people to existing leaders worthy of emulation or involving young people in constructive programs at the local level. It must bring together young leaders for the moral support they derive from each other and from their very numbers. It must work with colleges and schools to develop educational programs with more appeal and meaning for youth. This program would refuse to write off the talent and responsibility of Appalachian young people, but instead would challenge them to live up to their highest potential.

Solving the youth crisis in Appalachia will require a combination of imaginative program strategies. Some, such as high-risk college student programs, have already begun inside the regular educational system but need to be developed and expanded. Others, such as leadership training schools, must be operated in conjunction with the existing system.

We must come to recognize that the greatness of an educational system is measured not by how it rewards motivation and achievement, but rather by how it creates these qualities where they did not exist before. The challenge is not merely to educate in the usual sense, but to create "the most vital of men," persons capable of overcoming the "most deadly and prevalent of all diseases—poverty."

Into the 1970s

A BOLD IDEA FOR A NEW APPALACHIA
John Fetterman

Imagine a prim little old lady all lavender and lace and scented in lilac. She scrupulously deposits dividends from the common stocks of giant corporations she owns and busies herself admirably with adamant letters to her local newspaper complaining of the sickly condition of the petunias around the town square. She is, as her friends would quickly attest, a lover of nature. She has never checked carefully into the source of the dividends which sustain her and her beloved canary. It is well. The dividends may well be her reward for her share of what has been the most staggering destruction of land and water in the history of the nation. The destruction of land and water is taking place in Appalachia, where decades of hope for relief have been snugly entombed in the graveyards of local apathy and state and county bureaucracy.

Now, at long last, a handful of people are looking in an entirely new direction for help—to themselves. Appalachia, they contend, is the civilized world's last absolute stronghold of colonialism and exploitation by absentee owners. This yoke of colonialism, they say, has

From the Louisville *Courier-Journal and Times Magazine*, March 5, 1967. Used by permission of the author.

resulted in the paradox of the nation's poorest and most illiterate populace dwelling amid the nation's richest region in terms of natural resources. The most daring concept of self-help came into being on a recent wintry day in a 130-year-old, white columned inn in Abingdon, Virginia. The inn's dining hall, with its soaring ceiling, panoramic papering and ornate chandeliers, was filled with experts in many fields who have found a common fascination in Appalachia.

As men will, they organized and formed a group, which they named Congress for Appalachian Development. This naturally becomes CAD, and they will be called worse before their course is run. CAD, which is incorporated and chartered in West Virginia, offers a simple and singular proposition: That the millions of people who live in Appalachia retain a small part of the riches their region provides to the rest of the world.

This startling proposition did not send the attending observers from an array of government and social agencies scurrying for safety. They stayed and listened, on occasion nodding approval. There were people from the Interior Department, the Department of Housing and Urban Development, the Office of Economic Opportunity, the Council of the Southern Mountains, management consultants, ministers, state legislators, experts in the field of human and natural resources, and just plain Appalachian people.

CAD elected as chairman Harry Caudill, who has been the thorn in the side of coal operators and others who despoil the hills in removing the coal and other minerals. "We Kentucky mountaineers have used a supremely rich land to become a remarkably poor people," Caudill says. "We are on a road leading many areas to total ruin . . . some valleys already have come to total ruin. Our people have surrendered self-government. We have become a kept people." In a masterpiece of understatement, Caudill told the 200 or so in attendance, "This is no undertaking for the weak."

Indeed it is not. The course CAD has set for itself must in time bring it into confrontation with the greatest and best organized of American capitalistic structures—the corporations which own the land and coal, the private power industry, and many self-seeking lawmakers. Some men call the task impossible. But gathered on the genuine antique chairs and sofas of the old inn were men who had been through a similar struggle before and had emerged with victory. They were the infighters who brought the Public Utility District concept into being in the State of Washington, where men once fretted to the breaking point under economic strangulation. The Public Utility District, or PUD, as presented by these men is one of the ventures under discussion by CAD. There are others.

PUD was born in the State of Washington early in the century. When enabling legislation failed to pass the Washington Legislature in 1929, the issue was taken to the people in a referendum in 1930. It passed, largely with the support of bankrupt farmers. A Public Utility District can be authorized by a state legislature. It is a corporate body, owned and operated by the people, and it has the power to issue revenue bonds, purchase property and exercise the right of eminent domain. PUDs in Appalachia would concern themselves with the generating and distribution of cheap electric power. The State of Washington offers an intriguing precedent. Its 22 PUDs now operate a $120 million plant, serve 280,000 customers, and have an average revenue of 93 cents a kilowatt hour for residential users, about half the average price of power supplied by private utilities.

PUDs have turned Washington into the nation's leading aluminum reduction state. Each PUD operates within a county. Some PUDs are small, some are large. A typical one is in Lewis County. Lewis County, Washington, is rolling to level in the west, and in the east it soars toward the Cascade Mountains. It has no heavy industry. There are about 35,000 people in the county engaged in logging and the raising of cattle and berries and truck gardening. The Lewis County PUD has operating revenues of slightly over $2 million and returns $132 thousand in taxes. About $125,000 of these revenues support Lewis County's modern education system, including a two-year college. It is purely a distribution facility which buys its power from the Bonniville Power Administration. What happens in Lewis County, Washington, makes Appalachian people wonder as they see the wealth of their land extracted and removed and as they attempt to live amid the ruins that are left.

Gordon Ebersole, veteran of 30 years with the Bureau of Reclamation, now in private engineering practice, is only one of many experienced and talented men who have volunteered to help CAD. Ebersole puts it bluntly: "If we are serious about throwing off the yoke of colonialism, then attention should be directed to the Yankee-Dixie concept of mine-mouth electric-power generation." Executive director of Yankee-Dixie Power, Inc., is Joe Botto. He said: "The best way to sell coal is through power lines." The two statements form the nub of the major concept being studied by CAD.

Yankee-Dixie, with headquarters in Winchester, Kentucky, is a big plant, already in the engineering phase. It has 218 members in 22 states, including rural electric cooperatives, municipalities and even one investor-owned utility. It envisions a network of high-voltage lines from coal-powered generating facilities located atop their source of coal. Yankee-Dixie proposes a surcharge on wholesale power which it says will be applied back to a development fund for the region of between $10 million and $12 million a year. Yankee-Dixie is to be a 100 percent debt operation—financed entirely by revenue bonds. It proposes to serve any locally owned Public Utility Districts which may be set up in Appalachia. In short, the coal would be owned, mined and converted to power by local interests. It would remove the area from dependence on entirely extractive economy.

The exporting of power has other supporters with other arguments. One of the prime movers of CAD is E. S. Fraley, a 77-year-old spry and angry retired farmer and businessman who lives in Bristol, Virginia. "The relationship that exists between Appalachia and absentee owners is essentially a colonial relationship," he said. "They own the resources and live on the outside. They have little interest in the welfare of the people in the area. The taxes they pay to support such things as schools are trivial and insignificant." It is somewhat of a personal crusade for Fraley. "My father sold his coal—65 acres—for $32.50 about 1880." Fraley points up another argument for power generation in Appalachia: air pollution in the industrial cities of the northeast. In the New York area, more than 1,000 firms share the blame for some of the dirtiest air on the continent. Among the prime contributors are power generating plants.

CAD hopes to unite hundreds in the campaign. Unity has always been a problem in the mountains. Families traditionally are entities unto themselves and the destruction is visited upon the mountaineer with singular tragedy. One family here—then another there—is destroyed by the plundering of hill and stream. There is no sudden mass tragedy —to attract public outcry. The man, alone and unbefriended far up a hollow, can see little hope. He feels he is alone in a vast wasteland. But others, now looking closely at Appalachia, see a vision of something better. Kirby Billingsly, president of the American Public Power Association says flatly: "Appalachia has everything the urban problem-solver is seeking—cheap land and water and adequate rainfall."

Lewis G. Smith, a retired engineer and water resources expert who spent a career with the Bureau of Reclamation, has devoted months of his own time attempting to demonstrate this point. He has presented CAD with a huge map—30 feet long and four feet wide—showing what he thinks can be done with the urbanization of Appalachia. Smith would lace the ridges with roads to serve a region whose economic base would be light industry. He reasons that new towns will have to be built somewhere. Already, they are on the drawing boards for other regions. "An estimated $3 trillion is to be spent in this country on new housing by the turn of the century," Smith argues. Why not build where nature provides a region suitable for lakes and nearby playgrounds?

Would the mountaineer move from his hollows and up onto the ridge to work? Gus Norwood, executive secretary of the Northwest Public Power Association says he will. He cites Alaska. "Some Alaskan villages were practically in the stone age. Then they created a town with a Rural Electric Association, a hospital and schools. In about a generation's time, they begin the move to town and away from the villages." Gideon Yachin, Israeli-born civil engineer who already has offered relocation plans for the mountains, sees CAD as an opportunity for "the local people to reverse the trend of robbing by outsiders." The mere building of lakes, Yachin says, "can raise the value of land by a ratio of 20 to 1 in three or four years. Where else can you get that return?"

CAD, despite the examples already set by the utility district in Washington and the new-found support of men experienced in the development of natural resources, is confronted with a bitter, seemingly hopeless battle. For one thing, stockholders of large holding companies, can be expected to oppose bitterly. They disagree with Ebersole when he speaks of "profits drained off to build centers of luxurious living in Miami, Las Vegas and Palm Springs." And CAD raises the tattered banners of the old and savage "public-versus-private" power conflict. It is a fight that never fails to bring to the surface deep and bitter conflicts, and in some cases—as in Washington and the Tennessee Valley development—public interests have won.

At the inception of the Tennessee Valley Authority, the opposing symbolic battle cries were raised early by E. A. Yates, vice-president of Commonwealth & Southern, a vast power holding, and Sen. George Norris, author of the TVA bill. "I can see no market whatsoever for this power," Yates said. "It is emblematic of the dawning of that day when every rippling stream that flows down the mountainside shall be harnessed . . . for the welfare and comfort of man," Norris said. TVA, now 34 years old, speaks for itself. One needs only to cross the state line from Kentucky into Tennessee, where the same mountains and streams flow, to read the message in the hills.

CAD's charter pledges a fight against "a state of servile bondage to absentee industrial and financial interests." Against these giants, Caudill and CAD would pit "local leadership." Opponents of public development often raise the charge that local leadership is insufficient to look after local interests. But the young CAD already is mustering an impressive gathering of dedicated people.

The Public Utility Districts of Washington also appear to refute the claim that local leadership cannot manage local affairs. Ebersole points out that Washington turned to the people for leadership in developing the vast power complexes. In Chelyan County, he said, the three elected board members are all local farmers and the manager of that half-billion-dollar system is a former reporter for a small newspaper. Ebersole adds: "The people of Appalachia should remember that when they permit outside capital and outside management to come in and develop Appalachia's resources, then the profits will forever leave for the outside. When outside capital and local management are used, then part of the profits will go to the outside until the 'mortgage' is paid off. After that, all profits will stay at home." And always before CAD, as a symbol of promise, is the fight the financially-strapped apple growers of Washington waged and won when times were hard out there.

NATIONALIZING OUR RESOURCES
Philip Young

Nationalization of America's natural resources is not the kind of an issue around which concerned people are rallying. It does not move people to action as does racial or economic injustice; it has driven no one out of the country or to jail, as has America's military injustice. But the damnable thing about many of the social, economic, or military wrongs in this nation is that their current manifestations are more temporarily than permanently relevant to humanity.

A growing number of Americans, however, representing both the scientific elite and the poorest white mountain resident of Kentucky and West Virginia, are alarmed at the extensive corruption of what most of us have always taken for granted—the physical world around us.

For the scientist, and to an increasing extent the federal planner, random technological advancement is the most frightening thing we must face in the near future. There is no random way of dealing with our physical environment. To the contrary, there are delicate balances and natural forces which scientists now believe are upset only at great costs to all of life. Unfortunately, we have paid no attention to these balances. Lake Erie is a magnificent cesspool; the air over our major urban centers is substantially poisonous.

An increased demand for coal to feed power plants continues to threaten the very existence of thousands of families in Appalachia who happen to live in those areas where strip-mining now goes on. During the winter months, story after story is told of immense earth slides that carry away roads, fields, and occasionally inundate homes. All year round, sulphur-stinking water flows into wells and streams sickening people, killing wildlife, and destroying tomorrow's resources.

There are at least two significant reasons why full consideration should be given to the nationalization of our resources. First, because there is mounting concern among citizens and scientists, the federal government is going to do something about water and air pollution

From *The New South Student* and *The Appalachian South*, Spring and Summer 1967. Used by permission of the author.

very soon. Without some real protest, this federal regulation will be only that which is acceptable to the industrial concerns affected by controls. In his 1967 message to the industry, Joseph Moody, President of the National Coal Policy Conference, Inc., indicated clearly that the coal industry—both labor and management—is determined not to let the Department of Health, Education and Welfare "force on the nation an air pollution abatement program far more strict than medical evidence justifies and without due regard to . . . what their affect may be upon various fuel industries, such as coal."

From the automobile industry, and the drug industry, to name two of the more flagrant examples of industrial meddling in the setting of Federal standards, we have long since learned that industry has little concern for the best, long-range interests of the people, let alone their physical health and safety. It seems to me that a different premise must be injected into all of the discussion about pollution: all of the natural resources in this nation belong to the people. This means that no right of private ownership exceeds the right of the people to the best use of all their resources. It is quite clear that national planning is absolutely essential, whether we are talking about using our land to feed the world, or simply about using our air to draw a safe breath.

Secondly, no issue comes closer to being critical to the rural poor than the use of the land on which they live. If America is to be serious about rural poverty, it must recognize that there is a clear relationship between the land and the people who live on it. Understanding the people trapped in poverty in rural areas requires an understanding of their sense of belonging to the land.

To know that major floods occur in the mountains regularly, and that minor flooding is a semi-annual problem, is to recognize that we have not taken seriously either the people who live in these areas or the billions of gallons of water that are annually wasted by floods. It may be legal for strip miners to deprive families of the use of their land without remuneration or due process of law; but it is also wrong.

Successful organizational attempts in Appalachia must reflect these issues, or they will be irrelevant to the people who live in that region. Poor schools, inadequate health facilities, political chaos, no job opportunities, as intolerable as they may be, are not the kinds of issues to which poor white mountaineers are now responding. But they do have a sense of relationship to the land upon which they live, and an understandable horror of rising water or sliding mountains. If the people and the natural resources are related, it must be made clear that the people's rights exceed the broad-form deed in fact, as well as in theory.

I am well aware of the gap between morality and legality in America. If that were the only critical issue here, it could be bridged by simply legalizing what is apparently moral. Industry and government could be called upon to act responsibly in dealing with all of America's natural resources; and because they represent a portion of the people, they could be relied upon to deal fairly with the future of all the people and their resources.

Even swallowing that crass fiction, America's larger problem has always been a massive disjunction between what is right and what is economically and politically possible. Nothing less than the crisis which we have unwittingly brought upon ourselves—the impending collapse of the physical atmosphere in which we live—can make us deal realistically with the whole matter of what is right for America's future.

A suffocating thermal inversion over Los Angeles, the total pollution of Lake Erie, the destruction of a mountain town in West Virginia by flood or mud, any major failure of our natural environment can no longer be considered as only remote, isolated possibilities.

Some concept of national planning, built upon social values, is absolutely necessary. The crisis in our use of natural resources provides the occasion for working toward that end. Even if this were not so, the misuse of natural resources comes closest to being the natural issue around which the rural poor will organize.

JADED OLD LAND
OF BRIGHT NEW PROMISE
Harry M. Caudill

The decade of the 1960s was a time of rediscovery for Eastern Kentucky. The chronically sick economy of Central Appalachia became the subject of many state and Federal studies and reports. Scores of newspaper and magazine articles and dozens of television documen-

From *Mountain Life & Work*, March 1970. Used by permission of the author.

taries carried the Appalachian dilemma around the world and made it the subject of numberless campus seminars and symposia. Poverty-plagued Appalachia rose like a specter to haunt affluent suburbia with its smug assumption that all was well with all of America.

The attention thus focused on Kentucky's mountain counties almost invariably dealt with the formidable failures and shortcomings of the region. The grim data amassed by the Appalachian Regional Commission and other study groups etched a bleak picture that need not be restated here. Its parts consisted of relentless exploitation of land and people by absentee mining corporations, silted and polluted streams, ravaged hillsides, a high rate of adult illiteracy, generally poor schools, few and small colleges, high incidence of tuberculosis and other infectious diseases, weak county governments beset by perpetual fiscal crisis, high rates of unemployment, substandard wages, poor roads, dreadful housing, reactionary and unimaginative local leadership, and sustained outmigration. All these and other grave difficulties were discovered and studied but little attention was given to the other—and highly promising—face of Eastern Kentucky. For the eastern third of Kentucky is, in truth, poor in only a limited and quite superficial sense. When we look at the land itself we realize that it is extremely rich in many of the things most Americans cherish. If made known to modern corporate managers, the splendid attributes of this region might well bring an immense cycle of rejuvenation before the end of the 1970s. Paradoxically, the poor backward Kentucky mountains could become the setting for much of the nation's finest industrial and social development in the coming decade.

Let us examine some of the little-known assets that distinguish this ancient region:

Varied and Abundant Forests. Nine-tenths of the land is still in forest—perhaps the oldest surviving woodland on the planet. Botanists tell us it was in essentially its present form 70 million years ago. It is incredibly varied, with a dozen varieties of oaks alone. Builders of mobile homes, prefabricated housing and furniture are likely to discover a treasure trove in the fast-growing stands of timber.

Natural Beauty. It is doubtful that even the magnificent Great Smokies are lovelier than the Kentucky Cumberlands. From the fabled Red River Gorge on the north to the long crest of the Pine Mountain and the dark immensities of the Big Black in the south, the land is lovely.

In the spring the forests are gay with incense and bright with millions of wild flowers. In the fall the colors defy description—red, yellow, plum, gold, orange and brown in riotous combinations. Forests, crags, laurel thickets and rushing streams offer healing for the harried soul of every visitor.

Nor are the hills without broad, level, fertile bottoms. Along the Big Sandy, the Red Bird, the Cumberland and the three forks of the Kentucky are expanses of wide, flat, open land. Nearly all such places are bordered by railroads and highways, and all boast a history rich in botanical and zoological splendor, plus a marvelously varied human story. For 5,000 years men have built towns here, and this colorful region grips all who come to know it.

Strategic Location. It lies only 400 miles from the nation's capital and midway between the old population centers in the Northeast and the rapidly expanding cities of Florida. No costly continent-spanning flights will be necessary when executives take off for meetings in Washington and New York.

Abundant Water. The quest for fresh water is increasingly urgent in many parts of the nation, with enormously costly state and Federal projects required to bring enough of it into Texas, California, and a half-dozen other western states. Even the Atlantic seaboard suffers from occasional long, nerve-racking droughts. Only the rain forests of Washington and Oregon receive more precipitation than the Kentucky mountains. Our 45-50 inches of moisture per year assures ample supplies at relatively moderate costs—and in a pure state fresh from the skies.

Huge Labor Reserves. Thousands of mountain men and women are available to learn new skills and take up jobs wherever they may be offered. A string of new vocational schools will guarantee steadily upgraded aptitudes and proficiencies in both men and women, and in the cities of Maryland, Ohio, Indiana, Illinois and Michigan are tens of thousands of emigrants with highly valuable, city-learned techniques who are ready to return to their homeland as soon as the promise of decent jobs appears.

Immense Electricity Potential. A continuing shortage of railroad cars combines with a terrific increase in consumption to pose a long-term threat of electricity shortages for much of America. Eastern Kentucky's enormous coal reserves and abundant water could be translated into vast new power sources. The state could emulate the Public Utility Districts in the State of Washington, selling its capital-outlay bonds, building power plants and cooling-water reservoirs, and generating electricity for wholesaling to utility companies, REAs and municipalities. The state could thus assure power for its own development, guarantee ample sources for retail distributors and turn a handsome profit for support of its public facilities—and all without infringing on the business domain of any tax-paying firm. Such a state-sponsored little TVA could provide industrialists all the advantages afforded by the Tennessee Valley Authority without the bureaucratic folds that inevitably envelop a Federal agency and those dependent upon it.

Mineral Resources. Only a few Interior Department officials and some railroad and mining magnates fully comprehend the vast scope of the remaining mineral reserves. Perhaps three billion tons of coal have been mined, but at least 32 billion tons remain in the earth. Kentucky yields about 20 million barrels of petroleum annually and natural gas production in the mountains is steadily expanding. Wells on Bull Creek in Perry and Letcher counties are worth an estimated $50 million. The Pine Mountain is studded for 100 miles with thick outcroppings of hard, white limestone and silica-rich sandstone. There are modest deposits of iron ore and the extensive brine beds are yet to be tapped for any commercial purpose.

In addition to providing construction aggregates and fuel, these mineral lodes offer important opportunities to chemical and glass industries which may recognize the wisdom of making their finished product near the raw-material sources rather than paying to haul heavy raw materials to plants in distant cities.

Space. Finally, the exodus that has carried a million highlanders out of the hills since 1950 has created a situation hard to find in the world today. The nation's population has grown by nearly 70 million since World War II, and it need not be argued that congestion of people and their machines is a growing burden in most urban areas. But in Eastern Kentucky hundreds of valleys lie almost empty, crumbling shacks and vine-grown chimneys attesting to the departed multitudes who once called the territory their home. Forests reclaim the old fields and the land can be bought at relatively low prices. Here is elbow room, a commodity our ancestors esteemed highly but which most of our young will never experience. For a new breed of development-minded industrialists, here is a frontier of opportunity in many fields.

In the past the steep, rock-ribbed and crag-crested hills were a labyrinth that effectively isolated both land and people from the large outside world. Our mountain "quaintness" was simply a survival of old mores and attitudes after changing conditions elsewhere had eroded them away. Now new highways and the all-pervasive television are changing all of this. Within little more than four years the basic road system—Ky. 15, Ky. 80 and U.S. 119—will have been completely rebuilt and modernized, and every county seat will have access to a small airport. Isolation and isolationism are passing and most mountaineers now want—in the words of a discerning school superintendent—to "join the rest of the world."

A number of things can work to prevent the development of a new economic life. Strip mining is the worst enemy of progress because it ruins natural beauty, chokes streams, uproots forests, reduces the tax base and spurs more outmigration. If the state has any plans for the region's future apart from mining, this industry ought to be banned. In most instances the coal can be recovered by other methods and it is almost never sufficient in quantity to justify the environmental impairment it causes.

Weak government at state and local levels contributes enormously to decline, and it works to prevent developmental change. Strict law enforcement is needed in a number of long-neglected fields. Every county should be persuaded or compelled to establish sanitary collection and disposal systems in order to clean up the trash-coated countryside. After all, no self-respecting corporation will assign its personnel to an area where every stream is a sewer and every roadside a dump. An overhaul of the courts may have to come before this essential development can be realized.

Few things could have so beneficent an impact as the building of a full-scale university deep within the mountains. The University of Kentucky Extension at either Prestonsburg or Hazard should be scheduled for such development and its expansion promoted as rapidly as funds can be made available. Such an institution should not stop short of at least six colleges—including law, medicine and engineering—by the 1980s. Though the cost would be great, the investment would be an excellent one from the viewpoint of the state's taxpayers, because in the promotion of development and progress nothing succeeds like a dynamic campus—as the effect of the University of Kentucky on the city of Lexington so graphically illustrates.

All Kentuckians should study the example of Switzerland, a mountainous region the same size as Eastern Kentucky. It has no mineral deposits except brine beds, and a fifth of the surface is barren. It has little usable farmland. Yet there are 6,000,000 Swiss, in contrast to about 750,000 in our own hills. The Swiss have prospered while we have declined. They are watch-makers to the world and have eliminated unemployment and illiteracy. Labor is in such short supply that 600,000 foreigners have been permitted to enter the country to work in the humming factories. An estimated $70 billion reposes in Swiss banks. The country supports 22 great institutions of higher learning, including five world-famous medical colleges. Switzerland is a poor land whose people have grown rich; Eastern Kentucky is a rich land whose people have grown poor!

Americans concerned about the future of their country should ponder the following: If the U.S. were as highly developed as the Swiss republic, its population would equal that of China and India combined. There would be 1,200,000,000 of us but unemployment would be no problem. To the contrary, labor shortages would have compelled us to admit 120 million foreign nationals to work in our mines, mills and factories.

Unless the prospering urban areas of Kentucky see to it that Eastern Kentucky becomes prosperous too, they may eventually sink beneath the burden imposed by carrying two-score pauper counties. The school foundation law alone diverts enough money from city needs to mountain communities to break the state in time.

But this burden does not have to be a permanent one. With some creative imagination and a grasp of the possibilities, state policies can be formulated to emphasize the gigantic potential of the huge territory. Then, as the great boom of the 1970s gathers momentum, the Kentucky mountains can be discovered again in a cycle of development as sweeping as the decade preceding the First World War, when coal was king and hundreds of towns sprang up by hundreds of clattering new tipples.

Nor will the newcomers with their building plans be trailblazers. The first in this new wave are already on the scene—Control Data at Campton, Letcher Manufacturing in Letcher, Louisa Carpet Mills at

Louisa. These companies have already discovered the advantages of starting enterprises in an old land that is bright with new promise. Neither the land nor its inhabitants will disappoint them. Eastern Kentucky is like a somewhat seasoned but still lovely woman—she is eager to embrace all who will appreciate her charms. Clearly the time has come to stop treating her like a worn-out old bitch.

TOWARD A PEOPLE'S ARC
Robb Burlage

On the sixth floor of a modern insurance company building on Connecticut Avenue in Washington, D. C., is the ARC [Appalachian Regional Commission] headquarters. Modest offices sprawl through a number of corridors, panels, and floors. Grantsmen, political staffers, federal and state agency professionals, consultants, journalists, and students flow casually in and out. Few of the "people left behind" ever visit or petition these offices directly. Although projects are often informally initiated at the ARC staff level, such distant constituents are always sent back through their development districts and state capitals, which must endorse a project for ARC to consider it formally.

The ARC staff has fluctuated upward for more than five years (a rare personnel buoyancy in today's Washington). ARC Executive Director Ralph Widner, once administrative assistant and national manpower hearings quarterback for Pennsylvania's former U.S. Senator Joseph Clark, coaches a floating college of more than 100 staff professionals and generalists, many under age 40, some under 30. He constantly shifts them in and out of assignments, in and out of the Appalachian "field offices" on state and district turf. There are also dozens of "invisible college" consultants on whom he and they draw constantly, and hundreds of state, district and federal agency para-ARC-ers.

In less than five years this staff feels it has moved from being simply the Appalachian Governors Road Gang to being an exemplary federal-state "Regional Bureau of the Budget" for Appalachia (though

From *Peoples' Appalachia*, August-September 1970. Used by permission of the author.

many close analysts yet feel that its rush of road-mapping in 1965 was the major investment ball game). Led by Widner, many style themselves "rationalizers," "catalysts," and "brokers" whose job is to educate the politician state governors' offices—to work cooperatively and rationally from "inside the system" for positive "development," by which most very earnestly mean better things for people, at least at some point of "output." Few are from heartland Appalachia; most are prodigiously acquainted with the domestic diplomatic world of state capitols, federal agencies, and professional policy conferences. Even at lower technician levels, most are participating as evaluators and brokers of numerous projects. It is not surprising that many were "shocked" at conditions they observed evidently for the first time on their bus tour of Appalachia early this summer, to announce the "new human stage" of the ARC program.

ARC staff *esprit* is generally high and "loyal," not closed to criticism nor defensive about results. They are most proud of an engaging personal stake in a new "process." Though there is devastating evidence of program contradictions, political and corporate sabotage, and heavy failure to reach the region's neediest, most have a curious mixture of futuristic confidence, pre-emptive self-criticism (ideas are their product), deferred political responsibility and implicit skepticism that disarms the critic and totally frustrates the petitioner. This model of the almost totally "administrative" government offers the most sensitively educated "new class" person a new cut above bureaucratic rigidity, academic boredom and political pressure. Here one finds participatory intergovernmental brokerage experience without real, constituent accountability. It may be one of the most important "demonstrations" in the entire ARC program.

How did we get into the "development decade" in the first place? In late 1960, President-elect John F. Kennedy feared a national economic recession, which he thought could only be partly spiked by new military investment. Having successfully reached for the shaky electoral Southern states through their pocketbooks, and remembering his West Virginia primary-campaign promise, Kennedy called together governors, many from the Council of Appalachian Governors, to discuss what to do. The Area Redevelopment Act (ARA) resulted, emphasizing small business and public facility loans and grants.

Two years later, it was clear that the national map was littered with "pockets of poverty"; that scattered business development loans and grants had little real impact except to subsidize runaway sweatshops; and that poor black and white rebellions were escalating beyond Southern civil rights protest. In 1963, roving pickets in Hazard, Kentucky, seeking return of union medical cards (and trapped in a fight between big coal companies in conspiracy with the United Mine Workers against smaller, non-union companies) gained national attention and sympathy. Harry Caudill's *Night Comes to the Cumberlands* and Michael Harrington's *The Other America* also brought it home.

By then, Kennedy had called on Franklin D. Roosevelt, Jr., to head a President's Appalachian Regional Commission to develop a program in cooperation with Appalachian governors' representatives. The Commission staff was directed by Michigan's John Sweeney and stocked most notably with minor-league whiz kids from Pennsylvania. (Michael Harrington, who served as a consultant, quipped later that he was perhaps the first person the poverty program had brought out of poverty—a precedent for a major new pattern of professional and intellectual relief.)

The President's cabinet met with Appalachian governors in the spring of 1963 and outlined general program elements, including a federal-state commission with heavy federal financing and grant supplementation for the states and major investments in "development highways" to break down "regional isolation." Federal discussions were also beginning on a socially-oriented "poverty program" to complement the regional development approach.

The 1964 Commission report called Appalachia a "region apart," whose rich "natural endowment has benefited too few" and whose cities seriously lagged behind national economic growth. Using analogies of US foreign "underdeveloped country" aid, it called for a broad, experimental economic development program. The federal-state commission was to coordinate vast new highway linkages, public facilities, grass-rooted local entrepreneurial development organizations, public development programs for timber, livestock, water resources, electrical and nuclear power (including possible cooperative TVA and AEC programs), new coal and mineral processes and uses (including possible public "mine-mouth" power generation), and land reclamation. At one point, however, Mr. Roosevelt appeared in a press conference with a New York Consolidated Edison representative, to announce dynamic expansion plans by private power companies into Appalachia for Northeast and regional power needs. This heightened expectations that the "little TVA" locally-controlled public power alternative being pushed by Harry Caudill and others was steadily being shelved.

Most social program investments (health, education, community action) were to be deferred to the proposed national poverty program. An "interdependency" between a strictly "hard-core" rural development program and a broader (then touching 10 states) regional program, including urban areas, was emphasized. Its stated goal was ". . . the introduction of Appalachia and its people into fully active membership in the American society."

By the time the ARDA was passed by Congress and signed in March, 1965, it was essentially an "Appalachian governors' highways and public works act," stripped of almost all public competition with or regulation of private power and natural resource development. The Act explicitly forbade use of public funds to purchase or support public power and ignored most direct agency resource development and administrative powers. Water resources were given to the Congressional (and private power company) favorite, the Army Corps of Engineers, to study and plan with the states for five years. Timber, livestock, and mineral development programs were whittled away. Environmental control over coal was narrowed to a few restoration and study efforts.

Most actual programs were to operate through traditional, fragmented federal agencies. Overall plans and selection of development priority centers and areas was to be the loose prerogative of the states. Only a small research and planning budget was authorized for the Commission itself. Thus, "regional development" had come to mean "paving the way" for new industrial plant investments; local initiative and participation had come to mean conservative state and local political power structure veto.

Ohio, New York, and South Carolina were tacked on as Appalachian states. Mississippi became the 13th in 1967. New York is apparently in the program for the roads, and Ohio is considered a planning and administrative disaster area in the program. But South Carolina's Governor McNair has made his few Appalachian counties a basis for creating an aggressive state-wide planning and development program, including a "model" vocational education and placement system. (McNair had the professional work for his first "state plan" created by Wall Street's Moody's Investors Service, a group that knows the real corporate planning signals.) Even Mississippi has been more active in the program than the northern add-on states.

A six-year authorization for a Development Highway System received more than 80% of the initial billion dollar appropriation (thanks especially to the Highway Lobby and Public Works Chairman Sen. Jennings Randolph of West Virginia). Later appropriations, amendments and grant-supplementations have added almost a billion dollars for additional highway costs and local access roads, public airports, sewage and water treatment, multi-county health demonstrations, vocational and general education (especially to upgrade community colleges and rural schools), child development, hunger and nutrition, libraries, educational TV, public recreation facilities, and an Appalachian Housing Fund. More has also been made available to study and "demonstrate" solutions to problems of strip mining, solid waste management, environmental pollution, and occupational diseases, especially from coal. As ARC has moved toward becoming a kind of regional Bureau of the Budget with brokerage and expediting powers, still more supplemental funds have been provided for state-planned education and health facilities.

Early "professional" Appalachian economic development advice (most notably from a pre-ARC Litton Industries consulting study) was primarily to write off completely the rural areas, to build up a few perimeter metropolitan growth centers in or on the edge of broader Appalachia, and to encourage outmigration to them. When eastern Kentucky newspaper editor Tom Gish first saw the Litton "development map" late in December, 1964, he noted it had only "white space" for his area. He called it "Eastern Kentucky's White Christmas."

Traditional Congressional and state political pressures for such public works programs have been to spend as widely as possible; but experience with the wasteful scatter of the ARA days had created more state interest in the Commission for new, correlated-impact approaches. In its first six months, ARC had to expedite a "development corridors" highway plan, based on generally primitive, uncorrelated state advance planning data and on generally untested economic assumptions. Transportation access is clearly necessary, but hardly sufficient to induce balanced economic growth. Yet, this clearly has been the most important investment "plan" in the program.

ARC planners divided the 13-state area into "four Appalachias" (Northern, Central, Southern, and Highlands) with no clear policy implications except that major economic growth is planned for the perimeter areas. In turn, the 13 states created about 60 local development districts. They were projected around urban "growth centers" to be the focus of expenditures. The "four Appalachias" design clearly consigned densely-populated but essentially rural "Central Appalachia," as well as the recreational "Highlands," to a vague hinterland status with no apparent "take-off" handles for ARC's emerging "urbanizing" economic growth strategy.

ARC officials have looked for early silver linings. Carefully avoiding focussing their lens on Central Appalachia, they report that, overall, since 1965, outmigration is "tapering"; unemployment has declined (although there are now disturbing new signs in certain areas of sharp recession reversals); and per capita income is "increasing more rapidly than in the US as a whole" (although it is still less than 80% of the US average and is certainly declining relative to the US in most heartland areas).

Carefully selecting their points on the map, they find encouraging growth spots in such places as the South Carolina and Georgia spillovers of Piedmont and Atlanta growth, entering more "urban-stage" economies from mill-town origins, or in Alabama–east Tennessee beneficiaries of NASA, TVA, etc. They highlight, for example, the "miracles" being planned in the five-county eastern Kentucky Big Sandy Development District with 300,000 people around three mini-conurbations (total population 17,000). They are "model city" Pikeville, which is literally moving a mountain to divert the Big Sandy River out of downtown; Prestonsburg, whose doctor-mayor has emphasized medical programs as one key to development; and Paintsville, with its own urban renewal program and three new low-rent housing projects, whose mayor boasts his town has never turned down a bond issue and whose bankers' deposits have doubled in six years. This District has made "corporate folk heroes" out of a few new plants such as American Standard that have come to the area.

ARC insists that the new highways and vocational education programs have been the key to more than 1150 new plants locating in the 13-state area since 1965, and that their catalytic grant supplement funds have generated four federal dollars for each ARC one. Increased federal loans to housing have resulted in more than 6,000 units in two years. ARC's approach to environmental problems has induced studies on the costs of acid mine drainage and strip mining, some direct action against mine fires in Pennsylvania and solid waste disposal in Georgia; and small staff technical assistance to local and state planning, including encouragement of interstate compact approach to mining regulation. Appalachia is described as a "national laboratory" for "child development" and "youth leadership development" programs. Such ARC developmental brags even have included terms such as a note in the Wall Street Journal that new hospitals "might make vacationers more inclined to trek to a new ski lift" in the hills.

Now the Commission must defend the entire program, up for renewal the spring of 1971. With obvious central contradictions and failures looming, ARC leaders announced this summer that they will now move directly into "Stage II" on some of the previously-dodged hardcore problems. They explicitly mentioned new studies and action on disastrous coal industry environmental and occupational problems. To pay for some of its most blatant social costs, they say they're studying a possible national severance tax on coal, natural gas, and other extractable resources, shared with or reverted to states and localities (without harming "the competitiveness of Appalachian resources in national and world markets"). They say they now will also stress programs to reach the people left behind "up the hollows," whom some had assumed were the prime targets of the program in the first place. Says Director Widner: "Unfortunately, development makes its first impact on upper and middle income groups. It has a trickle-down effect to the really hardcore poor."

Now that they have built the "machine," ARC planners are considering holding town meetings up the hollows to ask people what choices they would make for social projects among scarce resources or even to give them some veto power over projects they do not want. But some grass roots leaders say this is only asking marginal permission after the basic decisions and impacts have already been made. Beyond new coal tax and environment and rural services re-considerations, intensive eleventh hour evaluations are going on (regarding health demonstration programs) and new program ideas are being developed (community corporations, youth self-expressive media, etc., to supplement established educational and commercial radio and television).

Thus, ARC is now heralding a "new Appalachian spring" with the glowing expectation of new highways, more industrial locations and a growing "service center network."

The people of heartland Appalachia are deeply skeptical. Once more they are being asked to eat promises. They find little satisfaction in sanguine generalizations about signs of progress in perimeters and spots of 13-state "Appalachia."

The glaring statistics of heartland failure thus far are legion. Even metropolitan "growth" areas in South and Central Appalachia overall showed only an eight percent population increase from '60–'70. Thirty percent of the increase came from NASA-land, Huntsville, Alabama, which is someone's concept of Appalachia. Some designated "growth centers" actually declined (Charleston, West Virginia, lost 9 percent). The entire state of West Virginia lost over six percent, leading the nation at the bottom; southwest Virginia lost six percent; eastern Kentucky, after the great coal miner displacement of the '50s, lost five percent more in the '60s. The most touted new manufacturing plant that has come to eastern Kentucky in recent years had more than 6,000 applicants for 45 trainee positions and ended up choosing only among high school graduates. The new private industrial investments ARC says have been induced to West Virginia are primarily coal mines and sweatshops.

ARC has revised its estimates of when net outmigration will "turn around" in Central Appalachia from 1980 to a year after 1984. (Is this when everyone is expected to have already been driven out, except for a few automated mine, chemical, and power plant technicians—who will commute with gas masks?) Widner has written: "Where coal mining is likely to continue to be one of the dominant sources of employment and income, we must assume a residual population of about 1.5 million will remain for some time to come."

Many ARC "pilot projects" thus far have only given more depth perception of the crying needs. For example, a home health program in Harlan County, Kentucky, showed widespread malnutrition. Mental retardation programs have showed half of the children with "learning problems" suffer from poverty-related physical or emotional illnesses.

Meanwhile, coal strip mining expands apace throughout the heartland, with only a requirement to post a "re-seeding bond" at best, in most states. Cities like Hazard may be inundated from resultant floods any day in a Johnstown-like horror. Doctors estimate that all citizens, especially the workers inside, have years taken off their life expectancies from the chemical air pollution of Charleston's Kanawha Valley. Some schools and hospitals in western Pennsylvania are actually imminently threatened by cave-ins from abandoned coal mines.

The *Wall Street Journal* recently summarized the environmental disaster setting: "Here in the mined out hills of Appalachia . . . the coal industry has long since left this land dead beyond all reasonable hope of reclamation. Many of the waterways are so polluted that they can't support fish and plants. . . . The costs and complexities of the environmental reclamation job are staggering . . . merely to clean up stream-polluting acid-mine drainage (affecting an estimated 10,500 miles of rivers and streams) might cost up to $10 billion. The costs of filling in old mines, smothering underground fires and removing the mountain of coal waste haven't even been guessed at. . . ."

Despite ARC flourishes about its local "miracles" in the making, the grating area development failures are more definitive than the exceptions thus far. For instance, the large, densely populated, eight-county Kentucky River Area Development District has many positive social assets, such as grass roots, poor peoples' economic development groups; lively youth leadership groups; the educated advocacy of lawyer-author Harry Caudill and editor Tom Gish; and a militant history of worker resistance to Big Coal. But the control by coal operators and rigid local power structures is still overwhelming. The Development District has been so resistant to poor peoples' groups that even their federal operating funds have been held in abeyance. The District board in July turned down a worker-owned housing project proposal (which was promised $780,000 from OEO) in favor of the possibility of a California-owned Lexington construction firm taking the contract instead.

The fickle effects of the tight national economy for such prospects became clearer in the District when the much-ARC-advertised Tandy Industries' (of Tulsa) pre-fabricated housing factory location in Letcher County was suddenly cancelled. Even with the guarantee of heavy federal plant and training subsidies, it split, evidently because of the tight housing finance market nationally, hitting hardest in the region.

As with much of the ARC program, "local initiative" evidently must be "local power structure initiative" to be deemed official. A major study done recently by the Spindletop Research Center in Lexington for the District has called for more "local development corporations," although the already-formed poor peoples' grass roots "development corporations" have been desperately trying to get recognition and assistance for three years.

Hazard, six years after its jilted miners' movement called national attention to the region, is now said by ARC to be "one and a half hours from Lexington by highway, rather than three and a half." But it is still hamstrung by coal and courthouse politics, with almost a 20% unemployment rate and a city government deeply in debt ($200,000) and an 18-month light bill. Rather than go after coal property, the city of Hazard passed a one-percent occupational tax on workers this summer. And there is still the continuing threat of floods, exacerbated by strip mining, that have caused $15 million damage in recent years.

To its credit, or creative oversight, the ARC program has made some inputs into the region, in addition to some desperately needed direct services for some people, which perhaps improve the chances of future political conflict emerging in a positive "developmental" way.

The "old feudalism," of regional coal capital and its kept, repressive county courthouse politics, is being gently challenged or co-opted in established circles. It was beginning to fall apart anyway through the new buy-up and broader interests of the international energy elite and through the permeation of national corporate "modernizing" politics into the local level. The latter is a Kennedy-Johnson legacy now being redefined by the Nixon Administration to match its tastes. However, grass-roots worker or community group challenges to that system at the local level usually run into a convergence of the "old" and the "new" feudalisms, rather than a decisive split of which to take advantage.

Indigenous youth leadership, even among high school drop-outs, is increasingly being encouraged—through district participation (much more than among poor peoples' and workers' groups), government program staff "apprenticeships," their own community action projects, and through Appalachian problem, policy, and history "emphasis" seminars. A handbook on environmental problems prepared by the ARC staff for these youth seminars is one of the best primers of its kind for any age group. Some are already asking deeply rooted and thoughtful questions about what's going on in the mountains, and about the ARC program itself. With real constituencies and increasingly independent conceptions about "development," they could become a whole new kind of critical "social investment" in the region.

Demonstration programs, primarily in health services planning and delivery and in educational program development, are beginning to offer some new "teams" of committed youth professionals and paraprofessionals, as well as some new community taste of different service standards. Although some such mountain practitioners and teachers are themselves deeply committed, they are now simply overwhelmed for lack of professional relief and paraprofessional and institutional support. The same could be true of some "new class" planners and community developers, now usually attempting to work out from under existing state and district planning and development establishments. However, unless they can relate themselves closely with potentially insurgent community support, they can only function as isolated and vulnerable outposts.

The executives, planners, and brokers of the ARC do not constitute a "People's ARC." Nor does ARC's federal-state "power structure" provide either the public sector leverage or the popular participation to do anything more than pave the way for many of the same absentee capitalist users of the region's land, people, and institutions. Major revolutions in the ARC must occur for the "new Appalachian Spring" to have any real chance of helping develop Appalachia for the benefit of its people.

There must be popular power to challenge the plans and exported profits of the existing private forces of extractive "development." These corporate developers are costing the people of the region much more than they are worth. People cannot wait for conservative state governors or private power company officials to take action in the public interest. To make the necessary great leap forward, public sector leadership will require major streams of guaranteed public revenues from the region's natural resources. It will also require a continuing federal commitment of reparations for having built the American metropolitan industrial empire out of the sweat and bounty of the region.

The public development of electric power has been dodged and sabotaged. Millions of dollars in potential development revenues are being lost, and private power companies are moving to capture remaining hydro, mine-mouth, and nuclear power sites as part of their comprehensive goals. A recently published, 25-volume "Appalachian Resources Plan," carried out over the last five years by the Army Corps of Engineers with authorization under the ARDA in cooperation with the ARC and other federal agencies, provides more evasion. Although the ARC, prohibited by law from engaging in public power projects, pushed the Corps to emphasize long-run "induced economic development" benefits, the plan did not even mention the alternative of public power. The report touches this issue only in passing: "The Appalachian Resources Plan has assumed that private power companies will provide the increased electric energy as fast as it is needed to meet the development goals of the plan." This assumption is intolerable, given the projected regional power needs, local development revenue needs, and the national energy crisis.

Action must be taken immediately to tax all private coal and resource extraction and absentee-owned production profit, to assure that necessary services and economic security are available for all in the Appalachian heartland and that a decent living income maintenance is guaranteed for all. Total community control of the general environment (against strip mining, industrial air and water pollution) and worker control of the workplace environment (to prevent black lung, chemical toxic synergisms, nuclear radiation, and managerial speed-ups) must be guaranteed with strong regional standards and enforcement assistance.

A keystone would be an enabling ARC framework for "Public Energy Utility Districts" (PEUDs) that generate public revenues from local, publicly-owned (one person, one vote) economic energy development, based on public natural resources—hydroelectric, mine-mouth, nuclear and other forms—to be newly developed and "recaptured." The public fight is thickening today within the Federal Power Commission and Congressional committees against private power company control of the region's vital remaining hydroelectric sites and water-based energy production locations. A national energy and power crisis of cost, availability, and environmental disaster is leading to undeniable public demand for a strong, comprehensive national public energy policy. This could delegate much resource control to such area PEUDs for more balanced energy production related to comprehensive development, public revenue generation, and sensitive environmental control. Until a comprehensive public-interest national policy is achieved, PEUDs can be prime area public demonstration units to achieve such general public control.

Finally, grassroots community development groups must be the building blocks of new development initiative in the region, creating new means of community-worker ownership and control of enterprise. All area development plans must emerge from participatory, democratic "development town meetings." ARC "new towns" and "model valleys" must emerge from people's initiatives and life plans, not as strategic hamlets for bulldozer, landgrab, and pollution refugees.

Biographical Notes

T. N. Bethell, a freelance writer-photographer, coordinates Appalachia Information, a news service in Washington, D.C.

James Branscome, a native of Hillsville, Virginia, a recent graduate of Berea College, and a former staff member of the Appalachian Regional Commission, is presently director of Save Our Kentucky.

David B. Brooks, formerly chief of the Department of Mineral Economics of the Bureau of Mines, is presently head of economic research for the Mineral Resources Branch of the Canadian Department of Energy, Mines and Resources.

James S. Brown is a professor of sociology at the University of Kentucky, author of numerous articles on Appalachian communities, and co-author of *Mountain Families in Transition*.

Robb Burlage is a writer-activist and a member of the Peoples' Appalachian Research Collective in Morgantown, West Virginia.

Harry M. Caudill, attorney-at-law in Whitesburg, Kentucky, is a noted lecturer on Appalachian problems and author of *Night Comes to the Cumberlands*.

Robert Coles, research psychiatrist at Harvard University Health Services, has written many articles and books on minority group children and social change.

Charles H. Drake edited *Mountain Life & Work* from 1950 to 1959.

Harry W. Ernst, a former newspaperman, is presently director of university relations for West Virginia University.

JOHN FETTERMAN is editor of the Louisville *Courier-Journal Sunday Magazine* and author of *Stinking Creek*.

BEN A. FRANKLIN is a Washington correspondent for the *New York Times*, and winner of the 1970 Weatherford award for the best published work on the Appalachian South.

PAT GISH directs the Eastern Kentucky Housing Development Corporation of Whitesburg, Kentucky.

TOM GISH edits the weekly Whitesburg *Mountain Eagle*.

PAUL GOOD is a freelance writer on social problems and author of *The American Serfs*.

JERALD TER HORST is chief of the Washington bureau of the *Detroit News*.

K. W. LEE, formerly a reporter for the *Charleston Gazette*, now works for the *Sacramento Union*.

JAMES C. MILLSTONE is a reporter for the *St. Louis Post-Dispatch*.

BILL MONTGOMERY was managing editor of *Mountain Life & Work* from 1968 to 1970.

ROBERT F. MUNN is director of libraries for West Virginia University.

THOMAS PARRISH edited *Mountain Life & Work* from 1968 to 1970.

JEANNE M. RASMUSSEN is a freelance writer-photographer living in Beaver, West Virginia.

PETER SCHRAG, contributing editor of *Saturday Review* and formerly editor of *Change*, writes frequently on educational problems and other social issues.

CALVIN TRILLIN writes the regular "U.S. Journal" articles for the *New Yorker*.

Rupert B. Vance, professor emeritus of sociology at the University of North Carolina, is the author of several classic regional studies of the South.

Dan Wakefield is a freelance writer, novelist, and contributing editor of *Atlantic*.

Don West, poet, preacher, farmer, labor organizer, and teacher, is the founder of the Appalachian South Folklife Center at Pipestem, West Virginia.

Philip Young, a Presbyterian minister living in Blacksburg, Virginia, was president of the Council of the Southern Mountains from 1967 to 1971.